JOURNAL FOR THE STUDY OF THE NEW TESTAMENT
SUPPLEMENT SERIES
147

Executive Editor
Stanley E. Porter

Sheffield Academic Press

The Story of Jesus according to L

Kim Paffenroth

Journal for the Study of the New Testament
Supplement Series 147

Copyright © 1997 Sheffield Academic Press

Published by Sheffield Academic Press Ltd
Mansion House
19 Kingfield Road
Sheffield S11 9AS
England

Printed on acid-free paper in Great Britain
by Bookcraft Ltd
Midsomer Norton, Bath

British Library Cataloguing in Publication Data

A catalogue record for this book is available
from the British Library

ISBN 1-85075-675-9

CONTENTS

PREFACE

C'est le plus beau livre qu'il y ait.
—Renan[1]

The genesis of this publication was my unremarkable senior essay written in the spring of 1988. Naive and uncritical, it was nonetheless my
first attempt at dealing with the Synoptic problem. Since then, I have
remained convinced that by closely examining the first three Gospels,
especially the differences between them, one can indeed find much truth
and beauty in these books; and I, like Renan, have found the Gospel of
Luke the most enlightening and beautiful. That essay was written at St
John's College, Annapolis, with the consultation of Dr John Verdi, and I
thank him again for his patience and assistance in directing my thoughts
in ways that otherwise would have been impossible or overlooked.
An unofficial advisor and mentor on that project was Revd Richard
Bumpass, whose untimely death in 1993 took from the St John's and
Naval Academy communities an exemplary minister and counselor to
generations of johnnies and midshipmen.

The present work was originally a doctoral dissertation written under
the guidance of Drs Gregory Sterling and Harold Attridge of the University of Notre Dame. I repeat my thanks for their encouragement and
assistance in building this analysis of the third Gospel.

I would like to thank my father for his support during all the years I
have been in school. I would never have embarked on this course if it
were not for the books that he surrounded me with as I grew up, and
the ideas and curiosity with which they filled me. For the last sixteen
years, the memory of my mother has always been with me; I wish I
could show her this work.

Finally, I dedicate this book with love and thanks to my wife Marlis.
For the last ten years she has constantly given me support and comfort

---

1. E. Renan, *Les évangiles et la seconde génération chrétienne* (Paris:
Calmann–Lévy, 1877), p. 283.

that I do not deserve, and for which I have too often been ungrateful; I will try to do better. I humbly thank her for her patience and love, and especially for the gift of little Charles, born contemporaneously with this work.

Kim Paffenroth
University of Notre Dame
Christmas 1996

ABBREVIATIONS

AJBI	Annual of the Japanese Biblical Institute
ANRW	*Aufstieg und Niedergang der römischen Welt*
AusBR	*Australian Biblical Review*
BETL	Bibliotheca ephemeridum theologicarum lovaniensium
Bib	*Biblica*
BJRL	*Bulletin of the John Rylands University Library of Manchester*
BTB	*Biblical Theology Bulletin*
BZ	*Biblische Zeitschrift*
CBQ	*Catholic Biblical Quarterly*
ConNT	*Coniectanea neotestamentica*
CurTM	*Currents in Theology and Mission*
EKKNT	Evangelisch-Katholischer Kommentar zum Neuen Testament
ETL	*Ephemerides theologicae lovanienses*
EvQ	*Evangelical Quarterly*
ExpTim	*Expository Times*
HeyJ	*Heythrop Journal*
HJ	*Hibbert Journal*
HTKNT	Herders theologischer Kommentar zum Neuen Testament
HTR	*Harvard Theological Review*
IBS	*Irish Biblical Studies*
Int	*Interpretation*
JBL	*Journal of Biblical Literature*
JR	*Journal of Religion*
JSJ	*Journal for the Study of Judaism in the Persian, Hellenistic and Roman Period*
JSNT	*Journal for the Study of the New Testament*
JSNTSup	*Journal for the Study of the New Testament*, Supplement Series
JSPSup	*Journal for the Study of the Pseudepigrapha*, Supplement Series
JTS	*Journal of Theological Studies*
Neot	*Neotestamentica*
NICNT	New International Commentary on the New Testament
NKZ	*Neue kirchliche Zeitschrift*
NovT	*Novum Testamentum*
NRT	*La nouvelle revue théologique*
NTD	Das Neue Testament Deutsch
NTS	*New Testament Studies*
RB	*Revue biblique*
ResQ	*Restoration Quarterly*

SANT	Studien zum Alten und Neuen Testament
SBL	Society of Biblical Literature
SBLDS	SBL Dissertation Series
SBLRBS	SBL Resources for Biblical Study
SBLSP	SBL Seminar Papers
SNTSMS	Society for New Testament Studies Monograph Series
SNTU	Studien zum Neuen Testament und seiner Umwelt
SO	Symbolae osioenses
ST	*Studia theologica*
TDNT	G. Kittel and G. Friedrich (eds.), *Theological Dictionary of the New Testament*
TGl	*Theologie und Glaube*
TSK	*Theologische Studien und Kritiken*
TynBul	*Tyndale Bulletin*
TZ	*Theologische Zeitschrift*
USQR	*Union Seminary Quarterly Review*
VT	*Vetus Testamentum*
WTJ	*Westminster Theological Journal*
WUNT	Wissenschaftliche Untersuchungen zum Neuen Testament
ZNW	*Zeitschrift für die neutestamentliche Wissenschaft*
ZTK	*Zeitschrift für Theologie und Kirche*

Chapter 1

INTRODUCTION AND STATE OF THE QUESTION

Inasmuch as *many* have undertaken to set in order a narrative of those
things which have been fulfilled among us... (Lk. 1.1).

1. *Introduction*

As recently as 1984, Dieter Lührmann wrote that an unaccomplished
and useful project of New Testament scholarship would be to distinguish how much of the so called 'L material' in Luke's Gospel is from a
source or sources, and how much of it is Lukan composition.[1] Such is
the goal of the present work.

It is widely acknowledged that much of the L material came to Luke
from some source or sources: the extreme position that the L material
is exclusively or primarily original Lukan composition has not been
deemed probable.[2] Luke's prologue (Lk. 1.1-4) certainly suggests that

---

1. D. Lührmann, *An Itinerary for New Testament Study* (trans. J. Bowden;
London: SCM; Philadelphia: Trinity, 1989), p. 44. I refer to the author or final redactor
of the third Gospel as 'Luke' out of convenience and convention, without any implications as to his possible identity. When discussing those scholars who do make statements as to his identity, I will be more specific: e.g. 'Luke, the companion of Paul'. I
use the masculine pronoun to refer to Luke because he refers to himself with such
(Lk. 1.3); this could conceivably be a misleading *nom de plume* (e.g. George Eliot), but
given the patriarchal culture of the first century, this seems less than likely. Similarly,
I will also use the masculine pronoun to refer to the other evangelists and authors of
pre-Gospel sources.

2. See the critique of such an extreme view in I.H. Marshall, *The Gospel of Luke:
A Commentary on the Greek Text* (NIGTC; Grand Rapids: Eerdmans, 1978), p. 31.
And although M.D. Goulder, *Luke: A New Paradigm* (JSNTSup, 20; 2 vols.;
Sheffield: JSOT Press, 1989), proposes his own solution to the Synoptic problem
different from that advocated here, he is similar in regarding the L material as being
Luke's reworking of older material.

he is relying on previous works.[3] Further, much of the L material has been judged as being from authentic traditions about the historical Jesus.[4] However, for reasons that I will examine below, further investigation into the pre-Gospel (but post-Jesus) form and history of this material has never been carefully attempted in a way that would stand up to scrutiny. For over a century it has been acknowledged that it is *possible* that a single source lies behind some of the L material. Depending on how much L material is considered, this may even be said to be *probable*, as the smaller the amount of material considered, and the fewer the form-critical types included in it, the greater the acknowledged possibility that it may be from a single source.[5]

My goal in this work is to make the situation of the L material less ambiguous by answering the following questions: Did some of the L material come to Luke gathered in a single source? What is the evidence for such a conclusion? What was such a source like? Before beginning to address these questions, it will be necessary to review previous research on the L material and to describe the methodologies that will be employed in the present work.

2. *Early Works on L*

Bernard Weiss seems to have been the first to label the material which is found only in the Gospel of Luke as L.[6] He believes that L was a single

3.   On the implications of Luke's reference to the 'many', cf. V.H. Stanton, *The Gospels as Historical Documents. II. The Synoptic Gospels* (Cambridge: Cambridge University Press, 1909), p. 135; and S.M. Gilmour, 'The Gospel According to St Luke' (IB, 8; New York: Abingdon Press, 1952), p. 14.

4.   For a recent evaluation of this material in the (new) historical Jesus debate, see J.D. Crossan, *The Historical Jesus: The Life of a Mediterranean Jewish Peasant* (San Francisco: HarperCollins, 1991), esp. Appendix 1, pp. 427-50, where Crossan judges nearly all the L parables as having originated with the historical Jesus.

5.   This has been acknowledged especially if one limits oneself to sayings material only. See J.M. Creed, '"L" and the Structure of the Lucan Gospel: A Study of the Proto–Luke Hypothesis', *ExpTim* 46 (1934–35), pp. 101-107; more recently, D.M. Parrott, 'The Dishonest Steward (Luke 16.1-8a) and Luke's Special Parable Collection', *NTS* 37 (1991), pp. 499-515; and K. Giles, '"L" Tradition', in J.B. Green, S. McKnight, and I.H. Marshall (eds.), *Dictionary of Jesus and the Gospels* (Leicester, UK: Inter-Varsity Press, 1992), pp. 431-32.

6.   B. Weiss, *Die Quellen des Lukasevangeliums* (Stuttgart: J.G. Cotta'schen Buchhandlung Nachfolger, 1907), and *Die Quellen der synoptischen Überlieferung* (Leipzig: J.C. Hinrichssche Buchhandlung, 1908).

written source that ran from the beginning of the infancy narrative to the end of the Gospel.[7] Unlike some later scholars (especially Feine), he does not suggest that this material had been combined with Q before it came to Luke.

Weiss gives three main reasons why this material should be considered as coming from a single source. First, he begins by noting, quite correctly, the difference in style between the prologue (Lk. 1.1-4) and the rest of the first two chapters of Luke.[8] Even if this is granted as indicative of a pre-Lukan source(s) for the infancy narrative, it does not make any sort of case for the rest of the material in Weiss's L; it especially neglects any consideration of whether or not the source(s) of the infancy narrative is (are) the same as the source(s) of the rest of Luke's special material.[9]

Weiss's second reason for assuming that L was a single written source is that the material is Jewish–Christian.[10] But as with the stylistic reason just noted, this observation applies mainly to material in the infancy narrative. Further, this does not show any real homogeneity among the material considered, but rather observes that *if* all the L material is from a single source, then that source could be characterized as Jewish–Christian. The Jewish–Christian character of this material may just as easily be attributable to several distinct but similar written sources, to general oral tradition, or even to Luke himself.[11]

---

7.   B. Weiss, *Die Quellen des Lukasevangelium*, pp. 195-276. He includes the following verses in this source: 1.5–2.52; 3.10-14, 23-38; 4.16-30; 5.1-11; 6.20-38, 46-49; 7.1-10, 11-17, 18-22a, 36-50; 8.1-3; 9.43-45, 51-56, 61-62; 10.1, 29-37, 38-42; 11.27-28, 37-52, 53-54; 12.1a, 33-34, 35-38, 49-53; 13.1-9, 10-17; 14.1-6, 7-14, 15-24, 25-27, 28-33; 15.1-3, 11-32; 16.14-15, 19-31; 17.3-10, 11-19; 18.9-14, 31-34; 18.43b-19.10; 19.11-28, 37-44, 47-48; 20.20-26, 34-38; 21.12-19, 20-24, 25-28, 34-36, 37-38; 22.1-6, 14-23, 31-34; 22.39–24.49; 24.50b-51. In *Die Quellen der synoptischen Überlieferung*, pp. 97-168, Weiss presents his source L as a continuous document.

8.   Weiss, *Die Quellen des Lukasevangelium*, p. 195; cf. his earlier *Lehrbuch der Einleitung in das Neue Testament* (Berlin: Hertz, 1886), pp. 542-50.

9.   See R.E. Brown, *The Birth of the Messiah: A Commentary on the Infancy Narratives in Matthew and Luke* (Anchor Bible Reference Library; New York: Doubleday, rev. edn, 1993), pp. 244-50, for a discussion of the possible source(s) of Luke's infancy narrative.

10.   Weiss, *Die Quellen des Lukasevangelium*, pp. 198-200; *Einleitung in das Neue Testament*, p. 543.

11.   See the critiques of this point by M.J. Lagrange, 'Les sources du troisième

Weiss's third reason for considering L to be a single source is particularly curious: he believes that it was because it contained so much material.[12] First, it should be noted that the amount of material in the putative source is precisely what is in question. Secondly, as noted above, the greater the number of different form-critical types included in the L material, the less likely it seems that L was a single source.[13] The weakness of Weiss's reasons makes it clear that an L source as extensive as the one he reconstructed is extremely unlikely.

At almost the same time, Paul Feine published the first complete treatment of L as a single source.[14] Feine's 'peculiar source' is very similar to Weiss's L, containing material from the infancy narrative through the resurrection account.[15] Like Weiss, Feine thinks of this source as Jewish–Christian.[16] Feine's contribution to the debate was to hypothesize that L and Q were combined before being incorporated into Luke's Gospel.[17] Although he believes that L and Q were combined before

Evangile', *RB* 4 (1895), pp. 5-22; *RB* 5 (1896), pp. 5-38, esp. pp. 32-38; and Stanton, *Gospels*, vol. 2, p. 223.

12. Weiss, *Einleitung in das Neue Testament*, p. 543.

13. See above, n. 5; also cf. H. Koester, *Ancient Christian Gospels: Their History and Development* (London: SCM Press; Philadelphia: Trinity, 1990), pp. 336-37.

14. See P. Feine, *Eine vorkanonische Überlieferung des Lukas in Evangelium und Apostelgeschichte* (Gotha: Perthes, 1891). He includes the following verses in this source: 1.5–2.52; 3.10-14, 23-38; 4.14-30; 5.1-11; 6.20-49; 7.1-10, 11-17, 36-50; 8.1-3; 9.51-56; 10.17-20, 25-37, 38-42; 11.5-8, 27-28, 37-52; 12.13-21; 13.1-9, 10-17, 22-30, 31-33; 14.1-6, 16-24; 15.4-10, 11-32; 16.1-13, 19-31; 17.11-19, 20-37; 18.1-8, 9-14; 19.1-10, 11-27, 39-44; 21.12-15, 37-38; 22.14-23, 31-38; 22.39–24.53. Feine refers to L material as Luke's 'peculiar source' (*eigentümlichen Quellenschrift* or *besondere Quellenschrift*). Although he does not use the term L, for convenience and continuity I will use it in my discussion of Feine. It antedates Weiss's later works, but is slightly later than Weiss's *Einleitung in das Neue Testament*, which gives the general outline of Weiss's later conclusions. On Weiss and Feine, see J. Moffatt, *An Introduction to the Literature of the New Testament* (International Theological Library; New York: Charles Scribner's Sons, 1911), pp. 276-78.

15. Weiss and Feine agree on the following verses: 1.5–2.52; 3.10-14, 23-28; 4.16-30; 5.1-11; 6.20-38, 46-49; 7.1-10, 11-17, 36-50; 8.1-3; 9.51-56; 10.29-37, 38-42; 11.27-28, 37-52; 13.1-9, 10-17; 14.1-6, 16-24; 15.11-32; 16.19-31; 17.11-19; 18.9-14; 19.1-10, 11-27, 39-44; 21.12-15, 37-38; 22.14-23, 31-34; 22.39–24.49; 24.50b-51 (536 verses). That is, 84 per cent of Weiss's list is found in Feine's; 85 per cent of Feine's is found in Weiss's; 74 per cent of the total verses (729 = 536 + 99 only in Weiss's + 94 only in Feine's) are found in both. Their agreement is thus quite close.

16. Feine, *Eine vorkanonische Überlieferung*, pp. 11-12.

17. Feine, *Eine vorkanonische Überlieferung*, pp. 124-26.

finding their way to Luke, Feine thinks that they can still be separated and analyzed individually. In his reconstruction, Feine's special Lukan source is subject to the same criticisms as Weiss's L.[18]

The works of Vincent Henry Stanton and J. Vernon Bartlet, appearing almost simultaneously, are essentially more careful and conservative versions of Feine's theory.[19] Both quite rightly note that Feine gave no adequate reason for considering Luke's infancy narrative as being from the same source as the rest of his special material.[20] Stanton goes further, admitting the likelihood that special material in Luke's Passion narrative is his own composition or has been gathered from a number of sources or traditions; he therefore excludes such material from his special source L.[21] The same possibility must be considered for all the rest of the L material.

Finally, there is the elegantly presented but extraordinarily complicated reconstruction of Ernest D.W. Burton.[22] In it there are several overlapping sources composed of L and Q material and it is this extensive overlap between hypothetical sources that makes the reconstruction especially problematic. Despite this however, several later reconstructions are quite similar to Burton's.[23]

None of these early reconstructions of L adequately considers the possibility of Lukan composition for this material, or its origin in a number of sources or traditions; in the present work I will attempt to consider these possibilities much more fully.

---

18. For an early critique of Weiss and especially Feine, see F. Dibelius, 'Die Herkunft der Sonderstücke des Lukas–evangeliums', *ZNW* 12 (1911), pp. 325-43.

19. J.V. Bartlet, 'The Sources of St Luke's Gospel', in W. Sanday (ed.), *Studies in the Synoptic Problem by Members of the University of Oxford* (Oxford: Clarendon Press, 1911), pp. 313-63; Stanton, *Gospels*, II, pp. 220-40. (Bartlet labels his special source S rather than L.)

20. See Stanton, *Gospels*, II, pp. 223-27, 239-40; Bartlet, 'The Sources', p. 358.

21. See Stanton, *Gospels*, II, p. 240.

22. See E.D.W. Burton, *Principles of Literary Criticism and the Synoptic Problem* (Chicago: University of Chicago Press, 1904), esp. his summary, p. 49. His student, A.M. Perry, later harmonized Burton's work with Streeter and Proto-Luke; see below.

23. E.g. B.W. Bacon, 'The "Order" of the Lukan "Interpolations". I. General Survey', *JBL* 34 (1915), pp. 166-79; 'II. The Smaller Interpolation, Lk. 6:20–8:3', *JBL* 36 (1917), pp. 112-39; 'III. The Longer Interpolation, Lk. 9:51–18:14', *JBL* 37 (1918), pp. 20-53; E. Schweizer, 'Eine hebraisierende Sonderquelle des Lukas?', *TZ* 6 (1950), pp. 161-85; W.L. Knox, *The Sources of the Synoptic Gospels. II. St Luke and St Matthew* (Cambridge: Cambridge University Press, 1957), pp. 60-120.

3. *Streeter and Taylor: L, Proto-Luke, and the Author's Identity*

Canon Burnett Hillman Streeter's work has become the best known and most widely accepted solution to the Synoptic problem, and his treatment of L was to have the widest and most lasting influence.[24] Streeter's theory is that Luke did indeed use Mark, but not as his primary source. Rather, Luke produced a first edition of his Gospel—Proto-Luke—out of the two sources L and Q. Only later did he insert material from Mark into this framework. Streeter's reasons for this proposal are suggestive even now: 1) non-Markan and Markan material occur in blocks in Luke, and there is more non-Markan material than Markan;[25] 2) Lk. 3.1 and the placement of Jesus' genealogy are curious as the Gospel now stands, but much more harmonious if it originally began at 3.1;[26] 3) Luke preferred L/Q material over Mark.[27] Proto-Luke stands or falls on the validity of these reasons, which I will briefly address here.

First, to note the quantity or alternation of Markan and non-Markan material is to an extent already to prejudge the issue. The volume of non-Q material in the Gospel is greater than that of Q material; the volume of non-L material is greater than the L. Non-Q material alternates with Q material; non-L material alternates with L material. None of this can be used to support the supposed link between L and Q or the secondary status of Mark.[28] Streeter's further observation that Luke begins and ends with non-Markan material is even less relevant to any theory of the secondary status of Mark. Mark's Gospel had no infancy narrative or resurrection appearances: since they necessarily could not be inserted anywhere else in the story, if Luke was to add them, he would have to begin and end with non-Markan material.

As for Streeter's second reason, I will say that the present placement of Lk. 3.1 does seem odd to me even now. But even if one were to grant that the infancy narrative may be secondary to Luke, this would say

---

24. For his earliest statement, see B.H. Streeter, 'Fresh Light on the Synoptic Problem', *HJ* 20 (1921-22), pp. 103-12; for his fullest presentation, see his *The Four Gospels: A Study of Origins. Treating of the Manuscript Tradition, Sources, Authorship, and Dates* (London: Macmillan; New York: St Martin's, 1924), pp. 199-222.

25. Streeter, 'Fresh Light', p. 106; *Four Gospels*, pp. 208-209.

26. Streeter, 'Fresh Light', pp. 106-107; *Four Gospels*, p. 209.

27. Streeter, 'Fresh Light', pp. 107-108; *Four Gospels*, pp. 209-12.

28. Cf. C.S. Petrie, 'The Proto-Luke Hypothesis', *ExpTim* 54 (1942–43), pp. 172-77.

nothing about the secondary nature of Mark, or of the combination of L with Q in a first edition of the Gospel.[29]

Finally, the idea that Luke prefers L/Q material over Mark when there is a parallel can never be more than an argument *ex silentio*, as we can never know how many times Luke has followed the Markan version and rejected the hypothetical non-Markan.[30] Further, many instances in which Luke differs from Mark may more likely be due to Lukan redaction than to parallel sources.[31]

After Streeter's initial statement of Proto-Luke, Vincent Taylor became the most frequent and vocal defender of the theory.[32] In all this, he does not substantially add to the reasons discussed above for believing in Proto-Luke. Taylor's particular contribution to the debate (and the point that he is repeatedly forced to defend) is to lay a much greater emphasis on L as the primary source for Luke's Passion narrative.[33] Taylor's main reason for maintaining the secondary status of Mark in

29. Cf. J.A. Fitzmyer, *The Gospel according to Luke* (AB, 28 and 28a; New York: Doubleday,1981–1985), p. 310.

30. Streeter admits as much: *Four Gospels*, p. 212.

31. This is especially likely in the Passion: see J. Neyrey, *The Passion according to Luke: A Redaction Study of Luke's Soteriology* (Theological Inquiries; New York: Paulist Press, 1985); and M.L. Soards, *The Passion according to Luke: The Special Material of Luke 22* (JSNTSup, 14; Sheffield: Sheffield Academic Press, 1987).

32. See V. Taylor, *Behind the Third Gospel: A Study of the Proto-Luke Hypothesis* (Oxford: Oxford University Press, 1926). Taylor repeatedly takes up the defense of Proto-Luke over a period of more than four decades (see bibliography). He is followed in the main by F.C. Grant, *The Gospels: Their Origin and Their Growth* (New York: Harper & Row, 1957), pp. 129-33.

33. For the case against Luke's use of a non-Markan (Proto-Lukan) Passion narrative, see J.M. Creed, *The Gospel according to St Luke: The Greek Text with Introduction, Notes, and Indices* (London: Macmillan; New York: St Martin's, 1930), p. lviii; *idem*, 'Study of the Proto-Luke Hypothesis', (see n. 5 above); *idem*, 'The Supposed "Proto-Lucan" Narrative of the Trial before Pilate: A Rejoinder', *ExpTim* 46 (1934–35), pp. 378-79; S.M. Gilmour, 'A Critical Re-examination of Proto-Luke', *JBL* 67 (1948), pp. 143-52; J.W. Hunkin, 'The Composition of the Third Gospel, with Special Reference to Canon Streeter's Theory of Proto-Luke', *JTS* 28 (1926–27), pp. 250-62; G.D. Kilpatrick, 'A Theme of the Lucan Passion Story and Luke xxiii. 47', *JTS* 43 (1942), pp. 34-36; C.S. Petrie, 'The Proto-Luke Hypothesis: Observations on Dr Vincent Taylor's Rejoinder', *ExpTim* 55 (1943-44), pp. 52-53. Taylor's supporters in this are much fewer: R.P.C. Hanson, 'Does δίκαιος in Luke xxiii. 47 explode the Proto-Luke Hypothesis?', *Hermathena* 60 (1942), pp. 74-78; P. Winter, 'Lucan Sources', *ExpTim* 68 (1956-57), p. 285; *idem*, 'Sources of the Lucan Passion Narrative', *ExpTim* 68 (1956-57), p. 95.

Luke's Passion narrative is that the verbal agreement is lower here than elsewhere in Luke's Gospel, while the agreement in order is closer than elsewhere in the Gospel.[34] Both of these reasons have been explained without recourse to a hypothetical non-Markan Passion narrative,[35] though it should be noted that many critiques of Proto-Luke were even more problematic.[36] When Taylor is finally forced to admit the possibility that Proto-Luke may not have contained a Passion narrative, one of the main reasons for supporting the hypothesis falls away.[37]

On one problematic point, Taylor does distance himself somewhat from Streeter. Streeter had speculated that L consists of the recollections of Luke, the travelling companion of Paul, who later produced Proto-Luke by combining his own work with Q.[38] Taylor, although he also endorses the indentification, distances himself and Proto-Luke from it by showing that such an identification is superfluous to the theory.[39] However, the damage was already done: Proto-Luke and L are still thought to stand or fall based on the validity of Streeter's identification of their author.[40] L has even been thought to be disproven as a source because the document could not have survived the shipwreck of Acts 27.[41] Since Streeter, his easily discounted speculation about the

34. See V. Taylor, 'Is the Proto-Luke Hypothesis Sound?', *JTS* 29 (1927–28), pp. 147-55, esp. pp. 148-51.

35. See the criticisms of Hunkin, 'Composition of the Third Gospel', pp. 256-57; and Creed, 'A Study of Proto-Luke', p. 104.

36. E.g. M. Goguel, 'Luke and Mark: With a Discussion of Streeter's Theory', *HTR* 26 (1933), pp. 1-55, who suggests a pre-Markan Passion narrative used independently by Mark and Luke. For a similar formulation, see also A.M. Perry, 'An Evangelist's Tabellae: Some Sections of Oral Tradition in Luke', *JBL* 48 (1929), pp. 206-32; *idem*, 'Luke's Disputed Passion Source', *ExpTim* 46 (1934–35), pp. 256-60. (See bibliography for other works by Perry.) See also the critique of Goguel and Perry by J.M. Creed, 'Proto-Lucan Narrative', pp. 378-79.

37. Taylor finally admits this in 'Important Hypotheses Reconsidered: The Proto-Luke Hypothesis', *ExpTim* 67 (1955-56), pp. 12-16.

38. See Streeter, *The Four Gospels*, pp. 218-22. On the identity of the author of L, see also E.P. Dickie, 'The Third Gospel: A Hidden Source', *ExpTim* 46 (1934-35), pp. 326-30, who identifies L as an *anti*-Christian source written by Pharisees; he is followed in this reconstruction by W.J. Fournier, 'The Third Gospel: A Hidden Source', *ExpTim* 46 (1934–35), p. 428.

39. Taylor, *Behind the Third Gospel*, p. 213.

40. E.g. Fitzmyer, *Luke*, p. 91.

41. H. Montefiore, 'Does "L" Hold Water?', *JTS* 12 (1961), pp. 59-60.

author of L has helped keep it from being seriously considered as a possible source.

Historically, connection with the two problematic hypotheses of Proto-Luke and the author's identity has doomed L from being taken seriously as a possible source. However, to deny these two hypotheses does not deny the possibility that some of the material found only in Luke is from a source. There is no intrinsic reason why denying that L material came from Paul's travelling companion would disprove an L source for Luke's Gospel, any more than denying the similar notion that the Gospel of Mark is based on the recollections of Peter would disprove it as a source for Luke (or Matthew): speculation as to the authorship of a hypothetical source is not intrinsic to the plausibility of that source. Similarly, to deny Proto-Luke would not seem to disprove an L source for Luke, any more than it would disprove Q as a source: one can deny Proto-Luke with no prejudice towards the existence or non-existence of either or both of its two possible components. The fact that Streeter and Taylor, whose work is the most well-known and influential dealing with L, came at the end of a century of often less than satisfying source criticism—both of the Gospels and the Pentateuch—certainly further diminished the chance that anyone would approach L anew.[42]

4. Easton, Rehkopf, and Jeremias: The Linguistic Evidence

Intermittently during this century, others have attempted to recover a special Lukan source by using linguistic evidence.[43] Such attempts have

42. Cf. the summary of Streeter by S. Neill and T. Wright, *The Interpretation of the New Testament 1861–1986* (Oxford: Oxford University Press, 2nd edn, 1988), p. 135.

43. The most notable attempts at such vocabulary studies have been B.S. Easton: 'Linguistic Evidence for the Lucan Source L', *JBL* 29 (1910), pp. 139-80; *idem*, 'The Special Source of the Third Gospel', *JBL* 30 (1911), pp. 78-103; *idem, The Gospel according to St Luke: A Critical and Exegetical Commentary* (New York: Charles Scribner's Sons, 1926), esp. pp. xxiii-xxx; more recently, F. Rehkopf, *Die lukanische Sonderquelle: Ihr Umfang und Sprachgebrauch* (Tübingen: Mohr, 1959); and J. Jeremias, *Die Sprache des Lukasevangeliums: Redaktion und Tradition im Nicht–Markusstoff des dritten Evangeliums* (Göttingen: Vandenhoeck & Ruprecht, 1980). Schweizer's 'Eine hebraisierende Sonderquelle' is also based primarily on linguistic data; see n. 23 above. All of these will be dealt with much more thoroughly in Chapter 3 below.

failed to convince, primarily because they consider far too much material: to say that some characteristic of vocabulary or style is pre-Lukan because it occurs nowhere else in Luke–Acts is only convincing if the block of material considered is fairly limited. If it is not, then the simple objection can be made that points of style or vocabulary that are scattered throughout the Gospel are more plausibly from Luke, the final redactor, than from a hypothetical source that included all of this disparate material.[44] The flaw in their methodology is made most explicit by one of their criteria for considering a word or construction pre-Lukan: they consider it pre-Lukan if it occurs only (or commonly) in the non-Markan material.[45] But this is already to assume two rather unlikely possibilities: that everything which is non-Markan is therefore pre-Lukan, and that a number of pre-Lukan sources coincidentally shared vocabulary and style.[46] In my treatment of vocabulary and style (Chapter 3), I will examine a much smaller body of material, and with the stricter criterion that points of style and vocabulary are likely to be pre-Lukan only if they are characteristics that Luke deliberately omits in his redaction of Mark and Q.

5. *Current Use of the Term L: A Representative Sample*

The use of the term L today is most often ambiguous. Some, such as C.F. Evans and S. Maclean Gilmour, state explicitly that L was probably not one single source.[47] However, they then go on to describe the characteristics of the material, as though it was from some single, homogenous source.[48] If it is probable that this material is from a variety of sources, why would one look for commonalities within the material? If L is a source, then it would have characteristics; but if it is a number of sources, then commonalities would more likely have been

44. This is the main point of the extended attack on Rehkopf and Jeremias in Goulder, *New Paradigm*, I, pp. 79-86. For another critique of Rehkopf, see H. Schürmann, 'Protolukanische Spracheigentümlichkeiten? Zu Fr. Rehkopf, Die lukanische Sonderquelle: Ihr Umfang und Sprachgebrauch', *BZ* 5 (1961), pp. 266-86.

45. See Rehkopf, *Die lukanische Sonderquelle*, p. 87, criterion 4; and Jeremias, *Die Sprache*, p. 8, criterion 5.

46. Cf. Goulder, *New Paradigm*, I, pp. 81-82.

47. C.F. Evans, *Saint Luke* (TPI New Testament Commentaries; London: SCM Press, 1990), p. 28; Gilmour, 'Luke', p. 14.

48. Evans, *Luke*, pp. 28-29; Gilmour, 'Luke', pp. 14-15.

imposed upon it by the final redactor.

Joseph Fitzmyer is more reticent about saying anything definite about L. In his commentary on Luke, Fitzmyer does give a list of L passages.[49] Furthermore, he often uses the term L in a way that seems to designate a real source of some kind, for example, 'In the main this episode is derived from Luke's private source, "L"'.[50] But this is only after he has given the caveat in his introduction that it is not to be thought of as a source in any real sense.[51] Nor does Fitzmyer give any characteristics of this 'source'. His use of the term is perhaps the most non-committal.

Koester does go further and specifically states that L does not designate a source. His main reason for denying that L may have been a source is because of the quantity of material he lists in L, both in sheer amount, but more especially because it is so formally heterogenous.[52] L stands for Luke's 'special material' rather than his 'special source' (*Sondergut*, not *Sonderquelle*). But if the amount and formal heterogeneity of the material are Koester's chief objections to the possibility of a single source, then these could be eliminated by considering a much smaller body of material. Koester in fact is quite ready to admit the probability that some of the L material existed in pre-Lukan collections, though he does not specify their contents.[53]

A critique of L for which there could be no such *rapprochement* is that of Michael D. Goulder, who denies the two-source hypothesis entirely.[54] His solution to the Synoptic problem is that Mark was indeed first; Matthew expanded on Mark; finally, Luke composed his Gospel with both Matthew and Mark in front of him.[55] Therefore everything in Luke's Gospel is explained by Goulder as Lukan redaction or midrashic

49. Fitzmyer, *Luke*, pp. 83-84.

50. Fitzmyer, *Luke*, p. 656. Even more provocative is the casual comment of E. Haenchen, *Die Apostelgeschichte* (MeyerK Abt. 3; 13th edn; Göttingen: Vandenhoeck & Ruprecht, 1961), p. 73, when he refers to a 'Gospel' behind the special material: '. . . jenem Evangelium, aus dem er sein Sondergut entnommen hat'.

51. Fitzmyer, *Luke*, p. 83.

52. Koester, *Ancient Christian Gospels*, pp. 336-37.

53. Koester, *Ancient Christian Gospels*, p. 337; similarly, cf. Marshall, *Luke*, p. 31; and Giles, '"L" Tradition', pp. 431-32.

54. See n. 2 above.

55. His solution is the same as that offered by A.M. Farrer, 'On Dispensing with Q', in D.E. Nineham (ed.), *Studies in the Gospels: Essays in Memory of R.H. Lightfoot* (Oxford: Basil Blackwell, 1955), pp. 55-88.

embellishment of Matthew, Mark, or the LXX. This hypothesis, it must be granted, does give Luke a high degree of authorial creativity and originality: we are asked to believe that Luke created the longest parable in the New Testament, the Prodigal Son (Lk. 15.11-32), out of Matthew's terse parable of a father with two children (Mt. 21.28-32), which also has a completely different point.[56] Despite such extreme examples, I am in general sympathetic to Goulder's hypothesis on this point: the Synoptics in general and Luke in particular have often been unfairly denied any originality. But Goulder's radical solution buys us Lukan creativity at the expense of Lukan sensibility and coherence. Awkward transitions, which are explained by most as redactional 'seams' where a source has been included but not fully adapted to the new work, are explained by Goulder simply as Lukan artlessness or 'muddle'.[57] For this reason, as well as the fact that the consensus has still not been noticeably shaken,[58] I here maintain and will work under the assumptions of the two-source hypothesis, though I will relate my work to that of Goulder where it is possible.

Recently, Petzke's commentary on 'S^{Lk}', although it has been taken to suggest the existence of a special Lukan source, in fact sidesteps the issue.[59] Petzke, like Fitzmyer and most others, does not decide on the origin of the L material.[60] Since he is primarily concerned with showing how the hand of Luke, the final redactor, can be seen in L material, his approach is certainly justified.[61]

---

56. Goulder, *New Paradigm*, II, pp. 609-18.

57. E.g. Goulder, *New Paradigm*, II, p. 490. It seems quite likely that one would become 'muddled' by trying to harmonize and integrate different traditions, but far less likely that one would become so in writing one's own original work.

58. On the continued momentum or unshakeableness of the two-source hypothesis, see M.D. Goulder, 'Is Q a Juggernaut?', *JBL* 115 (1996), pp. 667-81.

59. G. Petzke, *Das Sondergut des Evangelium nach Lukas* (Zürcher Werkkommentare zur Bibel; Zürich: Theologische Verlag, 1990); cf. F. Bovon, 'Studies in Luke–Acts: Retrospect and Prospect', *HTR* 85 (1992), pp. 175-96.

60. His discussion shows his ambiguity towards the *Sondergut*: he reproduces Streeter's chart, with S^{Lk} and S^{Mt} printed next to Mark and Q, implying that S^{Lk} is a source like Mark or Q, but goes on to explain that this is most likely not the case: 'Die Mehrheit der Forscher neigt heute zu der Auffassung, daß das Sondergut keine einheitliche Quelle war' (Petzke, *Sondergut*, p. 13).

61. See Petzke, *Sondergut*, pp. 209-54.

6. *A New Examination: Its Value and Methodology*

We are left then with an ambiguous use of the term L. Since Streeter and Taylor, L's connection with the problematic assumptions of Proto-Luke and the author's identity seems to have rendered it doomed not to be taken seriously as a source ever again. My proposal is that without this problematic baggage, and by limiting the examination to a much smaller body of material, we can now determine how much of the L material is pre-Lukan, how much of that material is probably from a single source, and the characteristics of that source. With such a source we will have recovered a voice from earliest Christianity effectively muted or transformed by its incorporation into the larger work of Luke. In short, one of the 'many' predecessors whom Luke acknowledges at Lk. 1.1 will finally be heard in his own right. We will recognize and better understand another trajectory or development of a tradition in earliest Christianity.

Further, although my interests are not primarily in the historical Jesus, a pre-Lukan source for some of this material will give us a source of Jesus traditions at least as old as Mark, and perhaps as old as Q. Those who do insist on pursuing the historical Jesus in the future will have to take note of this.[62]

To determine the probability that a source lies behind some of the L material, the material will be examined to determine two qualities: 1) the extent to which it differs from what we might have expected had Luke composed it himself; and 2) the degree to which the L material shows signs of internal similarities. The first of these qualities will be determined by comparison with Luke's authorial habits as observed

---

62. Although much of the L material is already judged as historically reliable, I believe that its origin in a very early source will help to counter the ascendancy of Q in historical Jesus reconstructions, especially Q as a depiction of Jesus the Cynic. On this view of Jesus and Q, see F.G. Downing, 'Quite Like Q—a Genre for Q: the Lives of the Cynic Philosophers', *Bib* 69 (1988), pp. 196-225; *idem, Christ and the Cynics: Jesus and other Radical Preachers in First Century Tradition* (Sheffield: Sheffield Academic Press, 1988); *idem, Cynics and Christian Origins* (Edinburgh: T. & T. Clark, 1992), esp. pp. 115-42; the respectability of this view has been greatly increased by its inclusion in Crossan, *Historical Jesus*, pp. 421-22. For critiques, see C.M. Tuckett, 'A Cynic Q?', *Bib* 70 (1989), pp. 349-76; and P.R. Eddy, 'Jesus as Diogenes? Reflections on the Cynic Jesus Thesis', *JBL* 115 (1996), pp. 449-69.

in his redaction of Mark, Q, and in his work in Acts. If an L pericope contains a characteristic that Luke routinely omits in his redaction of Mark (for example, the historical present, a reference to Jesus' emotions, and so on), this will be taken as increasing the likelihood that this L pericope is pre-Lukan; on the other hand, if an L pericope contains a theme that Luke shows a particular preference for throughout his work (for example, Jubilary theology), this will be taken as diminishing the likelihood that this L pericope is pre-Lukan. Throughout the examination, it will be assumed that Luke has treated this material (whatever its origin) in a similar way to material elsewhere in his double work. It is perhaps most important to note that all such dissimilarities to Luke's own writing will be taken as cumulative or corroborative throughout the work. Such a process of delimiting the L material—a kind of reversal of redaction criticism in the service of source criticism—will be the primary goal of Chapter 2, purely a matter of eliminating L material from consideration.

The homogeneity of the L pericopae will be considered alongside their dissimilarity to Luke's own hand in Chapters 3–5. These chapters will attempt to detect a 'family resemblance' among the L pericopae, while showing that Luke himself is most likely not the father of such similarities. Chapter 3 will still be primarily negative, in that it will eliminate from further consideration those L pericopae that show no noticeable stylistic differences from Luke's own style elsewhere. Chapters 4 and 5, however, will be primarily positive, examining similarities of form and content among the L pericopae. The *possibility* that a source lies behind some of the L material will be tilted in the direction of *probability* by highlighting similarity of style, vocabulary, form, and/or content in some L material, as long as it is also shown that these characteristics are not typical of the rest of Luke–Acts.

Even with such a 'family resemblance' among some of the L material, coupled with significant departures from Luke's own preferences, the question of the nature of such a source still needs to be addressed (Chapter 6). The source's structure and organization will be elaborated, the implications of its residual orality will be discussed and its generic resemblance to other works will be suggested. Finally, its probable origin will be reconstructed as far as possible.

To end this discussion of methodology, it may be appropriate to compare the present work with some other recent source-critical works. The proposed approach is similar to some of John S. Kloppenborg's recent work on Q.[63] In his *Formation of Q*, Kloppenborg attempted to find the consistency and redactional interests of a pre-Gospel tradition, and thereby to increase the probability of its existence. Although I do not accept all of his statements about the different redactional levels within Q (Q^1, Q^2, Q^3),[64] his work does show that observing a 'family resemblance' in a collection of material increases the likelihood of its being from a single written source. In the case of Q, this increased what was already acknowledged to be a probability for other reasons. In the case of L, the resemblance will necessarily have to function as the primary criterion to increase a possibility into a probability, as we have no other surviving document against which to check our reconstruction.

Finally, to compare the present work with another type of source criticism, the situation with Luke's sources is not nearly as precarious as it is with Pentateuchal source criticism, which has had to rely solely on internal observations, and is now in increasing disarray.[65] The fact that Luke used sources is virtually undisputed, and even the identity of two of those sources is widely accepted. Further, we have a second work written by Luke; although it most likely incorporates material from sources, those sources are certainly not the same as those of the Gospel, and therefore commonalities between the Gospel and Acts can be used to show us the characteristics of Luke's own hand. There was never anything analogous in Pentateuchal source criticism to this kind of consensus on sources; nor is there another extant work known to be written

63. J.S. Kloppenborg, *The Formation of Q: Trajectories in Ancient Wisdom Collections* (Studies in Antiquity and Christianity; Philadelphia: Fortress Press, 1987).

64. Although he distinguished the redactional strata of Q in his *Formation of Q*, Kloppenborg began using the superscript numbers only more recently: see his 'Literary Convention, Self-Evidence and the Social History of the Q People', *Semeia* 55 (1991), pp. 77-102. See also the critiques by C.M. Tuckett, 'On the Stratification of Q: A Response', *Semeia* 55 (1991), pp. 213-22; and H.W. Attridge, 'Reflections on Research into Q', *Semeia* 55 (1991), pp. 223-34. I will reassure the reader at the beginning that there will be no L^1, L^2, or L^3 in the present work.

65. The standard J/E/D/P source criticism was rejected at least as early as 1967 by M.H. Segal, *The Pentateuch: Its Composition and its Authorship* (Jerusalem: Hebrew University, Magnes Press, 1967), pp. 4-21. See more recently J. Blenkinsopp, *The Pentateuch: An Introduction to the First Five Books of the Bible* (AB Reference Library; Garden City, NY: Doubleday, 1992), pp. 19-28; also D. Garrett, *Rethinking Genesis: The Sources and Authorship of the First Book of the Pentateuch* (Grand Rapids: Baker Book House, 1991), pp. 18-33.

by the author of the Pentateuch.[66] By examining Luke's use of Mark and Q, as well as his authorial methods as shown in Acts, we can begin to know and then to isolate Lukan style and interests in a way that was never possible in Pentateuchal source criticism. Therefore, our conclusions on L should be considered more reliable than those that have long been accepted about J, E, D, or P.

66. The situation would only be analogous if two of the sources of the Pentateuch were known and existed independently, and the other two were reconstructed; and further, if we possessed a sequel to the Pentateuch which we knew was written by the same author, using sources different from J, E, D, and P.

Chapter 2

LIMITING THE MATERIAL TO BE CONSIDERED

First of all, we must never lose sight of the fact that the Bible is not a single nor even a homogeneous book. The Bible is, strictly speaking, not a book but a library.

—F.W. Farrar[1]

1. *Introduction*

As indicated in Chapter 1, one of the points that has greatly discouraged research into the origin of L material has been the improbably large amount of material that some have claimed for it. The goal of the present chapter is therefore to delimit the material that may then be considered as possibly from a single, pre-Lukan source.

This process of delimitation will proceed by eliminating all material that is more easily explained as Lukan redaction of Mark, Q, or Luke's free composition (or redaction so heavy that the pre-Lukan tradition is effectively irrecoverable); only in those pericopae where such an explanation is questionable or problematic will the material continue to be considered. The delimiting process will consider the Gospel in the following sections: the infancy narrative, the Passion and resurrection stories, and the remainder of the material in Luke 3–19.[2]

2. *Material in the Infancy Narrative*

As noted in Chapter 1, much of the early work on L (Feine and Weiss) relies heavily on the infancy narrative as part of the source; on the other

---

1.   F.W. Farrar, *The Bible: Its Meaning and Supremacy* (New York: Longmans, Green, 1897), p. 25.
2.   Cf. the similar division and discussion of L material in Gilmour, 'St Luke', p. 14; Stanton, *Gospels*, II, pp. 220-21; and Grant, *Gospels*, pp. 47-48, 61-62.

hand, later and equally important researchers (Streeter and Taylor) base their idea of L on the exclusion of material from the infancy narrative. Although both of these reconstructions have been shown to be ultimately unsatisfactory, the inclusion of material from the infancy narrative in a reconstruction of a source L is the more problematic.

Much of the infancy narrative most probably derives from Luke himself.[3] Luke's infancy narrative is a very long and carefully worked piece, both internally and in its integration into the larger work, and in this way it differs markedly from L material (whatever its origin) in the rest of the Gospel, which is brief, scattered, and often awkwardly inserted.[4] Whatever the source(s) of the infancy narrative, it is manifestly different in style and tone from the rest of the gospel, and there is therefore no reason to believe that it derives from the same source(s) as the rest of the material labelled L.[5] Where there are similarities between the material from the infancy narrative and L material in the rest of the Gospel, these would more plausibly be from the hand of Luke, rather than from a hypothetical source that included both an infancy narrative and an account of Jesus' ministry.[6] Further, without endorsing the Proto-Luke hypothesis, there is still the possibility that the infancy narrative was incorporated by Luke later than (and separate from) his other sources.[7] Material from the infancy narrative will thus not be considered as possibly from the same source(s) as the L material in the rest of the Gospel.

3.   On Lukan creativity in the infancy narrative and its integration into Luke's work, see P.S. Minear, 'Luke's Use of the Birth Stories', in L.E. Keck and J.L. Martyn (eds.), *Studies in Luke–Acts* (Nashville: Abingdon Press, 1966), pp. 111-30; Fitzmyer, *Luke*, p. 309; H. Hendrickx, *The Infancy Narratives* (Studies in the Synoptic Gospels; London: Geoffrey Chapman, rev. edn, 1984), pp. 1-7, 53-62; Brown, *Birth of the Messiah*, pp. 239-50. On the hymns as pre-Lukan, see S. Farris, *The Hymns of Luke's Infancy Narratives: Their Origin, Meaning and Significance* (JSNTSup, 9; Sheffield: JSOT Press, 1985), pp. 14-98.

4.   Cf. Grant, *Gospels*, p. 132.

5.   Cf. Fitzmyer, *Luke*, p. 83.

6.   On this point, I am essentially in agreement with Goulder, *New Paradigm*, I, pp. 81-82.

7.   See Fitzmyer, *Luke*, p. 310. The secondary nature of the infancy narrative solves the question of the placement of Lk. 3.1-2 and the genealogy (Lk. 3.23-38). It may also solve a perceived dissonance between Lk. 4.22 and Luke 1–2: see Grant, *Gospels*, p. 132; and Fitzmyer, *Luke*, p. 535.

3. *Material in the Passion and Resurrection Stories*

Much the same reasoning holds for special material in the Passion. Postulating a variant version of the Passion available to Luke would explain the differences between his Passion account and Mark's; but the independent conclusions of Neyrey and Soards that a variant Passion account is not necessary to explain the differences between the Lukan and Markan accounts should warn us that even a variant Passion source is a problematic assumption.[8] Further, a point in favor of a variant Passion account is that it could also explain agreements between Luke and John as their independent use of the same (or similar) source(s); the simpler explanation that John knew Luke directly, however, has been gaining new acceptance.[9] If this continues, another point in favor of a variant account behind Luke's Passion narrative will have dissipated.

It is more important for the present work, however, to note that even if Luke did make use of an account of the Passion other than Mark's, there is no reason to assume that such material is from the same source(s) as L material in the rest of the Gospel. Furthermore, L material, like Q, does not specifically refer to Jesus' suffering and death. Therefore, whether L material (or its audience) knew or included traditions about Jesus' Passion will probably have to remain an open question, much as it has remained undecided in Q research.[10] In short, Luke probably did not have any source other than Mark for his Passion narrative; and even if he did, it was more than likely from some other source(s) than that of the L material in the rest of the Gospel.

8.   See Chapter 1 n. 31.

9.   The suggestion of direct Johannine dependence on Luke goes at least as far back as Streeter, *Four Gospels*, pp. 401-408. More recently, see J.A. Bailey, *The Traditions Common to the Gospels of Luke and John* (Leiden: Brill, 1963); and T.L. Brodie, *The Quest for the Origin of John's Gospel: A Source-Oriented Approach* (New York: Oxford University Press, 1993). For the position of Luke and John independently using similar source(s), see R.E. Brown, *The Gospel according to John* (AB 29 and 29a; Garden City, NY: Doubleday, 1966), pp. xlvi-xlvii; and Fitzmyer, *Luke*, pp. 87-89. For a good history of the debate, see D. Moody Smith, *John among the Gospels: The Relationship in Twentieth Century Research* (Minneapolis: Fortress Press, 1992), pp. 85-110, 180-85.

10.   See the discussion by Kloppenborg, *Formation of Q*, pp. 8-40.

4. *L Material in the Rest of the Gospel (Luke 3–19)*

Having excluded material in the infancy narrative and the Passion, we are now left to consider how much of the L material in the rest of Luke's Gospel may be from a source(s). For the sake of simplicity, I have chosen to start by considering all verses in Luke 3–19 that are listed by Weiss or Feine as from the source L; since they are the most generous in assigning material to the hypothetical source, it is unlikely that they excluded anything that may be worthy of consideration.[11]

Delimiting this material will be done in three steps. First, some of the material will be examined to determine the likelihood that it is in fact Lukan redaction of Mark.[12] Similarly, some of the remaining material will be examined to determine whether it is more likely from Q than from elsewhere.[13] Finally, the remainder of the L material will be examined to eliminate those pericopae or parts of pericopae that are more likely Lukan composition, including those composed as redactional connections or transitions for pre-Lukan material.

4.1. *Lukan Redaction of Mark?*
Several pericopae or parts of pericopae attributed to L are possibly Lukan redaction of Markan material.[14] Some of these can quite easily be removed from consideration as part of a non-Markan source, because

11.   See Chapter 1 nn. 7 and 14. This gives a total of 407 verses: Lk. 3.10-14, 23-38; 4.14-30; 5.1-11; 6.20-49; 7.1-10, 11-17, 36-50; 8.1-3; 9.43-45, 51-56, 61-62; 10.1, 17-20, 25-37, 38-42; 11.5-8, 27-28, 37-54; 12.1a, 13-21, 33-34, 35-38, 49-53; 13.1-9, 10-17, 22-30, 31-33; 14.1-6, 7-14, 15-24, 25-27, 28-33; 15.1-3, 4-10, 11-32; 16.1-13, 14-15, 19-31; 17.3-10, 11-19, 20-37; 18.1-8, 9-14, 31-34; 18.43b–19.10; 19.11-28, 37-44, 47-48.

12.   On this material, see T. Schramm, *Der Markus-Stoff bei Lukas: Eine literarkritische und redaktionsgeschichtliche Untersuchung* (Cambridge: Cambridge University Press, 1971).

13.   See the reconstructions of Q in R.A. Edwards, *A Theology of Q: Eschatology, Prophecy, and Wisdom* (Philadelphia: Fortress Press, 1976), pp. xi-xiii; W. Schenk, *Synopse zur Redenquelle der Evangelien: Q-Synopse und Rekonstruktion in deutscher Übersetzung mit kurzen Erläuterungen* (Düsseldorf: Patmos, 1981); A. Polag, contained in I. Havener, *Q: The Sayings of Jesus* (Wilmington, DE: Michael Glazier, 1987), pp. 117-22; J.S. Kloppenborg, *Q Parallels: Synopsis, Critical Notes, & Concordance* (Foundations and Facets Reference Series; Sonoma, CA: Polebridge, 1988), pp. xxxi-xxxiii; and Koester, *Ancient Christian Gospels*, pp. 128-71.

14.   Those most likely to be part of this category are Lk. 4.16-30; 5.1-11; 7.36-50; 9.43-45; 10.25-37; 12.1a; 18.31-34; 19.34-44, 47-48.

they are widely acknowledged to be Lukan redaction of Mark.[15] Rather than treating the material strictly in order, I will eliminate these first. Those verses whose origin is more difficult to determine will follow.

4.1.1. *The Pericopae More Easily Removed from Consideration*

Lk. 9.43-45–the Second Passion Prediction. Weiss places this passage immediately after the ministering women (Lk. 8.1-3) in his reconstruction of L.[16] The placement is odd indeed when looked at closely: following on the actions of the women listed in Lk. 8.1-3, since Jesus has not done anything, at what are the people here 'astonished' (9.43a), and why are they 'marveling' (9.43b) at his actions? Lk. 9.43a is obviously the conclusion to the previous pericope (Lk. 9.37-43a), and shows signs of Lukan redaction in its similarities to other Lukan conclusions to miracles.[17] As for the other verses, there are noticeable differences between Luke's version of the second Passion prediction (Lk. 9.43b-45) and Mark's (Mk 9.30-32).[18] But the agreements in order—both of elements within the pericope and of the pericope's placement at this point in the narrative—show that Mark is still Luke's source here, and to postulate another is unnecessary.[19]

15. Lk. 9.43-45; 18.31-34; 19.34-40, 47-48.

16. Weiss, *Die Quellen der synoptischen Überlieferung*, pp. 118-19.

17. Note the reaction of the crowd (cf. Lk. 4.32; 8.25; 11.14), the glorification of God following a miracle (cf. Lk. 5.26; 7.16; 8.39), and the noun μεγαλειότης (Acts 19.27). See Fitzmyer, *Luke*, p. 810; Goulder, *New Paradigm*, I, pp. 447-48; and Evans, *Luke*, p. 424.

18. That Luke is using Mark here, see Fitzmyer, *Luke*, pp. 812-14; G. Schneider, *Das Evangelium nach Lukas* (Ökumenischer Taschenbuchkommentar zum Neuen Testament; vols. 3/1-2; 2nd edn; Gütersloh: G. Mohn; Würzburg: Echter, 1984), I, pp. 220-21; J. Nolland, *Luke* (WBC, 35a, 35b, and 35c; Dallas: Word Books, 1989) II, pp. 512-14. For a variant version of the pericope, see A. Schlatter, *Das Evangelium des Lukas* (2nd edn; Stuttgart: Calwer Verlag, 1960), pp. 106-107; K.H. Rengstorf, *Das Evangelium nach Lukas* (NTD, 3; Göttingen: Vandenhoeck & Ruprecht, 1967), pp. 126-27; Schramm, *Der Markus-Stoff*, pp. 132-33. Marshall, *Luke*, pp. 392-93, suggests the influence of continuing oral tradition. W.R. Farmer, 'The Passion Prediction Passages and the Synoptic Problem: A Test Case', *NTS* 36 (1990), pp. 558-70, concludes that Luke is following Matthew here and at Lk. 18.31-34.

19. Cf. Evans, *Luke*, p. 425; F. Bovon, *Das Evangelium nach Lukas* (EKKNT; 2 vols.; Zürich: Benziger Verlag, 1989), I, pp. 514-16. Goulder, *New Paradigm*, I, pp. 449-51, also treats this passage as primarily Lukan redaction of Mark (only one word taken from Matthew).

Lk. 18.31-34–the Third Passion Prediction. Much the same reasoning
holds for the third Passion prediction as for the second; again there are
significant differences from the Markan parallel (Mk 10.32-34).[20] However, here again there is agreement with the Markan order, there is
close agreement in wording between vv. 32-33 and Mk 10.33b-34, and
the mention of the Twelve in v. 31 is the first time they have been mentioned since Lk. 9.12, when Luke was following Mark.[21] Given Luke's
use of Mark, the burden of proof is on those who would postulate
another source, and here again that proof is lacking.

Lk. 19.37-40–Jesus' Triumphal Entry. For the first part of Jesus' entry
into Jerusalem (Lk. 19.28-38) there is again no compelling reason to
posit a source other than Mk 11.1-10.[22] The verbal agreement with
Mark is quite close through v. 36; and vv. 37-38, where the agreement
does drop, could hardly have stood on their own without the preceding
verses.[23] Verses 39-40 are more likely to be from a non-Markan
source for two main reasons:[24] 1) the rather abrupt reappearance of the
Pharisees (who have not been mentioned since Lk. 17.20 and disappear
after this for the rest of Luke's Gospel) seems awkward if Luke is freely
redacting Mark, but more understandable if from a source that included
them; 2) the existence of a similar saying in Mt. 21.15-16, though in a
form too dissimilar to attribute the episode to Q.[25] Although suggestive,
I do not think that these points can completely rule out the possibility

20.   For details, see Marshall, *Luke*, pp. 689-91; Fitzmyer, *Luke*, pp. 1207-1208;
Schneider, *Lukas*, II, pp. 372-73; Goulder, *New Paradigm*, II, pp. 672-74.
21.   Cf. Evans, *Luke*, p. 655; L. Sabourin, *L'Evangile de Luc: Introduction et
commentaire* (Rome: Editrice Pontificia Università Gregoriana, 1985), p. 306.
Schramm, *Der Markus-Stoff*, pp. 133-36, again suggests a variant version.
22.   *Pace* H. Patsch, 'Der Einzug Jesu in Jerusalem: Ein historischer Versuch',
ZTK 68 (1971), pp. 1-26, and Schramm, *Der Markus-Stoff*, pp. 145-49; cf. Rengstorf,
Lukas, p. 217; and Schneider, *Lukas*, vol. 2, p. 383.
23.   See Evans, *Luke*, p. 678. Goulder, *New Paradigm*, II, pp. 685-88, argues
that vv. 37-38 are influenced by Mt. 21.15-16: his conclusion is possible for vv. 39-40,
but not here.
24.   See Marshall, *Luke*, p. 709; Fitzmyer, *Luke*, p. 1243; Nolland, *Luke*, p. 922.
Others would also include vv. 37-38 in this: T.W. Manson, *The Sayings of Jesus*
(London: SCM Press, 1949), p. 317; Schlatter, *Lukas*, pp. 408-12.
25.   Or to direct Matthean influence, *pace* Goulder, *New Paradigm*, II, pp. 686-
90: there is no direct verbal agreement, only a general correspondence; nor are the
Pharisees present in Mt. 21.15-16. Also cf. Jn 12.12-16.

that vv. 39-40 are a free Lukan addition to Mk 11.9-10.[26] The likelihood that Lk. 19.39-40 was part of a pre-Lukan source will therefore be considered, although I will include it in brackets to indicate its questionable status.

Lk. 19.47-48, Jesus' Teaching in the Temple. These verses, although noticeably reworded by Luke, are widely ackowledged to be based on Mk 11.18.[27] The result is a typical Lukan summary.[28] The verses also serve the Lukan interest of placing primary responsibility for Jesus' death on the Jerusalem authorities, removing blame from the people at large and also from the Pharisees.[29]

4.1.2. *The Pericopae More Difficult to Determine*

Lk. 4.16-30–Jesus' Inaugural Sermon and Rejection. The sources of this pericope are difficult to determine precisely, because although the episode is obviously a composite, disentangling the various pre-Lukan strands has been done in a number of ways. The most extreme thesis is that of H. Schürmann, who attempts to show that almost all of Lk. 4.14-30 is from Q.[30] However, this and related reconstructions have never commanded significant support.[31] A consensus has therefore emerged, and remained basically unchanged (though not unchallenged) since

---

26. Cf. Creed, *Gospel*, p. 238.

27. Schramm, *Der Markus-Stoff*, p. 149; Marshall, *Luke*, p. 722; Fitzmyer, *Luke*, p. 1269.

28. Cf. Lk. 4.14-15, 31-32, 40; 6.17-19; 8.1; 21.37-38; Acts 2.42-47; 4.32-35; 5.12-16; 6.7; 9.31; 12.24; 16.5; 19.20; 28.30-31.

29. See Goulder, *New Paradigm*, vol. 2, p. 691; Nolland, *Luke*, pp. 939-40.

30. H. Schürmann, 'Der "Bericht vom Anfang": Ein Rekonstruktionsversuch auf Grund von Lk. 4, 14-16', TU 87 (1964), pp. 242-58; *idem*, 'Zur Traditionsgeschichte der Nazareth-Perikope Lk. 4, 16-30', in A. Descamps and A. de Halleux (eds.), *Mélanges bibliques en hommage au R.P. Béda Rigaux* (Gembloux: Duculot, 1970), pp. 187-205. His thesis has been revived by C.M. Tuckett, 'Luke 4,16-30, Isaiah, and Q', in J. Delobel (ed.), *Logia: Les paroles de Jésus—The Sayings of Jesus: Mémorial Joseph Coppens* (Leuven: Leuven University Press, 1982), pp. 343-54.

31. For a good summary of research on the pericope, see C.J. Schreck, 'The Nazareth Pericope: Luke 4,16-30 in Recent Study', in F. Neirynck (ed.), *L'Evangile de Luc: The Gospel of Luke* (rev. edn; BETL, 32; Leuven: Leuven University Press, 1989) pp. 399-471, esp. pp. 403-24. Although not specifically concerned with sources, J. Siker, '"First to the Gentiles": A Literary Analysis of Luke 4:16-30', *JBL* 111 (1992), pp. 73-90, is another good treatment.

Bultmann, that the pericope is adapted from Mk 6.1-6a, with vv. 25-27 as those most likely from another pre-Lukan source.[32] This has been reached more or less by elimination. The episode overall, and vv. 16, 22, and 24 in particular, are most easily explained as derived from Mark.[33] The end of the pericope, vv. 28-30, is widely acknowledged to be Lukan composition;[34] in particular, its language and style are markedly Lukan.[35] Verses 17-21 also exhibit Lukan vocabulary and style.[36] More importantly, they are built around the Isaiah quotation (Isa. 61.1-2; 58.6), and this was most likely done by Luke himself, since they serve the Lukan theme of the Jubilee.[37] Although v. 23 (especially the proverb) is quite likely pre-Lukan,[38] the verse stands somewhat apart conceptually from vv. 25-27: the former sets up a dichotomy between Capernaum and Nazareth, the latter between Israelite and non-Israelite, and the transition between them is unclear.[39] The pre-Lukan origin of vv. 25-27 is further shown by the fact that Luke makes no further use of the apocalyptic implications of the 'three and a half years' in v. 25.[40] Therefore, vv. 25-27 are the only part of Lk. 4.16-30 that can be considered as possibly from a pre-Lukan source with other L material.

32.   See R. Bultmann, *The History of the Synoptic Tradition* (trans. J. Marsh; Oxford: Basil Blackwell, 1963), p. 32. He is followed with little change by R.C. Tannehill, 'The Mission of Jesus according to Luke iv 16-30', in W. Eltester (ed.), *Jesus in Nazareth* (BZNW, 40; Berlin: de Gruyter, 1972), pp. 51-75; Fitzmyer, *Luke*, pp. 526-27; Schneider, *Lukas*, I, pp. 106-107; and Nolland, *Luke*, pp. 191-94.

33.   See Fitzmyer, *Luke*, p. 526.

34.   Goulder, *New Paradigm*, I, pp. 305-306; Nolland, *Luke*, pp. 193-94.

35.   See Tannehill, 'Mission', p. 61; Goulder, *New Paradigm*, I, p. 310.

36.   Tannehill, 'Mission', pp. 64-65.

37.   On this theme, see J.H. Yoder, *The Politics of Jesus* (Grand Rapids: Eerdmans, 1972) pp. 34-40; A. Trocmé, *Jesus and the Nonviolent Revolution* (trans. M.H. Shank and M.E. Miller; Scottdale, PA: Herald Press, 1973), pp. 27-40; R.B. Sloan, *The Favorable Year of the Lord: A Study of Jubilary Theology in the Gospel of Luke* (Austin, TX: Schola Press, 1977).

38.   Particularly since Jesus has not yet been to Capernaum according to Luke; cf. Mk 1.21. Goulder, *New Paradigm*, I, p. 303, attributes the mistake to Luke's 'handling multiple sources'.

39.   See Bultmann, *Synoptic Tradition*, p. 32; Tannehill, 'Mission', p. 59.

40.   See Dan. 7.25; 12.7; Jas 5.17; Rev. 11.2-3; 12.6, 14; 13.5. Cf. Fitzmyer, *Luke*, p. 538. Goulder, *New Paradigm*, I, p. 309, notes the Apocalyptic detail, but not its un-Lukan nature. Cf. also B. Thiering, 'The Three and a Half Years of Elijah', *NovT* 23 (1981), pp. 41-55.

Lk. 5.1-11–the Call of the First Disciples. This story is widely acknowledged to be based in part on Mk 1.16-20. A further source other than
Lukan redaction of Mark is postulated, however, because the episode
has been transposed from its Markan order,[41] and it contains significant
material not found in the Markan account.[42] Further, in the non-Markan
material there are fewer Lukanisms.[43] This hypothesis is further
advanced by the presence of a parallel account in Jn 21.1-14.[44] The
composite nature of the story in its present form is especially shown by
the transitions between various characters.[45] Who exactly is present: a
'crowd' (v. 1), 'fishermen' (v. 2), Simon (vv. 3-5, 8), or James and John
(v. 10)?[46] The simplest explanation of the sources in this pericope seems
to be that vv. 1-3 and 10-11 are based primarily on Mark.[47] To this has
been added a miracle story in vv. 4-9 whose primary character is Peter
(Simon) and whose companions are not named as the sons of Zebedee.[48]
Whether Luke composed this miracle story or inherited it from a non-
Markan source will be considered further.

Lk. 7.36-50–a Sinful Woman Anoints Jesus. Although obviously similar
to Mk 14.3-9, this story is different enough both in its placement and
content to lead to the hypothesis of a variant version available to Luke.[49]

---

41.   See Fitzmyer, *Luke*, p. 560. Goulder, *New Paradigm*, I, pp. 316-28, suggests
that here Luke is following Matthew's order (cf. Mt. 4.18-22). But Luke is following
Markan content and order in both the preceding and following pericopae; under either
hypothesis the order here is problematic.

42.   See Marshall, *Luke*, p. 199.

43.   See Goulder, *New Paradigm*, I, pp. 322-23.

44.   It is significant that Goulder, *New Paradigm*, I, pp. 322-26, concentrates on
showing that John could have borrowed from the Synoptics here: this is interesting, but
tells us nothing more about Luke's sources.

45.   Resulting in shifts between singular and plural verbs in vv. 4 and 5.

46.   Andrew is conspicuously absent from both the Lukan and Johannine
accounts; cf. Mk 1.16.

47.   See R. Pesch, *Der reiche Fischfang: Lk 5, 1-11/Jo 21, 1-14. Wundergeschichte–Berufungserzählung–Erscheinungsbericht* (Düsseldorf: Patmos, 1969),
pp. 53-76; Schramm, *Der Markus-Stoff*, pp. 37-40.

48.   See G. Klein, 'Die Berufung des Petrus', *ZNW* 58 (1967), pp. 1-44; cf.
Nolland, *Luke*, p. 220. Fitzmyer, *Luke*, p. 568, omits v. 9b from the source, because of
a perceived awkwardness in the Greek. I can find no support for this, and why should
Luke's Greek be more awkward than his source's?

49.   The transposition is particularly striking; since this would also be a transposition from the Matthean order, Goulder, *New Paradigm*, I, pp. 397-99, must rely on

The pericope is composite, containing a parable (vv. 41-43) within a controversy story (vv. 36-40, 44-50). Of these verses, vv. 48-50 are widely acknowledged to be Lukan composition based on reminiscences of Mark,[50] particularly because they serve the Lukan interest of transforming the story into a symposium.[51] Of the remainder, the debate has been over which part was added to which: was the parable inserted into the story setting,[52] or did the story grow around the parable?[53] Both of these suggestions have proven unconvincing, and it is now widely accepted that the two parts circulated together.[54] Even if the stories circulated independently at one time, in their present form the two parts seem to rely on one another: the parable needs some narrative setting, while the story without the parable does not address the questions of v. 39, and leaves the reader with the rather unflattering conclusion that Jesus forgives people who are nice to him. Therefore both the story and the parable (vv. 36-47) will be considered as possibly from a pre-Lukan source.

Lk. 10.25-37–the Good Samaritan. The story of the good Samaritan presents great difficulties for precise source determination.[55] Briefly,

his questionable lectionary hypothesis. The similarities to the Johannine tradition here (Jn 12.1-8) are again remarkable: see Brown, *John*, pp. 449-52.

    50.   Mk 2.5-7; cf. Lk. 5.20-21; 8.48. Cf. Schramm, *Der Markus-Stoff*, pp. 43-45.

    51.   For Luke's redactional interests here, especially his making the scene more like a symposium, see J. Delobel, 'L'onction de Jésus par la pécheresse', *ETL* 42 (1966), pp. 415-75; on this and the other symposia in Luke, see G. Sterling, *Historiography and Self-Definition: Josephos, Luke–Acts, and Apologetic Historiography* (Leiden: Brill, 1992), pp. 370-71.

    52.   For long the standard position, following J. Wellhausen, *Das Evangelium Lucae: Übersetzt und Erklärt* (Berlin: Georg Reimer, 1904), pp. 30-32; more recently, G. Braumann, 'Die Schuldner und die Sünderin Luk. vii. 36-50', *NTS* 10 (1963–64), pp. 487-93.

    53.   See Bultmann, *Synoptic Tradition*, pp. 20-21.

    54.   See U. Wilckens, 'Vergebung für die Sünderin', in P. Hoffmann, N. Brox, and W. Pesch (eds.), *Orientierung an Jesus: Zur Theologie der Synoptiker. Für Josef Schmid* (Freiburg: Herder, 1973), pp. 394-424; Marshall, *Luke*, pp. 304-307; Fitzmyer, *Luke*, p. 684; Nolland, *Luke*, pp. 351-52.

    55.   I will here refer to the story as a 'parable' out of convention, without prejudging the issue of formal differences between parable, illustration story, example story, response-parable, or guillotine question, all of which have been suggested in the present case: see Nolland, *Luke*, pp. 588-89. These will be dealt with more thoroughly in Chapter 4.

the origins of the pericope can be explained in the following ways:
1) vv. 25-28 are redacted from Mk 12.28-31 (there may also be influence from Mk 10.17-22) as an introduction to the parable proper, vv. 30-37, which is from some other source; v. 29 is also redactional to connect the two parts;[56] 2) there are enough points of contact with Mt. 22.35-40 in vv. 25-28 either to posit a Q version of the Great Commandment,[57] or direct Matthean influence in vv. 25-28;[58] as with the previous explanation, this has been connected by means of v. 29 to the parable proper; and 3) vv. 25-28 are not similar enough to Mark or Matthew to posit a common source; they are from some other source, although Luke was the first to join them to the parable following.[59]

But whether vv. 25-28 are from Mark, Q, or Matthew does not affect the present work: they are clearly not from another source that connected them with the following parable. There are two reasons for believing that Luke first joined the two parts: 1) if vv. 25-28 are from Mark, Q, or Matthew, then it is clear that none of these sources contained the parable of the Good Samaritan;[60] and 2) v. 29, which connects the two parts, creates a noticeable tension with the idea of 'neighbor' in v. 36.[61] The two parts of Lk. 10.25-37 are therefore most likely not from the same source; Luke was the first to join vv. 25-28 and vv. 30-37 together by means of v. 29.[62]

This eliminates vv. 25-28 from consideration as from a possible written source containing other L material. As for the rest of vv. 29-37, it has already been indicated that v. 29 is most likely redactional.[63] The end

56. Thus E.E. Ellis, *The Gospel of Luke* (NCB; London: Thomas Nelson and Sons, 1966), p. 158; Schneider, *Lukas*, I, p. 247.

57. Thus F.W. Beare, *The Earliest Records of Jesus* (Oxford: Basil Blackwell, 1964), pp. 158-59; Schramm, *Der Markus-Stoff*, pp. 47-49; and J. Lambrecht, *Once More Astonished: The Parables of Jesus* (New York: Crossroad, 1981), pp. 64-65. (The pericope is contained in neither Edwards's, Schenk's, Polag's, Kloppenborg's, nor Koester's reconstruction of Q, however.) There are the usual attempts to explain the versions as two separate sayings of Jesus: see M.J. Lagrange, *Evangile selon Saint Luc* (Paris: Gabalda, 1921), p. 310; Manson, *Sayings*, pp. 259-60; Marshall, *Luke*, p. 441.

58. Thus Goulder, *New Paradigm*, II, pp. 484-87.

59. Fitzmyer, *Luke*, pp. 877, 883.

60. Cf. Lambrecht, *Once More Astonished*, pp. 65-66.

61. Cf. Lambrecht, *Once More Astonished*, p. 66; and Fitzmyer, *Luke*, p. 883.

62. Cf. Nolland, *Luke*, p. 580.

63. Besides the ambiguous meaning of 'neighbor', there is the phrase δικαιῶσαι

of the pericope is harder to decide. For now, we will only eliminate 37b as the most obviously redactional.[64] This leaves Lk. 10.30-37a for later consideration as possibly originating in a non-Markan source.[65]

Lk. 12.1–a Warning to the Disciples. Based on linguistic evidence, the beginning of this verse is most probably Lukan composition.[66] The rest of the verse (strangely included by neither Weiss nor Feine in L) has variously been assigned to Lukan redaction of Mk 8.15,[67] Q,[68] or L.[69] The reason given for postulating its origin in L rather than Mark is the low agreement in words between Luke and Mark: but if one sets aside the beginning of the verse as Lukan composition, then in the actual saying of Jesus Luke reproduces five of the eleven words in Mark. This is 45 per cent, well within Luke's normal redactional habits;[70] there is no reason to postulate a source other than Mark.

Lk. 19.41-44–Jesus' Lament over Jerusalem. The story of Jesus' weeping over Jerusalem is found only here, and is widely acknowledged to

ἑαυτόν which is used again at Lk. 16.15, and the Lukan use of πρός + accusative after a verb of speaking: see H.J. Cadbury, *The Style and Literary Method of Luke* (HTS, 6; Cambridge, MA: Harvard University Press, 1920), p. 203; Fitzmyer, *Luke*, pp. 111, 116; Goulder, *New Paradigm*, II, p. 491; Nolland, *Luke*, p. 592.

64.   It contains the singular imperative πορεύου, found 12 times in Luke–Acts (Lk. 5.24; 7.50; 8.48; 10.37; 13.31; 17.19; Acts 8.26; 9.15; 10.20; 22.10, 21; 24.25), and 'do likewise' found also at Lk. 3.11 and 6.31, elements that also tie it to v. 28: see Lambrecht, *Once More Astonished*, p. 68, Fitzmyer, *Luke*, p. 888; Goulder, *New Paradigm*, II, p. 492; Nolland, *Luke*, p. 596.

65.   Although Lukan composition of vv. 30-37a will still be considered in what follows, I do not consider it likely that Luke composed this story on the basis of Mt. 12.1-14: the connections claimed by Goulder, *New Paradigm*, II, pp. 487-91, are of the most general thematic similarities.

66.   Cf. Lk. 11.29; ἐν οἷς is found only here and Acts 26.12 in the NT; πρός + accusative after a verb of speaking is typically Lukan: see Jeremias, *Die Sprache*, 211; Goulder, *New Paradigm*, II, p. 533.

67.   E.g. Creed, *Luke*, pp. 169-70; Evans, *Luke*, p. 514.

68.   Cf. Mt. 16.6, 11. Thus Schramm, *Die Markus-Stoff*, pp. 49-50; Marshall, *Luke*, p. 510; Schneider, *Lukas*, II, pp. 277-78; Havener (Polag), *Q*, p. 148. The reason given is that Matthew and Luke agree against Mark in their use of προσέχω. Goulder, *New Paradigm*, II, p. 528, attributes the verse to Matthean influence on Luke for the same reason.

69.   Manson, *Sayings*, p. 268; Fitzmyer, *Luke*, p. 953.

70.   Streeter, *Four Gospels*, p. 202, gives Luke's agreement with Mark as 37 per cent in the Passion, 53 per cent elsewhere in the Gospel.

be pre-Lukan tradition.[71] Verses 43-44 are especially un-Lukan in style: Luke regularly eliminates parataxis in his redaction of Mark, while here he has καί six times in two verses.[72] It has been suggested that v. 41 is Lukan because the style is not noticeably un-Lukan,[73] but the reference to Jesus' weeping would be highly uncharacteristic of Luke, who eliminates nearly all references to Jesus' emotions or even his touching of other people in his redaction of Mark.[74] Therefore, all of Lk. 19.41-44 should be considered as possibly from a pre-Lukan source.

4.2. L or Q?

Feine and Weiss are especially quick to assign Q material to L if the Matthean and Lukan versions differ somewhat. Therefore, a great deal of the L material listed above would now be seen by most as from Q.[75] As with the Markan material, I will first treat that which can more easily be removed from consideration,[76] and then consider that for which it is more difficult to decide.[77]

4.2.1. *The Pericopae More Easily Removed from Consideration*

Lk. 6.20-49–the Sermon on the Plain. Almost all of Luke's sermon on the plain is now acknowledged to be from Q, or to be Lukan redaction

71. Schramm, *Der Markus-Stoff*, pp. 146-47; Fitzmyer, *Luke*, p. 1253; Schneider, *Lukas*, II, pp. 388-89.

72. See Cadbury, *Style and Literary Method*, pp. 132-43; Schweizer, 'Eine hebraisierende Sonderquelle', p. 166; Jeremias, *Die Sprache*, pp. 281-82; Fitzmyer, *Luke*, p. 108. Goulder, *New Paradigm*, II, p. 690, does not offer much response with the observation that this passage is a 'sequence of prophecies' and therefore would include abundant parataxis.

73. Thus Marshall, *Luke*, p. 718; Nolland, *Luke*, p. 930; but cf. Jeremias, *Die Sprache*, pp. 281-82; and Fitzmyer, *Luke*, p. 1257.

74. E.g. Lk. 4.39; 5.13, 14; 6.10; 9.11, 22, 42, 48; 18.16, 17, 22; 22.40, 41, 47; 23.46; cf. Cadbury, *Style and Literary Method*, pp. 91-92; Fitzmyer, *Luke*, pp. 94-95.

75. The following verses deserve consideration as to whether they are Q or L: Lk. 3.10-14; 6.20-49; 7.1-10, 18-22a; 9.61-62; 10.1, 17-20; 11.5-8, 27-28, 37-54; 12.13-21, 33-34, 35-38, 49-53; 13.22-30; 14.15-27; 15.4-7, 8-10; 17.3-6, 20-37; 19.11-28.

76. These are Lk. 6.20-49; 7.1-10, 18-22a; 11.37-54; 12.33-34, 49-53; 13.22-30; 14.15-27; 17.3-6.

77. It will be clear that in this section, one's personal solution to the Synoptic problem makes little difference to the present argument: whether one sees Luke as redacting Q or Matthew does not matter, as long as it is agreed that he is probably not following another source L.

of Q.[78] However, there is significant disagreement about the woes (Lk. 6.24-26), which are attributed by some to a source L.[79] But there are a number of other explanations for these verses, any of which are more likely than a separate tradition: 1) the woes were in Q, but were omitted by Matthew;[80] 2) they were in Luke's version of Q (Q_{Lk});[81] 3) they were composed by Luke to complement the beatitudes.[82] All three of these explanations have points in their favor, enough to make the hypothesis of another source unnecessary.[83] Further, the close connection between the beatitudes and the woes makes their origin in two separate sources extremely unlikely.[84] For these reasons, nothing in Lk. 6.20-49 will be considered further.

Lk. 7.1-10–the Healing of the Centurion's Slave. There is almost universal agreement that this pericope came to Luke from Q,[85] although

78.   Thus Manson, *Sayings*, pp. 46-62; Fitzmyer, *Luke*, p. 627; Schenk, *Synopse*, pp. 24-35; D. Zeller, *Kommentar zur Logienquelle* (Stuttgarter Kleiner Kommentar Neues Testament, 21; Stuttgart: Katholisches Bibelwerk, 1986), pp. 26-37; Havener (Polag), pp. 125-27; Kloppenborg, *Q Parallels*, pp. 22-47; Evans, *Luke*, p. 21. Goulder, *New Paradigm*, I, pp. 346-76, must spend a lot of time arguing that Luke is here redacting Matthew's Sermon on the Mount: it is perhaps one of the hardest parts of his thesis to accept.

79.   See Easton, *Luke*, p. xxiii; more recently, Koester, *Ancient Christian Gospels*, p. 338.

80.   E.g. Manson, *Sayings*, p. 49; H. Schürmann, *Das Lukasevangelium* (HTKNT, Band III, t. 1 & 2; Freiburg, Basel, Wien: Herder, 1969), I, pp. 336-41; H. Frankenmölle, 'Die Makarismen (Mt 5, 1-12; Lk 6, 20-23). Motive und Umfang der redaktionellen Komposition', *BZ* 15 (1971), pp. 52-75; J.D. Crossan, *In Fragments: The Aphorisms of Jesus* (San Francisco: Harper & Row, 1983), pp. 169-70.

81.   E.g. C.S. Patton, *Sources of the Synoptic Gospels* (New York: Macmillan, 1915), pp. 194-95.

82.   E.g. J. Dupont, *Les Béatitudes: Le problème littéraire, le message doctrinal* (Bruges: Editions de l'Abbaye de Saint-André, 1954), pp. 104-13; Fitzmyer, *Luke*, p. 627; Bovon, *Lukas*, I, p. 298; Goulder, *New Paradigm*, I, pp. 354-60.

83.   Bovon, *Lukas*, I, p. 298, gives a good summary of the strengths of these solutions.

84.   Cf. Kloppenborg, *Q Parallels*, p. 26.

85.   Patton, *Sources*, pp. 143-45; Creed, *Luke*, p. 100; Manson, *Sayings*, pp. 62-66; S. Schulz, *Q: Die Spruchquelle der Evangelisten* (Zürich: Theologischer Verlag, 1972), pp. 236-46; Fitzmyer, *Luke*, pp. 647-50; Schenk, *Synopse*, pp. 36-39; Schneider, *Lukas*, I, p. 165; Zeller, *Logienquelle*, pp. 37-38; Havener (Polag), *Q*, pp. 127-28; Kloppenborg, *Q Parallels*, p. 50; Bovon, *Lukas*, I, p. 346; Evans, *Luke*, p. 342; Koester, *Ancient Christian Gospels*, p. 138. Dissenters are Easton, *Luke*,

disagreement over the amount of Lukan redaction. There is no solid reason to posit another source for this passage.

Lk. 7.18-22a–John's Question. John the Baptist's question is also almost universally thought to be from Q, although v. 21 is widely acknowledged to be Lukan, and v. 20 may be as well.[86] There is no need to posit another source here.

Lk. 11.37-54–Jesus Denounces Pharisees and Lawyers. Q is usually assumed to lie behind most of this passage, especially vv. 42-52.[87] The beginning (vv. 37-41) and end (vv. 53-54) are more questionable, with various suggestions being offered: 1) Lukan composition of vv. 37-38 and 41, heavy redaction in vv. 39-40, and composition of vv. 53-54;[88] 2) Lukan composition of vv. 37-38, some redaction in vv. 39-41, and Q material in vv. 53-54;[89] 3) Q material throughout vv. 37-54;[90] 4) L

---

pp. 94-97, and U. Wegner, *Das Hauptmann von Kafarnaum* (WUNT, 2.14; Tübingen: Mohr, 1985), who see the pericope as a combination of L and Q. Cf. Goulder, *New Paradigm*, I, pp. 376-80, for the pericope as originating from Matthew.

86.   Patton, *Sources*, p. 152; Easton, *Luke*, pp. 100-101; Creed, *Luke*, pp. 104-106; Manson, *Sayings*, pp. 66-67; Marshall, *Luke*, p. 287; Fitzmyer, *Luke*, pp. 662-63; Schenk, *Synopse*, pp. 40-41; Schneider, *Lukas*, I, pp. 169-70; Zeller, *Logienquelle*, pp. 39-45; Havener (Polag), *Q*, p. 128; Kloppenborg, *Q Parallels*, p. 52; Bovon, *Lukas*, pp. 369-70; Evans, *Luke*, p. 349; Koester, *Ancient Christian Gospels*, p. 138. Cf. Goulder, *New Paradigm*, I, pp. 387-95, on the Lukanisms here (though Goulder again has to rely on his lectionary hypothesis for the placement of this pericope).

87.   Excepting v. 45 as Lukan redaction; thus, with minor variations, Creed, *Luke*, p. 164; Bultmann, *Synoptic Tradition*, pp. 113-14; Marshall, *Luke*, p. 491; Fitzmyer, *Luke*, pp. 942-43; Schenk, *Synopse*, pp. 75-80; Zeller, *Logienquelle*, pp. 65-66; Kloppenborg, *Q Parallels*, pp. 106-15; Nolland, *Luke*, pp. 661-70; Koester, *Ancient Christian Gospels*, pp. 141-44. On the symposium setting, see above on Lk. 7.36-50; see also E.S. Steele, 'Luke 11:37-54: A Modified Hellenistic Symposium?', *JBL* 103 (1984), pp. 379-94. Cf. Goulder, *New Paradigm*, II, pp. 516-28, though the transposition from the Matthean order seems problematic, as does the 'limited' number of 'Matthaeanisms', and the overall conclusion that the Lukan version is 'a series of unhappy alterations' of the Matthean.

88.   Fitzmyer, *Luke*, p. 943; Schenk, *Synopse*, pp. 75-80.

89.   Nolland, *Luke*, pp. 662-69, following H. Schürmann, 'Die Redekomposition wider "dieses Geschlecht" und seine Führung in der Redenquelle (vgl. Mt. 23, 1-39 par Lk. 11, 37-54): Bestand–Akoluthie–Kompositionsformen', *SNTU* 11 (1986), pp. 33-81.

90.   Marshall, *Luke*, p. 491.

material in vv. 37-41 and 53-54.[91] Since Q is not our primary concern, only the last of these hypotheses would affect the present work. Against vv. 37-41 originating in another source, there is noticeable Lukan style in vv. 37 and 39,[92] and the hypothesis requires an extensive and unverifiable overlap between L and M in vv. 39-41. Once vv. 37-41 are eliminated, vv. 53-54 follow, because in the proposed reconstruction they serve as the conclusion to vv. 37-41. Although vv. 53-54 do not display Lukan language, they must be the conclusion to something, so they were either part of Q,[93] or added by Luke as a conclusion to the story;[94] with either explanation the verses were not part of L, and therefore nothing in Lk. 11.37-54 will be considered further.

Lk. 12.33-34–Sayings on Wealth. Although v. 33a is most probably Lukan composition (cf. Lk. 11.41), there is some verbal agreement between v. 33b and Mt. 6.20, while v. 34 and Mt. 6.21 are almost identical. For these reasons, most commentators attribute these verses to Q,[95] although most believe that the Matthean version is the more original.[96] The differences between the two versions are not sufficient to posit another written source.

Lk. 12.49-53–Divisions in Households. Of this pericope, vv. 51-53 are paralleled at Mt. 10.34-36 and are almost universally attributed to Q.[97]

91. Manson, *Sayings*, pp. 94-96; G. B. Caird, *The Gospel of St Luke* (Pelican Gospel Commentaries; Harmondsworth: Penguin, 1963), p. 158; Ellis, *Luke*, p. 108.

92. Verse 37: ἐν + articular infinitive (cf. Lk. 2.27; 3.21); v. 39: πρός + accusative after a verb of speaking; ὁ κύριος of Jesus in narrative; see Cadbury, *Style and Literary Method*, p. 203; Fitzmyer, *Luke*, pp. 116, 202-203; Goulder, *New Paradigm*, II, p. 526.

93. Marshall, *Luke*, pp. 507-508; Nolland, *Luke*, p. 669.

94. Fitzmyer, *Luke*, p. 943; Schneider, *Lukas*, II, p. 276.

95. Manson, *Sayings*, p. 114; Schulz, *Spruchquelle*, pp. 142-45; Marshall, *Luke*, p. 531; Fitzmyer, *Luke*, pp. 981-82; Schenk, *Synopse*, pp. 92-93; Crossan, *Fragments*, p. 344; Schneider, *Lukas*, II, pp. 286-87; Zeller, *Logienquelle*, pp. 78-81; Kloppenborg, *Q Parallels*, p. 134; Evans, *Luke*, p. 349; Koester, *Ancient Christian Gospels*, p. 145.

96. E.g. W. Pesch, 'Zur Exegese von Mt 6, 19-21 und Lk 12, 33-34', *Bib* 41 (1960), pp. 356-78; Marshall, *Luke*, p. 531; Fitzmyer, *Luke*, p. 981; Sabourin, *Luc*, p. 251. (Thus they would in this case be in some agreement with Goulder, *New Paradigm*, II, pp. 545-470).

97. Manson, *Sayings*, pp. 119-21; Schulz, *Spruchquelle*, pp. 258-60; Marshall, *Luke*, p. 545; Fitzmyer, *Luke*, p. 994; Schenk, *Synopse*, pp. 96-97; Crossan, *Fragments*, p. 345; Schneider, *Lukas*, II, p. 292; Zeller, *Logienquelle*, p. 74; Havener

Verses 49-50 are more difficult to decide. Verse 50 does contain noticeable Lukan style and is probably Lukan composition based on Mk 10.38.[98] Verse 49 on the other hand does not seem stylistically Lukan,[99] but is it from Q or some other source? The verbal similarity to Mt. 10.34 (Lk. 12.51), ἦλθον βαλεῖν... ἐπὶ τὴν γῆν, together with the parallel in *Gos. Thom.* 10 makes it seem more likely that this verse is from Q than from another source.[100]

Lk. 13.22-30–the Narrow Door and the First and the Last. Most of this passage is widely attributed to Q.[101] However, as with most of Q, there is considerable debate as to which parts are Lukan redaction and which were original to Q: vv. 22-23 are the most likely to be redactional, and v. 25 has also been questioned.[102] Athough its placement in the order of Q is unclear, its inclusion in that source seems likely;[103] there is no sufficient reason to posit its origin in another source.

(Polag), *Q*, pp. 139-40; Kloppenborg, *Q Parallels*, p. 142; Nolland, *Luke*, p. 707; Koester, *Ancient Christian Gospels*, pp. 146-47. Cf. Goulder, *New Paradigm*, II, p. 555, who admits that the Q hypothesis is not as problematic here as he deems it elsewhere.

98.   Lukan style in this verse includes ἔχειν + infinitive; συνέχειν; τέλειν; and ἕως ὅτου; see Goulder, *New Paradigm*, II, p. 556. See also C.P. März, '"Feuer auf die Erde zu werfen, bin ich gekommen..."': Zum Verständnis und zur Entstehung von Lk 12, 49', in *A cause de l'Evangile: Etudes sur les Synoptiques et les Actes: Mélanges offerts à Jacques Dupont* (Paris: Cerf, 1985), pp. 479-511, esp. pp. 483-84; and S.J. Patterson, 'Fire and Dissension: Ipsissima Vox Jesus in Q 12.49, 51-53?', *Forum* 5.2 (1989), pp. 121-39, esp. pp. 124-25. Some attribute the verse to Q despite this: Manson, *Sayings*, p. 120; Crossan, *Fragments*, p. 345; Havener (Polag), *Q*, p. 139.

99.   On the relative lack of Lukanisms, see Goulder, *New Paradigm*, II, pp. 555-56; Patterson, 'Fire and Dissension', p. 124.

100.   This is the position taken by all those listed in n. 97 above, excepting Fitzmyer and Schenk. Fitzmyer, *Luke*, p. 994, and Evans, *Luke*, p. 26, attribute the verse to L.

101.   Manson, *Sayings*, pp. 124-26; Schulz, *Spruchquelle*, pp. 309-12, 323-30; Marshall, *Luke*, pp. 563-64; Fitzmyer, *Luke*, pp. 1021-22; Schenk, *Synopse*, pp. 102-105; Crossan, *Fragments*, p. 345; Havener (Polag), *Q*, p. 141; Kloppenborg, *Q Parallels*, pp. 152-57; Koester, *Ancient Christian Gospels*, pp. 147-48.

102.   For the arguments, see the synopsis of secondary literature in Kloppenborg, *Q Parallels*, p. 154. Curiously, Fitzmyer, *Luke*, p. 1022, attributes v. 30 to L.

103.   See Mt. 7.13-14, 22-23; 8.11-12; 19.30; 20.16; 25.10-12. Also cf. Mk 10.31, *Gos. Thom.* 4. The disagreement in order seems more problematic for Goulder, *New Paradigm*, II, pp. 571-75, than it would be for the Q hypothesis.

Lk. 14.15-24–the Great Banquet. Although the stories of the banquet
here and at Mt. 22.1-14 are noticeably different, they are similar
enough that they are attributed by most to Q.[104] The further factor here
seems to be the presence in *Gos. Thom.* 64 of an apparently more prim-
itive (i.e. less allegorical) version of the story.[105] In this case at least, it
appears that *Thomas* is not dependent on the more allegorical versions
of Matthew and Luke, and this has increased the probability that a prim-
itive version of the story was included in Q.

Lk. 14.25-27–the Cost of Discipleship. Although the introductory v.
25 is most likely Lukan, almost all commentators now ascribe vv. 26-
27 to Q, especially because the two sayings (hating one's family,
carrying one's cross), occur in the same order.[106]

Lk. 17.3-4, 5-6–on Forgiveness and on Faith. Except for the transi-
tional verses (vv. 3a and 5-6a), which are probably supplied by Luke,
these sayings are widely attributed to Q.[107] Any differences can be easily
accounted for as redactional.

104. Manson, *Sayings*, pp. 128-30; Schulz, *Spruchquelle*, pp. 391-403; Marshall,
Luke, p. 584; Fitzmyer, *Luke*, p. 1052; Schenk, *Synopse*, pp. 107-109; Crossan, *Fragments*, p. 345; Havener (Polag), *Q*, pp. 141-42; Kloppenborg, *Q Parallels*, pp. 164-
67; Evans, *Luke*, p. 572; Koester, *Ancient Christian Gospels*, p. 147. Dissenters
include Patton, *Sources*, pp. 202-203; A. Plummer, *A Critical and Exegetical Commentary on the Gospel according to St Luke* (ICC, 28; Edinburgh: T. & T. Clark, 5th
edn, 1922), pp. 359-60; and Ellis, *Luke*, p. 194. On the symposium setting, see
above on Lk. 7.36-50 and 11.37-54. In this pericope, Goulder, *New Paradigm*, II,
pp. 588-93, must argue the same case as those who support Q: that the two stories,
with very low verbal agreement, are in fact quite similar.
105. See H. Montefiore, 'A Comparison of the Parables of the Gospel according
to Thomas and of the Synoptic Gospels', in H.E.W. Turner and H. Montefiore,
Thomas and the Evangelists (London: SCM Press, 1962), pp. 40-78, esp. 60-64.
106. Cf. Mt. 10.37-38; *Gos. Thom.* 55. See Manson, *Sayings*, p. 131; Schulz,
Spruchquelle, pp. 430-33, 446-49; Fitzmyer, *Luke*, p. 1060; Schenk, *Synopse*, pp. 109-
10; Crossan, *Fragments*, p. 345; Kloppenborg, *Q Parallels*, pp. 168-70; Nolland,
Luke, p. 761; Koester, *Ancient Christian Gospels*, pp. 147-48. Goulder, *New
Paradigm*, II, p. 596, observes that Luke's phrasing may be due to an ascetic intensi-
fication of the material; this is quite probable.
107. Cf. Mt. 18.15, 21b-22; 17.20; *Gos. Thom.* 48; also cf. Mk 11.22-23. See
Manson, *Sayings*, pp. 139-41; Schulz, *Spruchquelle*, pp. 320-22, 465-68; Marshall,
Luke, pp. 641-45; Fitzmyer, *Luke*, pp. 1139-43; Schenk, *Synopse*, pp. 117-19;
Crossan, *Fragments*, p. 345; Schneider, *Lukas*, II, pp. 345-48; Havener (Polag), *Q*,

4.2.2. *The Pericopae More Difficult to Determine*

Lk. 3.10-14–the Crowds Question John. A few commentators have included this passage in Q,[108] mainly because it now fits in quite smoothly with the surrounding Q material.[109] It seems unlikely that vv. 10-14 are from Q: the material's integration with Q material can more easily be explained by Lukan composition of vv. 10-14,[110] or as Luke's redaction of a pre-Lukan tradition in order to make it fit into the Q material,[111] thereby avoiding speculation as to Matthew's motives for omitting it. The likelihood seems to be inclined towards Lukan redaction of pre-existing material by two considerations: 1) the hypothesis of Lukan composition is based in part on the questionable dogma that the teaching is late Hellenistic, and not early Jewish-Christian;[112] 2) the language exhibits noticeable idiosyncracies.[113] For these reasons, the verses will be considered further as possibly from a source other than Q.

Lk. 9.61-62–a Potential Follower of Jesus. Despite the lack of a Matthean parallel, some attribute these verses to Q.[114] In this case their arguments seem convincing. The two verses cohere well with vv. 57-60,

p. 144; Kloppenborg, *Q Parallels*, pp. 184-87; Koester, *Ancient Christian Gospels*, p. 148. Here again, the disagreement in order seems to undermine Goulder, *New Paradigm*, II, pp. 640-42.

108. Plummer, *Luke*, p. 90; Schürmann, *Lukasevangelium*, I, p. 169; Marshall, *Luke*, p. 142.

109. Lk. 3.7-9, 16-17.

110. See F.W. Horn, *Glaube und Handeln in der Theologie des Lukas* (Göttingen: Vandenhoeck & Ruprecht, 1983), pp. 92-93; Goulder, *New Paradigm*, I, pp. 274-76.

111. E.H. Scheffler, 'The Social Ethics of the Lukan Baptist (Lk. 3:10-14)' *Neot* 24 (1990), pp. 21-36 (esp. pp. 28-29), effectively counters the claims of pure Lukan composition.

112. The dogma is inherited from Bultmann, *Synoptic Tradition*, p. 145. However, the Jewish character of the teaching has been noted by J. Sahlin, 'Die Früchte der Umkehr: Die ethische Verkündigung Johannes des Täufers nach Lk. 3:10-14', *ST* 1 (1948), pp. 54-68; T.W. Manson, 'John the Baptist', *BJRL* 36 (1953-54), pp. 395-412; Marshall, *Luke*, p. 142; and Fitzmyer, *Luke*, p. 465.

113. See Schürmann, *Lukasevangelium*, I, p. 169; Marshall, *Luke*, p. 142; Jeremias, *Die Sprache*, pp. 107-12.

114. Marshall, *Luke*, p. 408; Crossan, *Fragments*, pp. 243, 343; Havener (Polag), *Q*, p. 129; Kloppenborg, *Q Parallels*, p. 64; Koester, *Ancient Christian Gospels*, p. 140.

so well that their origin in two different sources seems less likely.[115] Further, the suggestion that Matthew omitted the verses as redundant and anti-climactic after Mt. 8.21-22 seems plausible: if the call supersedes filial obligations to the dead, then it would surely supersede saying goodbye. It is quite likely that Lk. 9.61-62 is from Q, and therefore it will not be considered further.

Lk. 10.1, 17-20–the Mission of the Seventy(-two). Where this story of the mission of the seventy(-two) came from is unclear. A small number have suggested that it stood in Q,[116] but this has received little support. The language of v. 1 is strongly Lukan,[117] as is admitted even by some who would attribute the passage to Q.[118] As for vv. 17-20, Fitzmyer's argument that the entire mission of the seventy(-two) is built up by Luke out of Q and Markan material (cf. Mt. 9.37-38; 10.7-16; 11.21-23; Mk 6.6b-13), seems proven by the reference at Lk. 22.35 to 'sandals' when he is speaking to the Twelve.[119] Although perhaps in part pre-Lukan, vv. 17-20 seem to be a composite of unrelated sayings together with Lukan composition;[120] we have no reason to consider them from another source.

Lk. 11.5-8–the Importunate Friend. Some have suggested that this story was originally in Q, the main reason being the pericope's close connection with the following Q material.[121] The suggestion is highly speculative for at least two reasons: 1) most importantly, the lack of a parallel in either Matthew or *Thomas*; 2) the connection with the fol-

---

115. They could be Lukan composition in imitation of the preceding: see Fitzmyer, *Luke*, p. 833; Goulder, *New Paradigm*, II, pp. 461-63. The verses are not noticeably Lukan in style, however, and the redundancy would seem strange if they are composed by Luke: Marshall, *Luke*, p. 408.

116. Patton, *Sources*, pp. 196-97; Easton, *Luke*, p. 163; Marshall, *Luke*, p. 427; Havener (Polag), *Q*, p. 130 (v. 1 only).

117. E.g. μετὰ δὲ ταῦτα (Lk. 5.27; 12.4; 17.8; 18.4; Acts 7.7; 13.20; 15.16; 18.1); ὁ κύριος; ἀναδείκνυμι (Acts 1.24; cf. Lk. 1.80). See Jeremias, *Die Sprache*, p. 183; Fitzmyer, *Luke*, pp. 202-203, 845-46; Goulder, *New Paradigm*, II, p. 473.

118. E.g. Marshall, *Luke*, p. 414.

119. Cf. Lk. 9.1-6; 10.4. See Fitzmyer, *Luke*, p. 843; cf. Goulder, *New Paradigm*, II, pp. 464-79, 737.

120. See Bultmann, *Synoptic Tradition*, p. 158; Fitzmyer, *Luke*, p. 859.

121. Easton, *Luke*, pp. 177-78; more persuasively, D.R. Catchpole, 'Q and "The Friend at Midnight" (Luke xi. 5–8/9)', *JTS* 34 (1983), pp. 407-24.

lowing Q material does not seem as close as is claimed: certainly the idea of persistence central to vv. 5-8 is missing from the subsequent Q material.[122] Therefore, excepting the introductory clause,[123] Lk. 11.5b-8 will be considered further as possibly from a pre-Lukan source other than Q.

Lk. 11.27-28–True Blessedness. A few commentators have included these verses in Q.[124] Certainly the sentiment of rejection of family fits in Q, but this can equally be said of other strands of Gospel tradition.[125] The argument from order is perhaps more persuasive: it is possible that Matthew omitted this Q saying in favor of Mk 3.31-35 (Mt. 12.46-50), because that Matthean passage occurs at the same relative position in Matthew as this pericope does in Luke. Further, in Luke the pericope occurs in the midst of a rather large block of probable Q material.[126] But in the end, the lack of a Matthean parallel must certainly diminish the likelihood that the pericope stood in Q. All in all, I am inclined against including it in Q, but the above considerations are certainly enough to raise the possibility. Therefore, although I will consider Lk. 11.27-28 as possibly from a source other than Q, I will bracket it to indicate its questionable status. Also, Lukan language predominates in the first half of v. 27,[127] so only vv. 27b-28 will be considered further.

Lk. 12.13-21–the Rich Fool. A few have attributed the parable of the rich fool and its introduction to Q.[128] Similar arguments have been

122. In this, Goulder, *New Paradigm*, II, pp. 498-501, is rather more to the point: he connects this parable to that of the Unjust Judge (Lk. 18.1-8). This shows that the parables are connected; it does not prove Lukan composition, however. See below, Chapter 5, section 4.5.

123. Luke's typical πρός + accusative after a verb of speaking (see above n. 92).

124. Manson, *Sayings*, pp. 85, 88; Caird, *Luke*, p. 156; Crossan, *Fragments*, p. 344; Koester, *Ancient Christian Gospels*, p. 143.

125. E.g. Mk 3.31-35.

126. Lk. 11.9–12.12. Also, note the parallel in *Gos. Thom.* 79: see Koester, *Ancient Christian Gospels*, p. 143.

127. E.g. ἐγένετο δέ+ finite verb; ἐπαίρω; Luke's preference for participial constructions such as this one: see Cadbury, *Style and Literary Method*, pp. 133-37; Fitzmyer, *Luke*, pp. 110, 119; Goulder, *New Paradigm*, II, pp. 509-11. The number of Lukanisms drops considerably in vv. 27b-28.

128. Thus, excluding v. 15 as redactional: Easton, *Luke*, p. 201; Kloppenborg, *Q Parallels*, p. 128; Koester, *Ancient Christian Gospels*, p. 145. This raises the possi-

advanced as those given for Lk. 11.27-28: it is in a large block
of Q material and is closely connected with what follows in Q.[129]
Kloppenborg makes the further claims that the criticism of the rich and
the chriic style of vv. 13-14 are similar to other Q passages.[130] Although
suggestive, these arguments are hardly decisive.[131] Its connection with
what follows surely accounts for its present placement in Luke, but gets
us no closer to Q. The chreia is hardly unique to Q.[132] Also, a negative
attitude towards wealth is found throughout the Gospel tradition.[133]
However, at least a plausible explanation for Matthew's omitting the
pericope has been given in this case: an apothegm and parable would not
have fitted in the Sermon on the Mount.[134] Again, the evidence seems
more in favor of excluding the passage from Q, but it does raise the
possibility, and we must therefore bracket Lk. 12.13-14, 16-21 when
we consider it further. Further, the introductions to the apothegm (v.
13a) and the parable (v. 16a) as well as the secondary ending (v. 21) are
probably Lukan, and will not be considered.[135]

Lk. 12.35-38–on Watchfulness. Although this passage is similar to
Matthew's parable of the ten virgins (Mt. 25.1-13) in its theme of vigi-
lance and its mention of a wedding, the two have no verbal agreement,

bility that the two parts did not circulate as a unit: thus Fitzmyer, *Luke*, p. 968; Nolland,
Luke, pp. 683-84. Manson, *Sayings*, pp. 270-72, and Marshall, *Luke*, p. 522, include
all of vv. 13-21 in Q. (Cf. the parallels in *Gos. Thom.* 72 and 63, though these may be
dependent on Luke: see Marshall, *Luke*, p. 521; Fitzmyer, *Luke*, p. 971; Goulder, *New
Paradigm*, II, p. 538).

129. Lk. 12.22-31.

130. Cf. Q 9.57-58, 59-60; 12.33-34; 16.13; see Kloppenborg, *Formation*, p. 216.

131. Goulder, *New Paradigm*, II, pp. 534-39, believes Luke has constructed this
story out of Mt. 16.24-28; 6.19, 25-26. Most problematic about this would be the disagreement in order, the lack of an explicit reference to money in Mt. 16.24-28 (cf. Mk
8.34-38; Lk. 9.23-27), and the fact that the verses from Matthew 6 are pushed into
double service (they have explicit parallels in what follows, though again with disagreement in order: Lk. 12.22-24//Mt. 6.25-26; Lk. 12.33//Mt. 6.19).

132. Cf. W.R. Farmer, 'Notes on a Literary and Form-Critical Analysis of Some
of the Synoptic Material Peculiar to Luke', *NTS* 8 (1961–62), pp. 301-16, who argues
that the chreia is more characteristic of L material, which he seems here to think of as
a source. (Besides, anything about chreiai would tell us nothing about vv. 16-21, unless
it is assumed that they circulated as a unit, which is far from clear if v. 15 is excluded.)

133. E.g. Mk 10.17-22; Lk. 16.19-31.

134. Cf. Mt. 6.25-33. See Easton, *Luke*, p. 201; Marshall, *Luke*, p. 522.

135. See Fitzmyer, *Luke*, pp. 969-73; Nolland, *Luke*, pp. 684-87.

and the plots of the stories are reversed. Ascribing it to Q seems unwarranted.[136] It will therefore be considered as possibly from some other pre-Lukan source.

Lk. 15.4-7–the Lost Sheep. Although vv. 1-3 are most likely Lukan composition and are therefore not included by any in Q,[137] most commentators do include the parable of the lost sheep in Q,[138] though a few do not.[139] The arguments against including it in Q are worth considering. It is argued that: 1) the agreement in language between Matthew and Luke is extremely low;[140] 2) the parable is closely tied to the following parable of the lost coin (vv. 8-10), making their origin in two separate sources seem less likely;[141] 3) it is also structurally similar to Lk. 13.1-9, a parallelism that makes no sense in the present plan of the

---

136. It is included in Q by Creed, *Luke*, p. 176; Bultmann, *Synoptic Tradition*, p. 118; Manson, *Sayings*, pp. 115-16; Crossan, *Fragments*, pp. 58, 344; Schneider, *Lukas*, II, pp. 288-89; and Havener (Polag), *Q*, p. 138. Marshall, *Luke*, p. 533, and Nolland, *Luke*, p. 699, summarize the two positions without deciding between them. The objections against its origin in Q would also stand against it being Lukan redaction of Mt. 25.1-13, *pace* Goulder, *New Paradigm*, II, pp. 543-45.

137. See below, section 4.3.1.

138. Creed, *Luke*, p. 196; Schulz, *Spruchquelle*, pp. 387-91; Fitzmyer, *Luke*, p. 1073; Schenk, *Synopse*, pp. 112-14; Crossan, *Fragments*, p. 345; Schneider, *Lukas*, II, pp. 324-25; Havener (Polag), *Q*, pp. 142-43; Kloppenborg, *Q Parallels*, p. 174.

139. The dissenters are notable: Patton, *Sources*, p. 203; Manson, *Sayings*, pp. 282-84; Farmer, 'Some of the Synoptic Material', pp. 301-16; Marshall, *Luke*, p. 600; C.L. Blomberg, 'Midrash, Chiasmus, and the Outline of Luke's Central Section', in R.T. France and D. Wenham (eds.), *Gospel Perspectives: Studies in Midrash and Historiography* (6 vols.; Sheffield: JSOT Press, 1983), III, pp. 217-61; Nolland, *Luke*, p. 769; Evans, *Luke*, p. 26.

140. Only 24 of the 81 words in Lk. 15.4-7 are found in Mt. 18.12-13; this is only 30 per cent. C.E. Carlston and D. Norlin, 'Once More—Statistics and Q', *HTR* 64 (1971), pp. 59-78, give the average agreement of Matthew and Luke in Q sayings material as 73.6 per cent. They give the agreement in this pericope as 63 per cent, but this is only accomplished by counting 'synonyms' and by dropping v. 6 from consideration; this would seem to be prejudging the issue. Again, the low agreement tells equally against the reconstruction of Goulder, *New Paradigm*, II, pp. 603-609.

141. The main reason given by Evans, *Luke*, p. 26. Lukan composition of the one parable in imitation of the other is still possible, though this likelihood is lessened by the relative lack of Lukan language, as shown by Farmer, 'Some of the Synoptic Material', pp. 303-305, and Jeremias, *Die Sprache*, pp. 245-48; (*pace* Goulder, *New Paradigm*, II, pp. 603-609).

Gospel, and therefore seems less likely to be from Luke;[142] 4) the parable has never fit well in any thematic grouping of Q material.[143] Although perhaps not enough completely to overthrow the consensus, the evidence against including the pericope in Q is enough to raise the possibility that the parable was available to Luke from another source. It will therefore be considered, although bracketed. Verse 7 will not be considered, because it appears secondary to the parable proper,[144] and the language of 'repentance' here inclines the likelihood rather towards Lukan addition,[145] as does the fact that the verse ties the parable back to the narrative introduction (vv. 1-3) which was composed by Luke.

Lk. 15.8-10–the Lost Coin. As noted above, this parable is closely tied to the preceding one and therefore some have included it in Q, despite the lack of a Matthean parallel.[146] The lack of any plausible explanation as to why Matthew would omit this parable, especially when it provides a female parallel to the preceding one makes this possibility extremely unlikely.[147] It will therefore be considered, excluding v. 10 for the same reasons as v. 7 was excluded above.

Lk. 17.20-21–the Coming of the Kingdom. Some commentators have attempted to link these verses with what follows and argue that all of Lk. 17.20-37 is from Q.[148] This has not proved convincing to many, as the

142. See Farmer, 'Some of the Synoptic Material', pp. 306-16, and Blomberg, 'Midrash, Chiasmus', pp. 217-61.

143. Kloppenborg, *Formation*, p. 100, sets it aside as unclassifiable, while in *Q Parallels*, p. xxxiii, he places it in the significantly entitled category of 'Miscellaneous Sayings'; Koester, *Ancient Christian Gospels*, pp. 147-48, places it in the umbrella category of 'Eschatological Didache'. (Q hardly seems like a tradition characterized by 'joy'.)

144. Thus Bultmann, *Synoptic Tradition*, p. 326, though the connection may be pre-Lukan: see Fitzmyer, *Luke*, p. 1073.

145. 'Repentance' is a favorite theme of Luke's: see Lk. 3.3, 8; 5.32; 10.13; 11.32; 13.3, 5; 16.30; 17.3, 4; 24.47; Acts 2.38; 3.19; 5.31; 8.22; 11.18; 13.24; 17.30; 19.4; 20.21; 26.20. See also Fitzmyer, *Luke*, p. 237; and J.L. Bailey, 'Repentance in Luke–Acts', Diss. University of Notre Dame, 1993, esp. pp. 185-228.

146. Thus Creed, *Luke*, p. 196; Crossan, *Fragments*, p. 345; Schneider, *Lukas*, vol. 2, pp. 324-25; Havener (Polag), *Q*, p. 143; Kloppenborg, *Q Parallels*, p. 176.

147. Cf. such parallelism at Mt. 13.31-33.

148. E.g. R. Schnackenburg, 'Der eschatologische Abschnitt Lk 17, 20-37', in A. Descamps and A. de Halleux (eds.), *Mélanges bibliques en hommage au R.P. Beda Rigaux* (Gembloux: Duculot, 1970), pp. 213-34; Schneider, *Lukas*, II, pp. 354-55.

differences outweigh the thematic similarities: the audience shifts from Pharisees (v. 20) to disciples (v. 22), while the eschatological subject shifts from the kingdom (v. 20) to the days of the Son of Man (v. 22).[149] These differences suggest the juxtaposing of originally separate material.[150] Luke may be responsible for the present placement of vv. 20-21 and for the reference to the Pharisees, but otherwise the verses are not noticeably Lukan.[151] Lk. 17.20-21 should therefore be considered as possibly from a pre-Lukan source other than Q.

Lk. 17.22-37–the Days of the Son of Man. The source(s) of these verses is extremely difficult to determine. Nearly all commentators attribute vv. 23-24, 26-27, 33, 34-35, 37b to Q;[152] some would also include vv. 22, 25 and 37a, although it is also possible that these are Lukan composition. This leaves vv. 28-32 as the most problematic. Almost all include v. 30 in Q.[153] Many include vv. 28-29, despite the lack of a Matthean parallel.[154] Far fewer include vv. 31-32.[155] I find the inclusion of vv. 28-29 in Q less than likely, because no good reason has been advanced for Matthew wanting to omit the mention of Lot, especially because the

149. Cf. Lagrange, *Luc*, p. 459; Fitzmyer, *Luke*, p. 1158.

150. In a very different way, this is what Goulder, *New Paradigm*, II, pp. 648-51, suggests, though for him the separate material is three Matthean passages: Mt. 16.1-4, 21-28, and Matthew 24 (though the wording and order are both problematic here).

151. Cf. A. Strobel, 'Die Passa-Erwartung als urchristliches Problem in Lc 17, 20f.', *ZNW* 49 (1958), pp. 157-96, who concludes that the verses are Lukan composition. His position has not received much support; see the criticism of it in N. Perrin, *Rediscovering the Teaching of Jesus* (New York: Harper & Row, 1976), pp. 69-72.

152. Thus Creed, *Luke*, pp. 217-18; Manson, *Sayings*, pp. 141-47; Schulz, *Spruchquelle*, pp. 277-87; Marshall, *Luke*, pp. 656-69; Fitzmyer, *Luke*, pp. 1164-65; Schenk, *Synopse*, pp. 120-23; Crossan, *Fragments*, pp. 176-79, 345; Schneider, *Lukas*, II, pp. 352-57; Zeller, *Logienquelle*, pp. 89-91; Havener (Polag), *Q*, pp. 144-45; Kloppenborg, *Q Parallels*, pp. 190-95; Nolland, *Luke*, pp. 856-57. For the passage as coming from Matthew, see Goulder, *New Paradigm*, II, pp. 651-55; as above, this would not affect the present work, as the material is clearly not from L.

153. Fitzmyer, *Luke*, p. 1165, is an exception.

154. Manson, *Sayings*, p. 143; Marshall, *Luke*, pp. 662-63; Schenk, *Synopse*, pp. 121-22; Crossan, *Fragments*, pp. 176-79, 345; Schneider, *Lukas*, II, pp. 352-57; Zeller, *Logienquelle*, p. 89 (uncertain); Havener (Polag), *Q*, p. 145; Kloppenborg, *Q Parallels*, pp. 192-94; Nolland, *Luke*, pp. 856-57.

155. Manson, *Sayings*, p. 144; Marshall, *Luke*, pp. 662-63; Crossan, *Fragments*, pp. 176-79, 345; Havener (Polag), *Q*, p. 145.

connection between Noah and Lot was apparently a popular one.[156] I
will therefore consider vv. 28-29 as possibly from a pre-Lukan source
other than Q below. I am more hesitant about vv. 31-32, because v. 31
has a parallel in Mk 13.15-16, and the wording does not appear as different as Fitzmyer claims.[157] His other arguments carry more weight,
however: the placement and the connection to the preceding material on
Lot might suggest a source other than Mark. I will therefore also consider vv. 31-32 below, although bracketed to show my hesitation.

Lk. 19.11-28–the Parable of the Pounds. Although the parable of the
pounds is attributed by many to Q,[158] the verbal agreement with the
Matthean parable of the talents (Mt. 25.14-30) is low indeed, leading
some to attribute the parables to different sources.[159] However, this
would leave a significant amount of agreement, especially in vv. 21-23,
24b, and 26, unexplained.[160] To account for these agreements, it would
seem most likely that some version of the parable existed in Q. Of the
other verses in Luke's version, it is significant that several concern the
separate motif of the rejection of the man as king.[161] Did these verses
constitute a separate parable combined with the parable of the pounds,
either by Luke or the tradition prior to him?[162] Even if these verses do

156. Cf. Wis. 10.4-8; 3 Macc. 2.4-5; *T. Naph.* 3.4-5; 2 Pet. 2.5-7; Jude 6-7;
Apostolic Constitutions 8.9.22. It should be noted that the popularity of this pairing
would also give Luke a reason to compose these verses: thus Goulder, *New Paradigm*,
II, pp. 653-54, 655-56. This part of Goulder's hypothesis is borne out below in
Chapter 3.

157. Fitzmyer, *Luke*, p. 1165.

158. Weiss, *Die Quellen der synoptischen Überlieferung*, p. 146, includes v. 28
to connect this pericope with his next L passage (Lk. 19.37-38), but it is obviously a
Lukan introduction to the next section (Lk. 19.28-40). Lk. 19.11-27 is included in Q
by Creed, *Luke*, pp. 231-32; Schulz, *Spruchquelle*, pp. 288-98; Schenk, *Synopse*, pp.
125-26; Fitzmyer, *Luke*, pp. 1230-32; Crossan, *Fragments*, p. 345; Sabourin, *Luc*,
pp. 310-11; Kloppenborg, *Q Parallels*, p. 200; Koester, *Ancient Christian Gospels*,
p. 149.

159. Thus Manson, *Sayings*, p. 313; Schneider, *Lukas*, II, p. 379. Carlston and
Norlin, 'Statistics and Q', do not mention the parable in their treatment of Q.

160. In these verses the agreement of Luke with Matthew is 50 out of 86 words,
or 58 per cent. Cf. Creed, *Luke*, p. 231; Fitzmyer, *Luke*, p. 1230.

161. Lk. 19.12, 14, 15a, 24a, 27. Matthew would hardly have omitted a royal
theme had he found it in Q (cf. Mt. 22.7).

162. Thus Caird, *Luke*, p. 210; Jeremias, *Parables*, p. 59; Ellis, *Luke*, p. 222;

represent the remnants of a separate parable, that parable is now unre-coverable; the narrative that one gets by combining them is too sketchy to make much sense.[163] In sum, part of Lk. 19.11-27 is probably from Q; as for the rest, it is either Lukan embellishment or the remnants of an unrecoverable parable. Therefore none of Lk. 19.11-27 will be considered below.

4.3. *Lukan Composition?*
The rest of the pericopae or parts of pericopae listed by Feine or Weiss above must now be considered to ascertain the extent to which they exhibit typical Lukan language or interests.[164] Although it is always possible that Luke and his sources overlapped in their language or interests, those parts that are demonstrably Lukan in these respects will not be considered further. As above, those that are more easily eliminated from consideration will be examined first.[165]

4.3.1. *The Pericopae More Easily Removed from Consideration*

Lk. 4.14-15–the Beginning of the Galilean Ministry. These verses are a Lukan composition loosely based on Mk 1.14-15. It is so loose, how-ever, that Schürmann has postulated the existence of the verses in Q.[166] This has not proved convincing. Delobel in particular has noted the Lukanisms and given explanations for Luke's changes in his Markan source here.[167] The result is a typically Lukan summary.[168]

P. Perkins, *Hearing the Parables of Jesus* (New York: Paulist Press, 1981), pp. 146-47; Nolland, *Luke*, pp. 910-11.

163. Cf. Creed, *Luke*, p. 232. On this point, the reconstruction of Goulder, *New Paradigm*, II, pp. 679-83, comes the closest to that of other scholars: they agree that the royal elements are Lukan embellishment on an earlier (Matthean or Q) parable.

164. The verses that remain are Lk. 3.23-38; 4.14-15; 8.1-3; 9.51-56; 10.38-42; 13.1-9, 10-17, 31-33; 14.1-6, 7-14, 28-33; 15.1-3, 11-32; 16.1-13, 14-15, 19-31; 17.7-10, 11-19; 18.1-8; 18.43b–19.10.

165. Though these are much fewer in this case: Lk. 4.14-15; 15.1-3.

166. See above n. 30.

167. J. Delobel, 'La rédaction de Lc., IV, 14-16a et le "Bericht vom Anfang"', in F. Neirynck (ed.), *L'Evangile de Luc: The Gospel of Luke* (rev. edn; BETL, 32; Leuven: Leuven University Press, 1989), pp. 113-33, 306-12. Cf. the similar conclusion (since here he sees little influence from Matthew) of Goulder, *New Paradigm*, I, pp. 299-300, 306-307.

168. On these, see above n. 28.

Lk. 15.1-3–Introduction to the Lost Sheep. With the exception of Farmer, who regards vv. 1-2 as pre-Lukan,[169] these verses are widely regarded as a Lukan composition to introduce the rest of chapter 15.[170] The consensus has emerged because of the Lukan language in these verses,[171] and the argument seems convincing in the case of these verses.

4.3.2. *The Pericopae More Difficult to Determine*

Lk. 3.23-38–the Genealogy of Jesus. Jesus' geneogy is still often attributed to L.[172] The ultimate source of the pericope is obviously the LXX.[173] But whether the names were assembled by Luke or someone previous to him seems impossible to determine, as the usual method of examining vocabulary or style is useless in a list of names such as this.[174] Inclining the probability in favor of Lukan composition are works that have shown how the genealogy fits into Luke's overall portrait of Jesus, culminating in 'son of God' (v. 38),[175] as well as its apologetic function;[176] Lukan language has also been shown in v. 23.[177] It is likely that Luke is responsible in large part for the form and content of the genealogy. Therefore it will not be considered further.

169. Farmer, 'Some of the Synoptic Material', p. 302.

170. Thus Marshall, *Luke*, pp. 598-99; Fitzmyer, *Luke*, p. 1072; Schneider, *Lukas*, II, p. 324; Goulder, *New Paradigm*, II, pp. 603-604; Nolland, *Luke*, p. 769.

171. Especially the echoes of Lk. 5.29-30 (Lukan redaction of Mk 2.15-17): see Jeremias, *Die Sprache*, pp. 243-45; Goulder, *New Paradigm*, II, pp. 603-604, 609.

172. Fitzmyer, *Luke*, p. 83; Evans, *Luke*, p. 26; Koester, *Ancient Christian Gospels*, p. 341.

173. See esp. καινάμ in v. 36, found only in the LXX and not the MT of Gen. 11.12 and 1 Chron. 1.18 (Alexandrine text). See also J. Willcock, 'Cainan (Luke III, 36)', *ExpTim* 30 (1918–19), pp. 86-87; A.R.C. Leaney, *A Commentary on the Gospel according to St Luke* (Black's New Testament Commentaries; London: A. & C. Black, 1958), p. 112; Fitzmyer, *Luke*, p. 503.

174. Cf. Fitzmyer, *Luke*, p. 491; Goulder, *New Paradigm*, I, p. 288.

175. See M.D. Johnson, *The Purpose of the Biblical Genealogies with Special Reference to the Genealogies of Jesus* (SNTSMS, 8; Cambridge: Cambridge University Press, 1969), esp. pp. 229-52; Goulder, *New Paradigm*, I, p. 283.

176. See Sterling, *Historiography*, pp. 383-84.

177. See H.J. Cadbury, 'Some Lukan Expressions of Time (Lexical Notes on Luke–Acts VII)', *JBL* 82 (1963), pp. 272-78; Goulder, *New Paradigm*, I, p. 290.

Lk. 7.11-17–the Raising of the Widow's Son. Lukan language is notice-able in this miracle story, especially at the beginning and the end.[178] Although there are some Lukanisms even in vv. 11b-15,[179] the possi-bility that they are from a pre-Lukan source should still be considered: the reference to Jesus' emotions (v. 13) and his touching the bier (v. 14) would be extremely surprising if the pericope were pure Lukan com-position.[180] Verses 11b-15 will therefore be considered, as well as the proper name 'Nain' (v. 11a), which Luke probably inherited from the tradition.[181]

Lk. 8.1-3–Women Followers of Jesus. The introductory verse (v. 1) to the list of Jesus' women followers is highly Lukan in language and most likely composed by him.[182] The list itself (vv. 2-3), however, should be considered as possibly from a pre-Lukan source.[183] Luke has added names that do not appear in the list from Mk 15.40. Also, the abruptness with which the women are mentioned here, then ignored throughout the

178. καὶ ἐγένετο + finite verb (v. 11a); ἑξῆς (v. 11a; only in Luke–Acts in the New Testament; see Lk. 9.37; Acts 21.1; 25.17; 27.18); φόβος as the crowd's reaction (v. 16; see Lk. 1.12, 65; 2.9; 5.26; 8.25, 37; Acts 2.43; 5.5, 11; 19.17); 'God has visited his people' (v. 16; cf. Lk. 1.68, 78; Acts 15.14); the report spreads all over (v. 17; cf. Lk. 4.14, 37); see Fitzmyer, *Luke*, p. 119.

179. ἐγγίζω (v. 12; see Lk. 10.9, 11; 12.33; 15.1, 25; 18.35, 40; 19.29, 37, 41; 21.8, 20, 28; 22.1, 47; 24.15, 28; Acts 7.17; 9.3; 10.9; 21.33; 22.6; 23.15); ὁ κύριος (v. 13); see Fitzmyer, *Luke*, pp. 202-203; Goulder, *New Paradigm*, I, pp. 386-87. In general, narrative material such as miracles is more heavily redacted than sayings mate-rial: see the percentages given in Carlston and Norlin, 'Statistics and Q', p. 71.

180. See above on Lk. 19.41-44.

181. See Fitzmyer, *Luke*, p. 656. Goulder, *New Paradigm*, I, pp. 382-85, believes that Luke's knowledge of Palestinian geography was sufficient to add this detail; this seems less than likely, and also overlooks Luke's tendency to remove such details from his material: see Chapter 5, section 2. Goulder's discussion of the pericope also relies again on his questionable lectionary hypothesis.

182. E.g. καὶ ἐγένετο + finite verb; καθεξῆς (Lk. 1.3; Acts 3.24; 11.4; 18.23); εὐαγγελίζω (10 times in Luke; 15 times in Acts); see Fitzmyer, *Luke*, pp. 119, 697; Goulder, *New Paradigm*, p. 410; Nolland, *Luke*, p. 365.

183. Cf. Marshall, *Luke*, p. 315; Fitzmyer, *Luke*, p. 695. Even Goulder, *New Paradigm*, I, p. 409, allows that the list is from L (!). On the pre-Lukan origins of the pericope, see also B. Witherington, 'On the Road with Mary Magdalene, Joanna, Susanna, and Other Disciples—Luke 8, 1-3', *ZNW* (1979), pp. 243-48; E. Schüssler Fiorenza, *In Memory of Her: A Feminist Theological Reconstruction of Christian Origins* (New York: Crossroad, 1983), pp. 138-40; D.C. Sim, 'The Women Followers of Jesus: The Implications of Luke 8:1-3', *HeyJ* 30 (1989), pp. 51-62.

following chapters, with only some of them reappearing (Lk. 24.10), suggests that Luke is probably working from some precedent.

Lk. 9.51-56–a Samaritan Village. Luke uses this pericope to begin his so-called travel narrative (Lk. 9.51-19.10). Since this large section is a Lukan construct built around Jesus' journey to Jerusalem, the references in Lk. 9.51-56 to Jerusalem and the journey (vv. 51, 53b, 56) are most likely from Luke.[184] Verse 51 also contains several Lukanisms.[185] Subtracting these verses, the remainder (vv. 52-53a, 54-55) still makes a coherent story, one without any intrinsic connection to Luke's larger narrative construct. They may be from a pre-Lukan source, and will therefore be considered further.[186]

Lk. 10.38-42—Martha and Mary. As noted above in the case of the raising of the widow's son at Nain (Lk. 7.11-17), narratives are usually more heavily redacted than sayings material. In the case of this pericope, Lukan language is found throughout;[187] it predominates in v. 38, to the point that only the name Martha is considered pre-Lukan.[188] If the pericope is pre-Lukan, its beginning is now unrecoverable, though it must have contained some reference to Martha. In the following verses Lukan usage is much less pronounced.[189] Verses 39-42, together with the name Martha from v. 38, will be considered further.[190]

184. Cf. Fitzmyer, *Luke*, p. 826; Nolland, *Luke*, p. 533.

185. E.g. the introduction ἐγένετο δέ + καί + finite verb; στηρίζω (Lk. 16.26; 22.32; Acts 18.23); πορεύεσθαι (51 times in Luke, 38 times in Acts); see Fitzmyer, *Luke*, pp. 119, 827-28; Goulder, *New Paradigm*, II, p. 463; Nolland, *Luke*, pp. 534-35.

186. Cf. Marshall, *Luke*, p. 404. Even Goulder, *New Paradigm*, II, p. 462, notes that the passage is 'counter-Lucan.' For the pericope as Lukan composition, see M.S. Enslin, 'Luke and Matthew, Compilers or Authors?', (*ANRW*, 2.25.3; Berlin: de Gruyter, 1985), pp. 2357-88, esp. pp. 2368-74.

187. See the thorough analysis of J. Brutscheck, *Die Maria–Marta–Erzählung: Eine redaktionskritische Untersuchung zu Lk 10, 38-42* (BBB, 64; Bonn: Peter Hanstein, 1986), esp. pp. 65-95. He attributes perhaps too many ambiguous words to Luke: cf. Jeremias, *Die Sprache*, pp. 193-95, and Nolland, *Luke*, pp. 602-605, who find far fewer Lukan words, and Fitzmyer, *Luke*, pp. 893-95, who finds practically none after v. 38.

188. Cf. Brutscheck, *Maria-Marta*, p. 74.

189. See Brutscheck, *Maria-Marta*, pp. 74-95; Jeremias, *Die Sprache*, pp. 193-95.

190. The discussion of the pericope in Goulder, *New Paradigm*, II, pp. 492-94, is primarily concerned with showing the similarities to Paul (1 Cor. 7.32-53) and the

Lk. 13.1-9–Disasters and a Barren Fig Tree. This pronouncement story (vv. 1-5) and parable (vv. 6-9) are widely attributed to L.[191] The language exhibits some Lukan characteristics throughout, but hardly enough to rule out a source.[192] Verses 1a and 6a do seem most likely to be Lukan compositions, v. 1a serving as a link to the preceding material, v. 6a linking the two parts of this passage.[193] This raises the possibility that they came to him from different traditions.[194] I will therefore consider vv. 1b-5 and 6b-9 separately.

Lk. 13.10-17–Jesus Heals a Crippled Woman. This pericope again shows that narratives are usually more heavily redacted than sayings material: some Lukan language is again found throughout.[195] But Jesus' touching the woman (v. 13) strongly mitigates against pure Lukan composition of this pericope,[196] and therefore the passage will be considered below. Verse 17c does appear to be a secondary ending composed by Luke and will not be considered.[197]

differences from Jn 11.1–12.11: the first is still highly dubious; the second I grant, though it does not affect the present reconstruction.

191. See Manson, *Sayings*, pp. 272-75; Fitzmyer, *Luke*, p. 1004; Evans, *Luke*, p. 26; Koester, *Ancient Christian Gospels*, pp. 337-38; Petzke, *Sondergut*, pp. 122-25. Goulder, *New Paradigm*, II, pp. 560-63, believes this is based on the story of the cursing of the fig tree (Mk 11.12-14, 20-26; cf. Mt. 24.32-35): besides the usual problem of order, the pericopae are similar in neither form nor content; there is no reason to connect them.

192. E.g. εἶπεν δὲ πρός in v. 7 (see Fitzmyer, *Luke*, p. 116; Goulder, *New Paradigm*, II, p. 563). Most of the Lukanisms are in vv. 1 and 6, however; see below.

193. The temporal note in v. 1 is Lukan, as is the verb ἀπαγγέλλω (Lk. 7.18, 22; 8.20, 34, 36, 47; 9.36; 14.21; 18.37; 24.9; Acts 4.23; 5.22, 25; 11.13; 12.14, 17; 15.27; 16.36; 22.26; 23.16, 17, 19; 26.20; 28.21); Luke is fond of labelling 'parables' as such, which he does at v. 6a (cf. Lk. 4.23; 5.36; 12.16, 41; 14.7; 15.3; 18.9; 20.9, 19); see Jeremias, *Die Sprache*, pp. 226-28; Fitzmyer, *Luke*, p. 599.

194. Cf. Fitzmyer, *Luke*, p. 1004.

195. See Jeremias, *Die Sprache*, pp. 228-30; Goulder, *New Paradigm*, II, p. 570.

196. See above on Lk. 19.41-44. Goulder, *New Paradigm*, II, pp. 564-67, notes the formal similarities to Mk 3.1-6 (Mt. 12.9-14): these are hardly enough to prove Lukan composition, especially in light of this un-Lukan depiction of Jesus' emotions; see also below on Lk. 14.1-6.

197. The reaction of the opponent(s) would end the controversy; Luke adds his favorite πάντες (πάς: 153 times in Luke; 170 times in Acts) and πᾶς ὁ ὄχλος (Lk. 6.19; Acts 21.27).

Lk. 13.31-33–Jesus Responds to Herod. Although some have suggested that these verses are purely Lukan composition,[198] there remains a consensus that some pre-Lukan kernel lies behind at least part of the pericope.[199] Verse 31a is heavily Lukan and most likely redactional.[200] Verse 33 appears also to be a Lukan addition: it is a secondary ending, it partly parallels v. 32, it ties the pericope into the context of the Lukan travel narrative, and it serves as a connector to vv. 34-35.[201] Removing these, vv. 31b-32 will be considered as possibly from a pre-Lukan source.

Lk. 14.1-6–Jesus Heals a Man with Dropsy. Again, this healing and controversy story exhibits some Lukan language throughout.[202] Some have suggested that Luke composed the pericope, based loosely on Mk 3.1-6.[203] Since Luke already has a parallel to Mk 3.1-6 (Lk. 6.6-11) it would create a doublet with material from the same source, and therefore seems less likely.[204] This increases the likelihood that some of the peri-

---

198. E.g. M. Rese, 'Einige Überlegungen zu Lukas XIII, 31-33', in J. Dupont (ed.), *Jésus aux origines de la christologie* (BETL, 40; Leuven: Leuven University Press, 1975), pp. 201-25; A. Denaux, 'L'hypocrisie des Pharisees et le dessein de Dieu: Analyse de Lc., XIII, 31-33', in F. Neirynck (ed.), *L'Evangile de Luc: The Gospel of Luke* (rev. edn; BETL, 32; Leuven: Leuven University Press, 1989), pp. 155-95, 316-23.

199. There would seem to be nothing to suggest the reappearance of Herod at this point in the narrative, *pace* Goulder, *New Paradigm*, II, pp. 575-77. On the pre-Lukan aspects of the pericope, see V. Taylor, *The Formation of the Gospel Tradition* (London: Macmillan & Co., 1933), p. 158.

200. E.g. ἐν αὐτῇ τῇ ὥρᾳ (cf. Lk. 10.21; 12.12; 20.19; 24.33); τις + noun (see Fitzmyer, *Luke*, p. 111); Luke's more favorable depiction of the Pharisees (cf. Acts 5.34). On this last point, see Nolland, *Luke*, p. 740; J.T. Carroll, 'Luke's Portrayal of the Pharisees', *CBQ* 50 (1988), pp. 604-21, esp. p. 616, gives the opposing interpretation.

201. Thus Fitzmyer, *Luke*, p. 1028; Schneider, *Lukas*, II, p. 310; Nolland, *Luke*, p. 739; but cf. Marshall, *Luke*, p. 570, who defends v. 33 as integral to the pericope.

202. E.g. πρός + accusative after a verb of speaking in vv. 3 and 5 (see n. 92, p. 42); see also Jeremias, *Die Sprache*, pp. 235-36.

203. See most recently, F. Neirynck, 'Luke 14, 1-6: Lukan Composition and Q Saying', in C. Bussmann and W. Radl (eds.), *Der treue Gottes trauen: Beiträge zum Werk des Lukas* (Freiburg, Basel, Wien: Herder, 1991), pp. 243-63. Cf. Goulder, *New Paradigm*, II, pp. 581-84.

204. See H. Schürmann, *Traditionsgeschichtliche Untersuchungen zu den synoptischen Evangelien* (Dusseldorf: Patmos, 1968), pp. 272-89; Fitzmyer, *Luke*, pp. 79-82.

cope came to Luke from another source, although as usual, the introductory and concluding verses (vv. 1 and 6) are more likely to be Lukan
framing.[205] Therefore only vv. 2-5 will be considered further.

Lk. 14.7-14–Sayings to Guests and Hosts. These sayings on banquets are
a composite of Lukan composition, Q, and material from elsewhere.
Verse 7 is a Lukan composition, tying the following sayings into the
dinner setting of v. 1.[206] Verse 11 is almost identical to Lk. 18.14, and is
also closely paralleled in Mt. 23.12; it is therefore most likely from
Q.[207] The remaining verses (vv. 8-10, 12-14) exhibit some un-Lukan
characteristics of style,[208] and will be considered as possibly from a
pre-Lukan source.

Lk. 14.28-33–the Tower and the King. These two parables are not
noticeably Lukan in language,[209] although v. 33 is most likely a Lukan
composition restating the point of v. 26 in Lukan terms.[210] Verses 28-32
will therefore be considered further.

---

205. In v. 1: καὶ ἐγένετο + finite verb (see Fitzmyer, *Luke*, p. 119), and the sympo-
sium-like setting. On the latter see X. de Meeûs, 'Composition de Lc., XIV et genre
symposiaque', *ETL* 37 (1961), pp. 847-70. In v. 6: opponents or spectators being
silenced (cf. Lk. 20.26; Acts 11.18; 12.17; 15.12; 22.2).

206. Also note Luke's labelling of what follows as a 'parable' (see above on 13.6);
πρός + accusative after a verb of speaking (see n. 92, p. 42).

207. Thus Fitzmyer, *Luke*, p. 1044; Schenk, *Synopse*, p. 106; Havener (Polag), *Q*,
p. 148; Kloppenborg, *Q Parallels*, p. 162.

208. See Jeremias, *Die Sprache*, pp. 237-39; note esp. the parataxis in v. 12 and
the dative instead of πρός + accusative in the same verse. Cf. Goulder, *New Paradigm*,
II, p. 585, who asserts these verses are thematically 'Lucan'. All his examples are from
other L material, however: this is obviously to prejudge the question of whether the L
material is Lukan or not.

209. See Jeremias, *Die Sprache*, pp. 242-43; Fitzmyer, *Luke*, pp. 1063-66;
Nolland, *Luke*, pp. 763-64. Even Goulder, *New Paradigm*, II, pp. 596-99, admits that
Luke feels 'discomfort' with these parables, especially the second, since their wealthy
and royal settings do not fit his more usual 'middle-class' characters (cf. Goulder, *New
Paradigm*, I, pp. 98-99).

210. Note especially the Lukan theme of renunciation of wealth (which is not present in the parables of vv. 28-32): cf. Lk. 12.33; 18.22. On this theme, see J. Dupont,
'Renoncer à tous ses biens (Luc 14, 33)', *NRT* 93 (1971), pp. 561-82.

Lk. 15.11-32–the Prodigal Son. The parable of the prodigal son contains a minimum of Lukanisms.[211] Attempts to divide the parable between vv. 24 and 25 have consistently been rejected,[212] as have been attempts to attribute all of the parable to Lukan composition.[213] This is because the linguistic evidence is not in favor of division or pure Lukan composition;[214] also the alleged thematic fit with Lukan interests is hardly perfect.[215] Therefore all of Lk. 15.11-32 will be considered further.

Lk. 16.1-13–the Dishonest Steward. The parable of the dishonest steward and the following verses are widely acknowledged as predominately pre-Lukan, but the lines have been drawn quite differently by various scholars. Nearly all are agreed that v. 1a is a Lukan introduction,[216] and that v. 13 is derived from Q.[217] Although vv. 1b-12 exhibit few Lukanisms and therefore may be pre-Lukan,[218] it is not clear at what

211. Though there are some: note esp. the optative in v. 26; cf. Jeremias, *Die Sprache*, pp. 248-54.

212. A recent proponent of division is J.T. Sanders, 'Tradition and Redaction in Luke xv.11-32', *NTS* 15 (1968–69), pp. 433-38. The unity is defended by most: Bultmann, *Synoptic Tradition*, p. 196; Manson, *Sayings*, p. 285; Marshall, *Luke*, pp. 605-606; Fitzmyer, *Luke*, pp. 1084-85; Nolland, *Luke*, pp. 780-81.

213. In favor of Lukan composition, see L. Schottroff, 'Das Gleichnis vom verlorenen Sohn', *ZTK* 68 (1971), pp. 27-52; also J. Drury, *Tradition and Design in Luke's Gospel: A Study in Early Christian Historiography* (Atlanta: John Knox, 1976), p. 158. Goulder, *New Paradigm*, II, pp. 615-16, must argue against both division and pure Lukan composition in order to see the parable as based on Mt. 21.28-32 (with which it has very few points of similarity).

214. As shown by J.J. O'Rourke, 'Some Notes on Luke xv. 11-32', *NTS* 18 (1971–72), pp. 431-33; and more fully by C.E. Carlston, 'Reminiscence and Redaction in Luke 15:11-32', *JBL* 94 (1975), pp. 368-90, esp. pp. 368-83.

215. The Lukan themes of repentance and forgiveness are not explicit in the parable proper: see Carlston, 'Reminiscence and Redaction', pp. 383-89; Nolland, *Luke*, p. 781. Goulder, *New Paradigm*, II, pp. 609-14, again identifies similarities between this and other L parables, but this does not prove Lukan authorship. (Note especially Chapter 4, section 2.1, below on monologue.)

216. Note esp. πρός + accusative after a verb of speaking (see n. 92, p. 42).

217. Cf. Mt. 6.24; see Creed, *Luke*, p. 202; Manson, *Sayings*, p. 133; Marshall, *Luke*, p. 622; Fitzmyer, *Luke*, p. 1106; Schenk, *Synopse*, p. 114; Crossan, *Fragments*, p. 345; Schneider, *Lukas*, II, p. 334; Havener (Polag), *Q*, pp. 143-44; Kloppenborg, *Q Parallels*, p. 178.

218. See Jeremias, *Die Sprache*, pp. 255-57; Fitzmyer, *Luke*, p. 1095. Note esp. the historical present in v. 7; on Luke's strict avoidance of the historical present in his

point vv. 1b-8a, 8b, 9, and 10-12 were joined.[219] Since no specifically Lukan interest is served by joining these verses, it is possible that vv. 1b-12 were a pre-Lukan unit. They will be considered further, although vv. 8b-12 will be bracketed to indicate that they may or may not have formed a unit with the preceding verses.

Lk. 16.14-15–a Saying against the Pharisees. The mention of the Pharisees, which ties this saying back to the narrative framework of Lk. 15.2,[220] together with the presence of Lukan language,[221] show that v. 14 is most likely a Lukan composition. Verse 15, however, may be pre-Lukan and will be considered further.[222]

Lk. 16.19-31–the Rich Man and Lazarus. Although the parable of the rich man and Lazarus is clearly not incompatible with Lukan interests,[223] two factors have convinced most that it is pre-Lukan: the placement is awkward,[224] and non-Lukan language is still noticeable.[225] A

redaction of Mark, see Cadbury, *Style and Literary Method*, pp. 158-59; Jeremias, *The Parables of Jesus* (trans. S.H. Hooke; New York: Charles Scribner's Sons, 1963), pp. 182-83; Fitzmyer, *Luke*, p. 107.

219. D.O. Via, *The Parables: Their Literary and Existential Dimension* (Philadelphia: Fortress Press, 1967), pp. 155-57; and Nolland, *Luke*, p. 805, argue that Luke attached vv. 9-12. Manson, *Sayings*, p. 293, believes he attached vv. 10-12; Fitzmyer, *Luke*, p. 1105, also allows for this possibility. Goulder, *New Paradigm*, II, pp. 618-26, sees all of vv. 1-13 as Lukan composition based on Mt. 18.23-35; again, the content of the two parables is similar only in the most general way. Finally, D. J. Ireland, *Stewardship and the Kingdom of God: An Historical, Exegetical, and Contextual Study of the Parable of the Unjust Steward in Luke 16:1-13* (NovTSup, 70; Leiden: Brill, 1992), pp. 48-115, argues that vv. 9-12, and perhaps even v. 13, came to Luke attached to the preceding.

220. See above on Lk. 15.2; on the Pharisees here, see Goulder, *New Paradigm*, II, pp. 628-29.

221. E.g. ἀκούω as a connective (Lk. 7.3, 9, 29; 8.50; 18.22; 23.6); ὑπάρχω (15 times in Luke, 25 times in Acts); see Jeremias, *Die Sprache*, p. 258; Goulder, *New Paradigm*, II, p. 632.

222. On the verse as pre-Lukan, see Bultmann, *Synoptic Tradition*, p. 335; Marshall, *Luke*, pp. 624-25; Fitzmyer, *Luke*, p. 1112. Goulder, *New Paradigm*, II, p. 629, believes it is Lukan redaction of Mt. 6.1, though this is again based in part on the questionable 'Paulinism' of Luke.

223. Again, Goulder, *New Paradigm*, II, pp. 635-36, points to the similarities between this and other L parables, but these similarities are not therefore 'Lucan'.

224. It seems awkward after the comment on divorce in v. 18: see Fitzmyer, *Luke*, p. 1125. John Donahue's attempt to make of the section a chiasmus seems forced,

further problem, however, is that the parable may be separable into two parts (vv. 19-26, 27-31), though this has been persuasively argued against.[226] All of Lk. 16.19-31 will therefore be considered further.

Lk. 17.7-10–on Servants. The short saying on unprofitable servants (slaves) contains a minimum of Lukanisms.[227] Further, it has often been noted that it is rather ill-suited to its present Lukan context as addressed to disciples (Lk. 17.1, 5).[228] This certainly is enough to raise the possibility that it is from some pre-Lukan source, and vv. 7-10 will be considered further.

Lk. 17.11-19–the Cleansing of Ten Lepers. Once again, this miracle exhibits more Lukan redaction than sayings material. Verse 11 is most likely Lukan composition, especially since it ties the episode into the Lukan setting of the journey to Jerusalem, and echoes the beginning of the travel narrative (Lk. 9.51). At least part of v. 19 is probably pre-Lukan, but if so, it has been redacted by Luke to the point of unrecover-

relying on v. 16 balancing all of vv. 19-31: see J. Donahue, *The Gospel in Parable: Metaphor, Narrative, and Theology in the Synoptic Gospels* (Philadelphia: Fortress Press, 1988), p. 173. Cf. Drury, *Tradition and Design*, p. 161, for the parable as Lukan composition.

225. See Jeremias, *Die Sprache*, pp. 260-62; Fitzmyer, *Luke*, p. 1125; Schneider, *Lukas*, II, p. 340. Note esp. the two historical presents in vv. 23 and 29: see Fitzmyer, *Luke*, pp. 107, 1132-34. Even Goulder, *New Paradigm*, II, pp. 636-37, acknowledges that these are a problem for Lukan authorship; his citation of the few other historical presents in Luke–Acts hardly counterbalances Luke's overwhelming distaste for them. Further, he does not note that what few there are occur almost exclusively in the L material we are examining: see below, Chapter 3, section 3.4.

226. See K. Grobel, '. . . Whose Name Was Neves', *NTS* 10 (1963–64), pp. 373-82; Marshall, *Luke*, pp. 633-34; and H. Hendrickx, *The Parables of Jesus* (London: Geoffrey Chapman; San Francisco: Harper & Row, 1986), pp. 210-11. Bultmann, *Synoptic Tradition*, p. 178, believes that the two parts had been joined by the pre-Lukan tradition.

227. See Jeremias, *Die Sprache*, pp. 263-64; Fitzmyer, *Luke*, p. 1145; Nolland, *Luke*, pp. 841-42.

228. See Jeremias, *Parables*, p. 193; P. Minear, 'A Note on Luke 17:7-10', *JBL* 93 (1974), pp. 82-87. Even Goulder, *New Paradigm*, II, p. 643, acknowledges that the passage seems to lack real connection with the preceding; see also above on Lk. 17.3-4, 5-6. Also on the audience, cf. K.E. Bailey, *Through Peasant Eyes* (Grand Rapids: Eerdmans, 1980), pp. 114-15.

ability.[229] Of the remaining (vv. 12-18), opinions vary.[230] The linguistic evidence is ambiguous, with Lukan language distributed unevenly.[231] The chief objection against Lukan composition is that the pericope would then be based on Mk 1.40-45, which has already been paralleled at Lk. 5.12-14.[232] This is the main reason I will consider the possibility that vv. 12-18 may be from a pre-Lukan source.

Lk. 18.1-8–the Widow and the Judge. The parable of the unjust judge (persistent widow) is widely acknowledged to be pre-Lukan in part,[233] although vv. 1 and 8b are most probably Lukan composition.[234] Verses

229. Nolland, *Luke*, p. 847, defends it as pre-Lukan. Certainly the direct dative instead of Luke's more typical πρός + accusative is suggestive, but Jesus' reply seems too Lukan (cf. Lk. 7.50) to speculate what might have stood behind it: cf. Fitzmyer, *Luke*, p. 1156.

230. Those who favor Lukan composition include W. Bruners, *Die Reinigung der zehn Aussätzigen und die Heilung des Samariters Lk 17, 11-19: Ein Beitrag zur lukanischen Interpretation der Reinigung von Aussätzigen* (Forschung zur Bibel, 23; Stuttgart: Katholisches Bibelwerk, 1977); Enslin, 'Matthew and Luke', pp. 2378-84. Those who favor some pre-Lukan origin of the pericope include R. Pesch, *Jesu, ureigene Taten? Ein Beitrag zur Wunderfrage* (QD, 52; Freiburg: Herder, 1970), pp. 114-34; H.D. Betz, 'The Cleansing of the Ten Lepers (Luke 17:11-19)', *JBL* 90 (1971), pp. 314-28; Marshall, *Luke*, p. 649; R. Glöckner, *Neutestamentliche Wundergeschichten und das Lob der Wundertaten Gottes in den Psalmen: Studien zur sprachlichen und theologischen Verwandtschaft zwischen neutestamentlichen Wundergeschichten und Psalmen* (Walberger Studien; Theologische Reihe, 13; Mainz: Grünewald, 1983), pp. 125-60; Schneider, *Lukas*, II, p. 350; Nolland, *Luke*, p. 844. Fitzmyer, *Luke*, pp. 1149-50, although inclined toward the latter, is unsure.

231. See Jeremias, *Die Sprache*, pp. 264-66; Nolland, *Luke*, p. 844.

232. On Luke's avoidance of doublets, see above on Lk. 14.1-6; see also Marshall, *Luke*, p. 649. Goulder, *New Paradigm*, II, p. 647, discounts this without noting the Lukan omissions.

233. An exception is E.D. Freed, 'The Parable of the Judge and the Widow (Luke 18.1-8)', *NTS* 33 (1987), pp. 38-60, who argues for Lukan composition throughout. E. Linnemann, *Jesus of the Parables: Introduction and Exposition* (trans. J. Sturdy; New York: Harper & Row, 1966), p. 121, argues that the parable does not go back to the historical Jesus. Goulder, *New Paradigm*, II, pp. 658-62, rightly notes the similarities between this parable and Lk. 11.5-8, but this does not prove Lukan authorship; see above, pp. 47-48.

234. Verse 1 includes the Lukan habit of labelling what follows as a 'parable' (see above on Lk. 14.7) and of making the point of the story explicit. Verse 8b, with its abrupt introduction of ideas absent in the rest of the parable (i.e. Son of Man, faith) is almost universally seen as a Lukan addition: thus Creed, *Luke*, p. 222; Ellis, *Luke*, p. 213; Fitzmyer, *Luke*, p. 1176; Schneider, *Lukas*, II, p. 360; Nolland, *Luke*, p. 870.

2-8a are not characterized by Lukan language,[235] and will be considered as possibly from a pre-Lukan source.

Lk. 18.9-14–the Pharisee and Tax Collector. The parable of the Pharisee and the tax collector is almost universally thought to be pre-Lukan,[236] although vv. 9 and 14b are most likely Lukan additions.[237] Verses 10-14a will therefore be considered further.

Lk. 18.43b–19.10–Jesus and Zacchaeus. The story of Zacchaeus (Lk. 19.1-10)[238] is widely acknowledged to be pre-Lukan in part. As usual in narratives, the language is partly Lukan throughout, but the abundance of parataxis is so un-Lukan that it is most probable that Luke is here preserving tradition,[239] although v. 1 is probably a Lukan introduction.[240] Also, the fit with Lukan theology is again not

But cf. D.R. Catchpole, 'The Son of Man's Search for Faith (Luke xviii 8b)', *NovT* 19 (1977), pp. 81-104; and J.M. Hicks, 'The Parable of the Persistent Widow (Luke 18:1-8)', *ResQ* 33 (1991), pp. 209-23, who argue that v. 8b is original to the parable.

235. ὁ κύριος in v. 6a is an exception; see Jeremias, *Die Sprache*, pp. 271-72.

236. E.g. Linnemann, *Jesus of the Parables*, pp. 58-64; Crossan, *In Parables: The Challenge of the Historical Jesus* (New York: Harper & Row, 1973), pp. 68-69; Donahue, *Gospel in Parable*, p. 187; all three exclude vv. 9 and 14b as Lukan additions (see below). For a critique, see L. Schottroff, 'Die Erzählung vom Pharisäer und Zöllner als Beispiel für die theologische Kunst des Überredens', in H.D. Betz and L. Schottroff (eds.), *Neues Testament und christliche Existenz: Festschrift für Herbert Braun zum 70. Geburtstag* (Tübingen: Mohr–Siebeck, 1973), pp. 439-61. Goulder, *New Paradigm*, II, pp. 668-69, again notes similarities between this and other L parables, but such similarities are not therefore 'Lucan'; see Chapter 4, sections 2.1 and 2.4.

237. In v. 9: πρός + accusative after a verb of speaking (see n. 92, p.42); Luke's habit of labelling what follows a 'parable' (see above on Lk. 13.6 and 14.7). Verse 14b is nearly identical to Lk. 14.11 (Q); see Schneider, *Lukas*, II, p. 365; Nolland, *Luke*, p. 878. See also Jeremias, *Die Sprache*, pp. 272-74; Goulder, *New Paradigm*, II, pp. 669-70.

238. Weiss again includes material from the preceding pericope (Lk. 18.43b) to link this with his preceding L section (Lk. 18.31-34). In *Die Quellen der synoptischen Überlieferung*, p. 143, he modifies this slightly, using a combination of Lk. 18.35a and 18.43b to connect the two L passages. Both verses are obviously Lukan redaction of Mark: see Fitzmyer, *Luke*, pp. 1214, 1217.

239. καί appears 13 times in vv. 2-10: see Jeremias, *Die Sprache*, pp. 275-77. Goulder, *New Paradigm*, II, p. 678, does not respond adequately to this.

240. It ties it to the preceding pericope (cf. Lk. 18.35) as well as to the journey motif in general; note also διέρχομαι (10 times in Luke, 20 times in Acts); see Fitzmyer, *Luke*, pp. 1222-23; Nolland, *Luke*, p. 904.

perfect.[241] The origins of vv. 8 and 10 are much harder to determine. Certainly the story can function without either, and v. 8 also makes v. 9 seem awkward. Both verses contain some language that seems Lukan and some that does not, therefore both sides have been argued persuasively.[242] For now I will consider all of Lk. 19.2-10, though vv. 8 and 10 will be bracketed.

5. The L Material to be Considered

Of the 407 verses in Luke 3–19 the origins of which I have considered, only 197 have been judged as possibly from a pre-Lukan source other than Mark or Q.[243] I will now consider the likelihood that these verses are from a single source by examining them for further dissimilarities of vocabulary, style, form, and content from Luke's own preferences, as well as beginning to discern internal similarities among these pericopae.

241. The explicit language of repentance is again absent: see above on Lk. 15.11-32.

242. Thus Fitzmyer, *Luke*, p. 1219, argues that v. 8 is a Lukan addition and v. 10 is pre-Lukan, while E. Schweizer, *The Good News according to St Luke* (trans. D.E. Green; Atlanta: John Knox, 1984), p. 290, argues that v. 10 is a Lukan addition and v. 8 is pre-Lukan.

243. These are Lk. 3.10-14; 4.25-27; 5.4-9; 7.11b-15, 36-47; 8.2-3; 9.52-53a, 54-55; 10.30-37a, 39-42; 11.5-8, [27b-28]; [12.13b-14, 16b-20], 35-38; 13.1b-5, 6b-9, 10-17b, 31b-32; 14.2-5, 8-10, 12-14, 28-32; [15.4-6], 8-9, 11-32; 16.1b-8a, [8b-12], 15, 19-31; 17.7-10, 12-18, 20-21, 28-29, [31-32]; 18.2-8a, 10-14a; 19.2-7, [8], 9, [10], [39-40], 41-44.

Chapter 3

VOCABULARY AND STYLE

Style. When we see a natural style we are quite amazed and delighted, because we expected to see an author and find a man.

—Pascal[1]

1. *Introduction: The Vocabulary and Style of L Material*

Chapter Two has already removed much material (especially the introductory or concluding verses of pericopae) from further consideration because it was predominantly Lukan in language. Of course, this only means that what remains is not overwhelmingly Lukan, not that it is necessarily pre-Lukan in vocabulary or style, and much less that it is homogenous. Again, although it is always possible that Luke and his sources overlapped in their use of language, we can only proceed by noting words and constructions in the L material that are dissimilar to Luke's usage elsewhere in his work. This results in a continuum of probability. Any word or construction in Luke–Acts may possibly be pre-Lukan, even if Luke has shown a preference for it; one that occurs only in L material is more likely to be pre-Lukan, insofar as Luke has not shown a preference for it by adding it in his redaction of Mark or Q, or in his composition of Acts; finally, one that appears only in L material and that Luke has deliberately omitted in his redaction of Mark and Q has the greatest probability of being pre-Lukan.

The attempts of Easton, Rehkopf, and Jeremias to discern pre-Lukan vocabulary in the L material of Luke's Gospel have thus far proved unconvincing to most scholars. There are two main reasons for this: 1) they considered too much material from throughout the Gospel which was probably from a variety of sources or traditions, and therefore any vocabulary found to be common to several parts of it is more

1.   B. Pascal, *Pensées* (trans. A.J. Krailsheimer; Harmondsworth: Penguin, 1966), p. 242.

likely to be from Luke himself than from accidental overlap between different sources; 2) words that Luke did not add in his redaction of Markan material were counted as pre-Lukan, even if the words also occur in Q or Acts; this is problematic because in the case of Q (unless there is direct verbal agreement with Matthew) and Acts,[2] it is just as likely that Luke added these words. Only in cases where Luke has demonstrated an aversion to a word or construction by omitting it in his redaction of Markan material can the probability be said to incline in favor of the language being pre-Lukan.

This chapter will attempt to proceed in a more careful way. Already the majority of L material has been removed from consideration. There is a possibility that some of what remains is from a single source, and that possibility will be enhanced if there are demonstrably un-Lukan peculiarities of vocabulary and/or style in this material. Further, similarity in vocabulary or style between this material and any other material in Luke–Acts—whether from Luke's redaction of Mark or Q, or from the infancy narrative or Acts—will be counted as seriously diminishing the likelihood that the usage is here due to a source. I will first try to determine to what extent the vocabulary of the L material differs from other material in Luke–Acts; I will then search the material for un-Lukan elements of style.

2. *Vocabulary*

I will begin by examining the vocabulary of the L material under consideration to determine how many words are more likely pre-Lukan than Lukan; and in particular, how many words may still show pre-Lukan connections between pericopae. I will begin with a consideration of those words that occur only in this L material and nowhere else in all of Luke–Acts (*hapax legomena*).[3] I will then consider those words which, although they may occur (infrequently) in other parts of Luke's

---

2.   Cf. the critique by Goulder, *New Paradigm*, I, pp. 73-78. On the sources of Acts, see J. Dupont, *Les sources du livre des Actes: Etat de la question* (Bruges: Desclée de Brouwer, 1960); F.F. Bruce, *The Acts of the Apostles: The Greek Text with Introduction and Commentary* (rev. edn; Leicester, England: Apollos; Grand Rapids: Eerdmans, 1990), pp. 40-46.

3.   Throughout this discussion, I use *hapax* to designate words that occur only in the sample under consideration and nowhere else in the given corpus, rather than words that occur literally just once. (To use the terms *dis legomena*, etc., would seem less relevant in this discussion.)

work, are omitted by him in his redaction of Mark or Q, and are therefore less likely to have been added by him here.

2.1. *Unique Vocabulary*: Hapax Legomena

The appearance of an unusual (or even unique) word in a text almost always attracts the reader's attention. The study of these unusual words has been practiced in biblical studies for so long that some consideration of it would seem appropriate as the first step in trying to understand the analysis of vocabulary.[4] Further, it is hoped that the consideration of the two extremes of vocabulary study—the examination of the most unusual vocabulary by counting *hapax legomena* and the examination of the commonest vocabulary and usage by means of stylometry—will serve to complement one another.

Probably the best known and most thorough analysis of *hapax legomena* in New Testament studies is that of P.N. Harrison, who used the high number of *hapax legomena* in the Pastorals to argue against their Pauline authorship.[5] For many, this proved to be a more conclusive argument than others against Pauline authorship, and although it has been criticized, its influence and even persuasiveness must still be acknowledged.[6]

Harrison's argument is not as simple as stating that a high number of *hapax* in an epistle suggests non-Pauline authorship, and then producing the data. This is because Paul (or any other author subjected to the same test) may have been a writer who preferred and utilized a widely diverse vocabulary in general, or whose vocabulary changed according

---

4. Cf. A. Kenny, *The Computation of Style: An Introduction to Statistics for Students of Literature and Humanities* (New York: Pergamon Press, 1982), pp. 67-68; idem, *A Stylometric Study of the New Testament* (Oxford: Clarendon Press, 1986), pp. 2, 117.

5. See his *The Problem of the Pastoral Epistles* (Oxford: Oxford University Press, 1921). See also K. Grayston and G. Herdan, 'The Authorship of the Pastorals in the Light of Statistical Linguistics', *NTS* 6 (1959–60), pp. 1-15, based on Harrison's work.

6. For critiques of Harrison's work, see B.M. Metzger, 'A Reconsideration of Certain Arguments Against the Pauline Authorship of the Pastoral Epistles', *ExpTim* 70 (1958–59), pp. 91-94; J.J. O'Rourke, 'Some Considerations about Attempts at Statistical Analysis of the Pauline Corpus', *CBQ* 35 (1973), pp. 483-90; D. Guthrie, *The Pastoral Epistles: An Introduction and Commentary* (Tyndale New Testament Commentaries; Leicester, England: Inter-Varsity; Grand Rapids: Eerdmans, rev. edn, 1990), p. 55.

to subject matter, or at different times in his life. Perhaps an undisputably Pauline epistle has proportionately as many *hapax legomena* as the Pastorals. Therefore, in order for his data to carry any conviction, Harrison had to assemble not only lists of *hapax legomena* in the Pastorals, but also similar lists for each Pauline epistle.[7] His data showed that the Pastorals do fall noticeably outside of Pauline usage. The number of *hapax* in the Pastorals is more than twice the Pauline average, and is 87 per cent higher than the highest occurrence in an undisputed epistle (Philippians). Therefore, Harrison's data does seem to have increased the probability that the Pastorals are non-Pauline.

There are, however, two important ways in which the situation of the Pastorals differs from the situation of possible source material embedded in Luke, and these will undoubtedly lessen the amount of proof we can expect from counting *hapax legomena* in Luke. The first is the obvious observation that in the Pastorals, one only has to show that they are un-Pauline. In other words, the objective is to show that Paul had nothing (directly) to do with their writing.[8] In the case of Luke, this can never be shown, because everything in the Gospel and Acts is the product of Luke to one degree or another. Luke redacted Mark, Q, whatever source(s) lie behind the notation L, and whatever source(s) lie behind the narrative in Acts. Paul did not redact the Pastorals: he either did or did not write them. In the Pastorals, the epistles are examined to see if they are un-Pauline; in Luke, we are asking *to what extent* the material is un-Lukan. For this reason, we cannot expect as sharp a difference between Lukan and pre-Lukan material as Harrison found between the Pauline epistles and the Pastorals.

The second difference is related to the first. Just as it is impossible to prove that anything in Luke–Acts is purely un-Lukan, it is also difficult to know what is purely Lukan. To get an idea of Pauline usage, one would examine the undisputed Pauline epistles; but because of his use of source material, there is nowhere in Luke–Acts from which one could get such an unadulterated view of Lukan usage. The examination must

7.   See Harrison, *Problem of the Pastorals*, Appendix 1, pp. 137-48; cf. Kenny, *Stylometric Study*, p. 14.

8.   Paul was indirectly involved with the writing of the Pastorals in that they obviously know of him, and even reproduce authentic Pauline writings: see A.E. Barnett, *Paul Becomes a Literary Influence* (Chicago: University of Chicago Press, 1941), pp. 251-77; A.T. Hanson, *The Pastoral Epistles* (NCB Commentary; Grand Rapids: Eerdmans; London: Marshall, Morgan, & Scott, 1982), pp. 28-31, 199.

The Story of Jesus according to L

therefore proceed in a more circuitous way.

I have tried to do for Luke–Acts something similar to Harrison's analysis of the Pastorals by counting the *hapax legomena* (words that occur nowhere else in Luke–Acts) in five approximately equal blocks of material (ca. 200 verses): Lukan parallels to Markan material;[9] Q material in Luke;[10] and three randomly chosen blocks of material,[11] one from the Gospel,[12] one from Acts 1–12,[13] and one from Acts 13–24.[14] Although the random samples cannot show us pure Lukan usage, they should give us an idea of how many *hapax legomena* to expect in a body of Lukan material that is not from a single source; the Markan and Q samples should show us how many to expect when Luke is following a

9.   The following material was considered: Lk. 3.4-6, 15, 18, 21-22; 4.14-15, 31-44; 5.12-39; 6.1-19; 8.4-56; 9.1-50; 18.15-43. To make the Markan block approximately equal to the others, as well as to avoid any questions of variant source(s) in the Passion, I excluded material from later in the Gospel.

10.   For convenience, I have used Kloppenborg's estimation of Q given in his *Q Parallels*, pp. xxxi-xxxiii, excluding any verses that were bracketed or in parentheses, without necessarily agreeing with him. This yielded the following: Lk. 3.7-9, 16b-17; 4.1-13; 6.20b-23, 27-33, 35c, 36-37b, 38c, 39b-40, 41-49; 7.1b-2, 6-10, 18-19, 22-28, 31-35; 9.57-60; 10.2-16, 21-22, 23b-24; 11.2-4, 9-18a, 19-20, 23-26, 29-35, 39b-44, 46-52; 12.2-12, 22-34, 39-40, 42b-46, 51-59; 13.18-21, 24, 26-30, 34-35; 14.11, 16-24, 26-27, 34-35; 15.4-7; 16.13, 16-18; 17.1b-2, 3b-4, 6b, 23-24, 26-27, 30, 33-35, 37b; 19.12-13, 15b-26; 22.28-30. I was greatly assisted with the Q data by Kloppenborg's concordance to Q in *Q Parallels*, pp. 213-35.

11.   I did not use the scientifically pure process of consulting a random number chart to select these verses; I wrote down the verse numbers of all pericopae in the three sections (Gospel, Acts 1–12, Acts 13–24), handed the paper to my wife, and asked her to pick approximately 200 verses from each in any way she liked. This seems random enough, and the results came out quite close to a stratified random sample (i.e. there are some of each form-critical type, and the samples are spread, not in blocks). See the discussion of sampling practices in Kenny, *Computation of Style*, pp. 161-69.

12.   Lk. 1.39-45, 57-66; 2.8-21, 41-52; 3.10-14; 4.1-13, 31-37; 5.1-11; 6.17-19, 32-36; 7.11-17; 8.26-39; 9.28-36, 49-50; 10.38-42; 11.24-26; 12.22-34; 13.6-9; 14.12-14; 15.3-7; 16.1-9; 17.5-10; 18.15-17; 19.41-44; 20.34-40; 21.29-33; 22.39-46, 66-71; 23.13-16; 24.50-53.

13.   Acts 1.15-26; 2.14-42; 3.11-26; 4.23-31; 5.1-11; 6.1-7; 7.1-53; 8.4-25; 9.23-25, 36-43; 10.34-43; 11.19-30; 12.20-25.

14.   Acts 13.1-12; 14.8-28; 15.22-35; 16.1-10, 16-40; 17.16-34; 18.5-11, 24-28; 19.1-20; 20.17-38; 21.27-36; 22.22-29; 22.30–23.11; 24.1-9. I did exclude Acts 25–28 to avoid the nautical terminology of Acts 27; such heavy use of jargon does not seem representative of Luke's style, and would skew the results.

source. (The Markan and Q samples will also show how many of the *hapax legomena* are from Luke himself.)[15] If the data are similar in all the samples, it will show us that Luke has redacted Mark and Q to the point where they are indistinguishable from the rest of his work (at least in this one regard).[16] In addition to simple occurrences of *hapax legomena*, I have also noed how many occur in more than one pericopae within the sample, and calculated the percentage of total words that are *hapax legomena*. The results are given in Table 1.[17]

The findings are inconclusive. The random average calculation gives us the best and most accurate estimate of how many *hapax legomena* to expect from Luke in randomly chosen material: it is the most representative in that it is drawn from all parts of Luke's work, and the most accurate in that it is drawn from the results of the three random surveys (a total of 10,480 words), making its standard error lower.[18] But in order to include twice the standard error, this number must be expressed as an interval: this is from 3.6–4.4 per cent. Although both the Markan material and Q material fall outside of this interval (3.1 per cent and 4.7 per cent, respectively), both of these statistics must also be expressed as intervals (2.5–3.7 per cent and 4.1–5.3 per cent, respectively);[19] with this taken into consideration, it is seen that they overlap

15.   Which words are original to Mark will be clear. I have followed Kloppenborg in assuming that most of the words on which Matthew and Luke agree are original to Q; some of the rest probably are as well, but I will set that possibility aside. Cf. Kloppenborg, *Q Parallels*, pp. 207-208. Since Goulder regards Q material as coming from Matthew, he too would grant that where Matthew and Luke agree in this material, Luke is following his source (Matthew).

16.   This is the process described by Kenny, *Computation of Style*, p. 165, 'In an authorship study . . . we are comparing statistics of fragments which we know were *not* chosen as random samples to see how far they differ from statistics to be expected *if they had been*. If they do not significantly differ, then we know that we do not need to look for particular kinds of explanation of the statistics we find' (emphasis in original).

17.   The numbers in parentheses are twice the standard error for each amount calculated, thus giving the intervals at 95 per cent confidence limits within which to expect data to fall: see Kenny, *Computation of Style*, pp. 92-95. The formula for calculating the standard error is to take the square root of the following quantity: p (the rate of occurrence of the phenomenon) × q (its non-occurrence) ÷ N (the number of items in the sample).

18.   In the previous equation, since N is in the denominator, the higher its value goes, the lower the total quantity represented by the equation.

19.   That both members of the comparison must be represented as intervals is easily seen by the fact that otherwise two of the three random surveys (3.5 per cent and

the expected interval for randomly chosen material, and are in this respect indistinguishable from it. As noted above, this is probably not surprising: if I had proved that the same person could not have written the Markan and Q sections in Luke and the randomly chosen sections, this would certainly have created more problems than it solved. What is perhaps most surprising is that the interval for the Q material (4.1–5.3 per cent) falls near the high end of the expected interval, while the interval for the Markan material (2.5–3.7 per cent) near the low end, and the two do not overlap. Although both were redacted by Luke, it would be possible to distinguish between Markan material and Q material in Luke using this method.[20]

Table 1: *Comparison of Occurrences of* Hapax Legomena *in Sections of Luke–Acts*

	# of verses	# of words	# of *hapax*	# of *hapax* from source	# of *hapax* in multiple pericopae	per cent of total words that are *hapax*
Markan material (Luke 3–9, 18)	202	3720	117	59	5	3.1(± .6)
Q (Luke)	232	3933	185	108	8	4.7(± .6)
Random (Gospel)	206	3545	125	?	2	3.5(± .6)
Random (Acts 1–12)	198	3607	138	?	3	3.8(± .6)
Random (Acts 13–24)	194	3328	154	?	4	4.6(± .7)
Random (Average)	199	3493	139	?	3	4.0(± .4)

The number of *hapax legomena* that occur in more than one pericope within the sample considered may offer us one measure that does distinguish between samples drawn from a known source and those selected

4.6 per cent) would also fall outside the expected interval for randomly chosen material.

20.   Cf. Kenny, *Stylometric Study*, p. 27: 'When we are asking if two texts are by the same author, we raise first the question whether they can both be regarded as samples drawn randomly from the same stylistically homogeneous population... If the answer is in the negative, this again does not disprove common authorship; but it means that some explanation of the difference is called for (which might be, for instance, difference of subject matter, or chronological difference, or the influence of source matter)'. In the case of the Markan and Q material in Luke, both the sources and subject matter are different.

randomly. As can be seen, the three random samples yielded between 2 and 4 *hapax legomena* that occurred in more than one pericope. The number of these was noticeably higher when Luke was definitely following a source, especially in the case of Q. This makes a certain sense: the numbers of these *hapax legomena* found in the random samples should indicate how many we can expect from coincidental overlap between sources, or from Luke unconsciously adding peculiar vocabulary to different parts of his work; if the number rises above this, the increase is probably from the influence of a source.[21]

With all this in mind, how does the L material under consideration compare to other parts of Luke's work with respect to *hapax legomena*? The answer is that it comes out quite close to the results for Q, showing a higher percentage of *hapax legomena* than one would have expected, but not beyond twice the standard error. Of these, a much higher number occur in more than one pericope than one would have expected from a random sample.[22] The results are summarized in Table 2.

Table 2: Hapax Legomena *in L Material*

	# of verses	# of words	# of *hapax*	# of *hapax* in multiple pericopae	per cent of total words that are *hapax*
L Material	197	3421	166	13	4.9 (±.7)

As noted above, those *hapax legomena* that occur in more than one L pericope are more likely indicative of a pre-Lukan source than are the sheer number of total *hapax legomena*.[23] (Also, since I am ultimately

---

21. This is because it seems an unlikely redactional habit that Luke would deliberately add peculiar words only to material from a particular source and deliberately refrain from adding them anywhere else in his Gospel or Acts (assuming he could know in advance what vocabulary he would use in Acts). When he does make such additions, they should be as unconscious, and therefore about as numerous, as they would be in randomly chosen samples.

22. In the initial results I have included ὄνος at Lk. 14.5 (it is definitely at Lk. 13.15). The manuscript evidence is ambiguous: see Ellis, *Luke*, pp. 192-93; Marshall, *Luke*, pp. 579-80; Fitzmyer, *Luke*, pp. 1041-42; Schneider, *Lukas*, II, pp. 311-13; Sabourin, *Luc*, p. 267; J.D.M. Derrett, 'Positive Perspectives on Two Lucan Miracles', *Downside Review* 104 (1986), pp. 272-87; Nolland, *Luke*, p. 744; Evans, *Luke*, p. 570.

23. Some of the other *hapax* will be considered later in this chapter with other pre-Lukan vocabulary. Also, some pericopae should be noted as containing a particularly high percentage of *hapax*: Lk. 10.30-37a (16 out of 131 words; 12.2 per cent); 10.39-

interested in possible pre-Lukan connections between pericopae in the L material, these will be the more relevant.) Further, if these are words that Luke has omitted in his redaction of Mark, this will increase the likelihood that they are the remnants of the peculiar vocabulary of a pre-Lukan source. I will now examine each of these words.

1. βρέχω (Lk. 7.38, 44; 17.29). The verb does not occur in the Markan version of the anointing (Mk 14.3-9). It does occur at Mt. 5.45, a Q passage (cf. Lk. 6.35), but we do not know what the original Q version was like, and therefore we have no reason to believe Luke omitted it from his version.[24] However, Mt. 5.45 does alert us to the peculiar use of the verb at Lk. 7.38, 44: this is the only place in the New Testament where the word does not mean 'to rain'.[25] Nor is the usage here Septuagintal.[26] The absence of the verb anywhere else in Luke–Acts and its non-biblical usage here may incline the probability slightly in favor of the word being pre-Lukan; although this may be a connection to Lk. 17.29, its different meaning there shows that something else would have to be found to increase the likelihood of such a connection.

2. γάμος (Lk. 12.36; 14.8). This noun does not occur in Mark. It occurs nine times in Matthew;[27] although eight of these occurrences are in the Q passage of the great banquet,[28] the Matthean version is regarded as secondary,[29] and therefore we cannot

42 (7 out of 72 words; 9.7 per cent); 16.1b-8 (13 out of 161 words; 8.1 per cent); 16.19-31 (19 out of 244 words; 7.8 per cent). Although this may increase the likelihood of their being pre-Lukan, it cannot show connections between L material.

24.   It is hard to believe that Luke would break up the neat parallelism of the Matthean version: cf. Schenk, *Synopse*, p. 26. But Goulder, *New Paradigm*, I, pp. 364-65, thinks that this is exactly what Luke has done, resulting in typical Lukan 'prosiness'.

25.   See Mt. 5.45; Lk. 17.29; Jas 5.17; Rev. 11.6.

26.   'To rain' is also the meaning in the majority of occurrences in the LXX: Gen. 2.5; 19.24; Exod. 9.23; Ps. 77 (78). 24, 27; Amos 4.7; Joel 2.23; Isa. 5.6; Ezek. 22.24; 38.22. Only at Ps. 6.6 and Isa. 34.3 does it have the meaning 'wet' or 'drench'.

27.   Mt. 22.2, 3, 4, 8, 9, 10, 11, 12; 25.10; see also Jn 2.1, 2, 3; Heb. 13.4; Rev. 19.7, 9.

28.   Mt. 22.1-14; cf. Lk. 14.15-24; cf. *Gos. Thom.* 64. See also Chapter 2, section 4.2.1, on Lk. 14.15-24.

29.   See esp. Manson, *Sayings*, p. 129. But if the reconstruction of Goulder, *New Paradigm*, II, pp. 588-94 is correct, this would strengthen the case that Luke prefers δεῖπνον over γάμος.

speculate that Luke omitted the word from his parallel. Inclining the probability slightly more in favor of the word being pre-Lukan is that Luke has available several synonyms: 1) δεῖπνον, which he uses in similar contexts in Markan material,[30] Q material,[31] as well as other L material;[32] 2) ἄριστον, which he uses in his own composition and in L material;[33] 3) δοχή, which he inserts into Markan material and which is found in L material.[34] Luke's more frequent use of these synonyms makes the word γάμος more likely to be pre-Lukan here.

3. γείτων (Lk. 14.12; 15.6, 9). This noun occurs in neither Matthew nor Mark.[35] The fact that Luke more often uses the synonym πλησίον, which he has inherited from Mark,[36] inclines the probability slightly in favor of the word being pre-Lukan here.

4. δεκαόκτω/δέκα καὶ ὀκτώ; (Lk. 13.4, 11, 16). The number 'eighteen' occurs nowhere else in the New Testament. It is not one of the stereotyped numbers used so often in the Gospels,[37] and it would seem gratuitous for Luke to add such a detail to either of these pericopae. Further, Luke frequently changes the word order in his source so that the numeral follows the noun,[38] while in v. 16 the numeral precedes the noun. For these reasons, the number seems most likely to be pre-Lukan here.

5. ἔλαιον (Lk. 7.46; 10.34; 16.6). Luke omits this noun from his parallel to Mk 6.13 (Lk. 9.6),[39] a healing. Although he does not

---

30. Lk. 20.46//Mk 12.39.

31. Lk. 14.16, 17, 24.

32. Lk. 14.12.

33. It is used in Lukan composition at Lk. 11.38 (also see the verb at 11.37), and in L material at Lk. 14.12.

34. Luke inserts the word at Lk. 5.29 (cf. Mk 2.15), and it is in L material at Lk. 14.13.

35. The only other occurrence in the New Testament is at Jn 9.8.

36. See Lk. 10.27, 29 (cf. Mk 12.31, 33); 10.36; Acts 7.27.

37. E.g. forty (Lk. 4.2; Mk 1.13); seven (Lk. 17.4; Mt. 18.22); ten (Lk. 19.13).

38. Lk. 9.13//Mk 6.38; Lk. 9.14//Mk 6.44; Lk. 9.17//Mk 6.43; Lk. 9.33//Mk 9.5; Lk. 11.26//Mt. 12.45; see Cadbury, *Style and Literary Method*, pp. 153-54. Also cf. passages such as Acts 25.6.

39. Elsewhere in the New Testament at Mt. 25.3, 4, 8; Heb. 1.9; Jas 5.14; Rev. 6.6; 18.13.

deem 'oil' as appropriate in this healing story, it is later used by the Samaritan to treat the wounded man in Lk. 10.34.[40] The word's occurrence in three L passages and its omission by Luke in a similar passage elsewhere make it likely that it is pre-Lukan here.

6.   ἐνενήκοντα ἐννέα/ἐννέα (Lk. 15.4, [7]; 17.17). The number 'ninety-nine' occurs only in the parable of the lost sheep, and the number 'nine' only in the healing of the ten lepers in Luke–Acts.[41] Again, as in the case of 'eighteen', 'nine' is not one of the typical numbers in the Gospels, and either pericope could function without it.[42] Because it does not seem likely that Luke would add this detail, the number seems likely to be preLukan.

7.   κόπος (Lk. 11.7; 18.5). The expression παρέχειν κόπον occurs in the Markan version of the anointing (Mk 14.6), but not in the Lukan, so Luke has indirectly omitted it by using his variant version. It is one of the parallels often noted between the parable of the persistent friend and the parable of the unjust judge, a parallelism that does not seem borne out in the present plan of Luke's Gospel,[43] thereby lessening the likelihood that Luke constructed or imposed the parallelism himself. It is more likely that this expression is a pre-Lukan similarity between these two parables, rather than a Lukan insertion, especially as he does not include it in his version of the anointing.

---

40.   For this treatment as indicative of Luke's medical training, see W.K. Hobart, *The Medical Language of St Luke* (Dublin: Hodges, Figgis & Co, 1882), pp. 28-29; see the critique in Cadbury, *Style and Literary Method*, pp. 45-51.

41.   The numeral is one of the very few links with the Matthean version: Mt. 18.12, 13; cf. *Gos. Thom.* 107. Although the number '(ninety)-nine' occurs at Lk. 15.7, which is redactional, Luke would have had to reproduce it there for his secondary application to work with the parable (vv. 4-6).

42.   Cf. Lk. 15.8-10, which functions without specifying the number of the remnant, or Lk. 19.11-27 (cf. Mt. 25.14-30) where the contrast is between 1, 5, and 10. Cf. Goulder, *New Paradigm*, I, pp. 104-105: I grant that fives and tens are common in Luke–Acts, but not nines.

43.   See Leaney, *Luke*, p. 188; Blomberg, 'Midrash, Chiasmus', pp. 240-41; Nolland, *Luke*, pp. 865-70. Cf. the structure proposed by K.E. Bailey, *Poet and Peasant* (Grand Rapids: Eerdmans, 1976), pp. 79-85, who suggests that it is pre-Lukan, but does not elaborate.

8. ὄνος (Lk. 13.15; 14.5). This noun occurs in the Matthean and Johannine versions of Jesus' entry into Jerusalem.[44] Although it may well have existed in the pre-Lukan versions of these two L healings, the two pericopae are close enough together in Luke's work that he may have redacted them to be more similar, adding a word such as ὄνος to one or the other of the pericopae.[45] There seems to be nothing to mitigate against this possibility, and the word cannot be deemed pre-Lukan.

9. περιζώννυμαι (Lk. 12.35, 37; 17.8). This verb occurs nowhere else in the Gospels.[46] The fact that Luke uses the more general verb for 'clothe' (περιβάλλω) several times in both his Gospel and Acts may incline the probability slightly in favor of περιζώννυμαι being pre-Lukan.[47] On the other hand, given how close the wording is between Exod. 12.11 (LXX) and Lk. 12.35, this could well be an addition by Luke himself. More evidence would be needed before this word could be considered as probably pre-Lukan.[48]

10. πύργος (Lk. 13.4; 14.28). Luke omits this noun from his parallel to Mk 12.1 (Lk. 20.9) as an unnecessary detail.[49] 'Tower' is intrinsic to the story at Lk. 13.1b-5, and Luke is unlikely to have composed the entire story from scratch; on the other hand, in Lk. 14.28-32, where the 'tower' could have been added to the story,[50] the addition of such a detail would seem as superfluous as Luke perceived it to be in Mk 12.1. The word is therefore probably pre-Lukan here.

11. σπλαγχνίζομαι (Lk. 7.13; 10.33; 15.20). Luke omits this verb from his parallels to Markan material three times.[51] This makes it less likely that Luke has added it three times to other material. Further, Luke's aversion to depicting Jesus' emotions

---

44.   Mt. 21.2, 5, 7; Jn 12.15.

45.   Cf. Nolland, *Luke*, p. 746.

46.   It occurs elsewhere in the New Testament at Eph. 6.14; Rev. 1.13; 15.6.

47.   περιβάλλω is found at Lk. 12.27; 23.11; Acts 12.8.

48.   It is included in pre-Lukan vocabulary by Easton, 'Linguistic Evidence', p. 157.

49.   It is retained by Matthew in his parallel (Mt. 21.33) but occurs nowhere else in the New Testament.

50.   The specific structure being built is not mentioned in vv. 29-30.

51.   Luke has no parallel to Mk 8.2; Luke omits from his parallels to Mk 1.41 (Lk. 5.13); Mk 6.34 (Lk. 9.11); and Mk 9.22 (Lk. 9.42).

has often been noted,[52] and makes it even more unlikely that he would add the verb with reference to Jesus at Lk. 7.13. The word is thus most likely pre-Lukan.[53]

12.   συκοφαντέω (Lk. 3.14; 19.8). This verb occurs nowhere else in the New Testament. Inclining the probability slightly in favor of the word being pre-Lukan is that an echoing of John the Baptist's preaching at Lk. 19.1-10 makes little sense in the present plan of the Gospel.[54]

13.   χρεοφειλέτης (Lk. 7.41; 16.5). Although this word ocurs nowhere else in the New Testament, the related nouns ὀφειλέτης and ὀφείλημα occur in Q,[55] where Luke has felt it necessary to substitute ἁμαρτίαι for 'debts'.[56] The related verb ὀφείλω is also almost exclusive to L passages.[57] Since Luke is not fully satisfied with speaking of 'debts', it seems likely that this complex of words is pre-Lukan.

Of the thirteen *hapax legomena* that occur in more than one L pericope, ten have been found to be more probably pre-Lukan than from

52.   See above, Chapter 2, section 4.1.2, on Lk. 19.41-44; see Cadbury, *Style and Literary Method*, pp. 91-92; Fitzmyer, *Luke*, p. 94-95.

53.   For similar conclusions, cf. Easton, 'Linguistic Evidence', p. 158; Rehkopf, *Die lukanische Sonderquelle*, p. 97; Farmer, 'Some of the Synoptic Material', p. 304; Fitzmyer, *Luke*, p. 656. On the other hand, for the verb (or at least its placement) as Lukan, see M.J.J. Menken, 'The Position of σπλαγχνίζεσθαι and σπλάγχνα in the Gospel of Luke', *NovT* 30 (1988), pp. 107-14. Menken's analysis relies on an extremely subtle use of word counts, and does not adequately deal with the Lukan omissions of the verb: cf. the similar critique in Nolland, *Luke*, p. 594.

54.   John the Baptist has not been mentioned since Lk. 9.19, and the two pericopae do not form an *inclusio* of any identifiable section in Luke. Cf. Manson, 'John the Baptist', pp. 411-12. Less likely is the suggestion of Bailey, *Poet and Peasant*, pp. 80-82, that the Zacchaeus pericope is parallel to the sending of the seventy (Lk. 10.1-20). συκοφαντέω is listed as possibly pre-Lukan by Easton, 'Linguistic Evidence', p. 165, and Schweizer, *Luke*, p. 290.

55.   Mt. 6.12; cf. Lk. 11.4.

56.   That 'debt' is the original Q reading is widely accepted: see Fitzmyer, *Luke*, p. 906; Schenk, *Synopse*, p. 61; Havener (Polag), *Q*, p. 132. Luke is fond of the word ἁμαρτία: 11 times in Luke, 8 times in Acts. (Since 'debts' is in Matthew, it will not affect the present point if Luke is using him as a source: Goulder, *New Paradigm*, II, p. 497, admits Luke's preference for speaking of 'sins' rather than 'debts'.)

57.   See below; Lk. 7.41; 16.5, 7; 17.10. It is in Q at Lk. 11.4 (cf. Mt. 6.12), and once in Acts 17.29.

Luke himself.[58] I turn now to determine how much other vocabulary found in the L material under consideration is more likely to be pre-Lukan, and whether there are any possible pre-Lukan links between the material.[59]

2.2. *Other Vocabulary in L Material*

Of the words listed by Easton, Jeremias, and Rehkopf, (and some that are not), the following words that occur in more than one L pericope show the highest likelihood of being pre-Lukan, either because they are omitted by Luke in his redaction of Mark or Q, or because he uses them with a different meaning, or because he elsewhere prefers a synonym. Of course, in trying to avoid the pitfalls of these works, the number of words listed here is much less than that claimed by them.[60]

1. αἰσχύνη/αἰσχύνομαι/καταισχύνω (Lk. 14.9; 16.3; 13.17). These words for 'shame' occur nowhere else in Luke–Acts. Luke retains the synonymous compound ἐπαισχύνομαι in his redaction of Markan material,[61] but uses a different expression for 'shame' in his infancy narrative.[62] The repeated occurrences of these words only in L material and Luke's use elsewhere of synonyms make these words more likely to be pre-Lukan here.[63]

2. ἄνθρωπός τις (Lk. 10.30; 12.16; 14.2; 15.11; 16.1b, 19;). This phrase begins five of the L parables, and one of the L healings. It occurs elsewhere in Luke–Acts only twice, once in Q,[64] and once at Acts 9.33. It would seem best explained as a combination of Lukan formulation, but with an underlying

58. These are γάμος, γείτων, δεκαόκτω, ἔλαιον, ἐνενήκοντα ἐννέα/ἐννέα, κόπος, πύργος, σπλαγχνίζομαι, συκοφαντέω, and χρεοφειλέτης.
59. Despite our differences, on this point my reconstruction is not completely irreconcilable with that of Goulder: of the *hapax* above he lists only γείτων as part of 'Lucan' vocabulary; of the words following in section 2.2, he lists only ἄνθρωπός τις and εὐφραίνω as 'Lucan'. See Goulder, *New Paradigm*, II, pp. 800-809.
60. Cf. Easton, 'Linguistic Evidence', pp. 145-58, who claims 71 words as 'especially characteristic' or 'probably characteristic' of L; or Rehkopf, *Die lukanische Sonderquelle*, pp. 91-98, who notes 78 words in his list.
61. Lk. 9.26//Mk 8.38.
62. Lk. 1.25 (ὄνειδος); see J. Schneider, ὄνειδος, *TDNT* 5 (1967), pp. 238-42.
63. Goulder, *New Paradigm*, II, p. 585, lists 'shame' as a Lukan theme, but he only lists these L passages and overlooks Lk. 1.25 and 9.26.
64. Lk. 19.12, where the ἄνθρωπος is probably original to Q (cf. Mt. 25.14).

pre-Lukan wording. On the one hand, it clearly seems an example of Luke's frequent use of τις + a noun.[65] On the other hand, Luke shows a preference for ἀνήρ over ἄνθρωπος in general,[66] and in particular, for ἀνήρ τις over ἄνθρωπός τις.[67] The fact that this phrase occurs almost exclusively in the introductions to L material, together with Luke's preference for another equivalent phrase make it seem likely that it is pre-Lukan here.

3. δαπάνη/δαπανάω (verb with accusative) (Lk. 14.28; 15.14). Luke uses the verb with the dative once in Acts 21.24, and omits it from his parallel to Mk 5.26 (cf. Lk. 8.43). This omission and the use of the verb with a different case incline the probability in favor of these words being pre-Lukan here.[68]

4. διασκορπίζω (Lk. 15.13; 16.1). Luke uses this verb once in his infancy narrative (Lk. 1.51) in imitation of the LXX,[69] and once in Acts 5.37; in both these casezs, the verb is related to people rather than capital, and therefore carries the rather different meaning of 'scatter'. Further, Luke omits the verb from his parallel to Mk 14.27 (cf. Lk. 22.31). These two considerations make it likely that the verb is pre-Lukan here.

65.   38 times in the Gospel, 63 times in Acts; see J.C. Hawkins, *Horae Synopticae: Contributions to the Study of the Problem* (Oxford: Clarendon Press, 2nd edn, 1909), pp. 19, 37-38; Jeremias, *Die Sprache*, p. 15; Fitzmyer, *Luke*, p. 111; M.E. Boismard and A. Lamouille, *Le texte occidental des Actes des Apôtres: Reconstitution et réhabilitation*. I. *Introduction et textes*. II. *Apparat critique, index des caractéristiques stylistiques, index des citations patristiques* (Paris: Editions Recherche sur les Civilisations, 1984), II, p. 208; F. Neirynck and F. Van Segbroeck, 'Le texte des Actes des Apôtres et les caractéristiques lucaniennes', *ETL* 61 (1985), pp. 304-39; Goulder, *New Paradigm*, II, p. 809.

66.   The noun ἀνήρ occurs 27 times in Luke and 100 times in Acts, cf. only eight times in Matthew and four times in Mark. See Cadbury, *Style and Literary Method*, p. 189; A.C. Clark, *The Acts of the Apostles: A Critical Edition with Introduction and Notes on Selected Passages* (Oxford: Clarendon Press, 1933; repr. 1970), p. 398; Farmer, 'Some of the Synoptic Material', p. 304; J. Dawsey, 'The Literary Unity of Luke–Acts: Questions of Style—A Task for Literary Critics', *NTS* 35 (1989), pp. 48-66.

67.   The former occurs at Lk. 8.27 (where Luke has substituted ἀνήρ for ἄνθρωπος; cf. Mk 5.2), and at Acts 5.1; 8.9; 10.1; 13.6; 14.8; 16.9; 17.5, 34; 25.14. The latter occurs only twice in Acts (Acts 9.33; 25.16).

68.   Cf. Easton, 'Linguistic Evidence', p. 160.

69.   Ps. 88 (89).10.

5. ἐλεέω (Lk. 16.24; 17.13). Luke reproduces this verb in his
    parallel to Mk 10.47, 48 (Lk. 18.38, 39), although he omits it
    once from his parallel to Mk 5.19 (Lk. 8.39). It occurs
    nowhere else in Luke–Acts. Luke's omission increases the like-
    lihood that the verb is pre-Lukan here.[70]

6. εὐφραίνω (Lk. 12.19; 15.23, 24, 29, 32; 16.19). This verb
    occurs elsewhere in Luke–Acts only at Acts 2.26 and 7.41.[71]
    Inclining the probability in favor of its being pre-Lukan here
    is Luke's preference for the synonym χαίρω, which he uses a
    total of eighteen times throughout his double work: in his
    infancy narrative,[72] in his redaction of Mark,[73] in Q material,[74]
    in L material,[75] in verses that are probably Lukan com-
    position,[76] in the Passion account,[77] and several times in Acts.[78]
    This preference for the verb χαίρω shows that εὐφραίνω is
    not Luke's preferred language, and makes it more probable
    that the verb is pre-Lukan here.[79]

7. ἡμέρα τοῦ σαββάτου (singular) (Lk. 13.14, 16; 14.5). This
    construction with the singular occurs nowhere else in Luke–
    Acts. Luke's use of the plural ἡμέρα τῶν σαββάτων several
    times in his work makes it more probable that the construction
    here is pre-Lukan.[80]

8. καταφιλέω (Lk. 7.38, 45; 15.20). Although Luke uses this
    verb once in Acts 20.37, he omits it from his parallel to Mk
    14.45 (Lk. 22.47). This makes it more likely that the verb here
    is pre-Lukan.[81]

70.   Cf. Easton, 'Linguistic Evidence', p. 153.

71.   Though the first is a LXX quotation (Ps. 15.9).

72.   Lk. 1.14, 28.

73.   He adds it in his redaction of Mark at Lk. 19.37 (cf. Mk 11.9); he retains it in
his parallel to Mk 14.11 (Lk. 22.5).

74.   Lk. 6.23; Mt. 5.12.

75.   Lk. 15.5, 32; 19.6.

76.   Lk. 10.20; 13.17c.

77.   Lk. 23.8.

78.   Acts 5.41; 8.39; 11.23; 13.48; 15.23, 31; 23.26.

79.   The verb is listed as pre-Lukan by both Easton, 'Linguistic Evidence',
pp. 154-55; and Rehkopf, *Die lukanische Sonderquelle*, p. 94.

80.   Luke has the plural at Lk. 4.16; Acts 13.14; 16.13. Cf. Easton, 'Linguistic
Evidence', p. 155.

81.   Cf. Easton, 'Linguistic Evidence', p. 156; Boismard and Lamouille, *Texte*

9. λέπρος (Lk. 4.27; 17.12). This noun occurs once in Q.[82] Luke makes a substitution in his parallel to Mk 1.40 (Lk. 5.12), and it is absent in Luke's version of the anointing (cf. Mk 14.3). It occurs nowhere in Acts. These omissions make it more probable that the word is pre-Lukan here.[83]

10. λιμὸς ἐγένετο (Lk. 4.25; 15.14). This phrase occurs nowhere else in Luke–Acts. Given Luke's use of other verbs to express the occurrence of a 'famine', especially his avoidance of this phrase at Acts 7.11,[84] it seems probable that here this phrase is pre-Lukan.[85]

11. μακρόθεν (Lk. 16.23; 18.13). Luke reproduces this adverb in his parallels to Mk 14.54 (Lk. 22.54) and Mk 15.40 (Lk. 23.49). He omits it from his parallel to Mk 5.6 (Lk. 8.28), and lacks parallels to the other two Markan occurrences (Mk 8.3; 11.13). It occurs nowhere in Acts. Luke's omission makes it probable that this word is pre-Lukan.[86]

12. ὀφειλέτης/ὀφείλω/χρεοφειλέτης (Lk. 7.41; 13.4; 16.5, 7; 17.10). As noted above, Luke omits the noun ὀφείλημα from Q.[87] Besides one occurrence in the same Q passage (Lk. 11.4), the verb occurs outside of L passages only at Acts 17.29. Given Luke's preference for speaking of 'sins' rather than 'debt', it does not seem that this is his own phrasing, and these words thus seem more likely to be pre-Lukan.[88]

13. πόρρω/πόρρωθεν (Lk. 14.32; 17.12). Although πόρρω occurs in Luke's resurrection account (Lk. 24.28), he omits it from his parallel to Mk 7.6 (cf. Lk. 11.41). Neither word occurs anywhere in Acts. Luke's omission makes it more likely that these words are here pre-Lukan.[89]

---

occidental, II, p. 203; Neirynck and Van Segbroeck, 'Le texte des Actes', p. 323.

82.   Lk. 7.22; cf. Mt. 11.5.

83.   Cf. Easton, 'Linguistic Evidence', p. 163.

84.   Luke uses λιμός with εἰμί at Lk. 21.11(// Mk 13.8) and Acts 11.28; and with ἔρχομαι at Acts 7.11, where he has *not* reproduced the LXX version, ἐγένετο λίμος (Gen. 41.54).

85.   Cf. Easton, 'Linguistic Evidence', p. 163; Jeremias, *Die Sprache*, pp. 126-27.

86.   Cf. Rehkopf, *Die lukanische Sonderquelle*, p. 95.

87.   Lk. 11.4; cf. Mt. 6.12.

88.   Cf. Farmer, 'Some of the Synoptic Material', p. 314; Nolland, *Luke*, p. 718.

89.   Cf. Easton, 'Linguistic Evidence', p. 157.

14. χορτάζω (Lk. 15.16; 16.21). Luke reproduces this verb in his redaction of both Mark and Q,[90] but he uses it nowhere in Acts. Lk. 15.16 and 16.21 are even more similar than just the use of the same verb: both use the aorist passive infinitive of χορτάζω after ἐπιθυμέω.[91] Luke's much more frequent use of the verb ἐσθίω also inclines the probability in favor of χορτάζω being pre-Lukan in these two parables.[92]

2.2.1. *Other Possibly Pre-Lukan Vocabulary*
In addition to those already mentioned, several words and expressions deserve to be noted as quite possibly pre-Lukan. They occur so seldom in Luke–Acts that they are obviously not specifically Lukan in any sense, but because Luke does not avoid them or show a preference for other words, we cannot conclude that they are probably pre-Lukan.[93]

1. τὸ ἀγαθόν/τὰ ἀγαθά (substantive) (Lk. 12.18; 16.25). This substantive does not occur in Mark,[94] and occurs once in Q.[95] Luke never uses the adjective in this way in Acts.[96]
2. ἀφαιρέω (Lk. 10.42; 16.3). Luke reproduces this verb in his parallel to Mk 14.47 (Lk. 22.50), and uses it once in his infancy narrative in imitation of the LXX.[97] It occurs nowhere in Acts.[98]
3. ἐπιμελέομαι/ἐπιμελῶς (Lk. 10.34, 35; 15.8). Neither of these words occurs anywhere else in Luke–Acts, although the

90. Lk. 9.17//Mk 6.42; Lk. 6.21 (cf. Mt. 5.6). Luke lacks parallels to the other three occurrences of the verb in Mark (Mk 7.27; 8.4, 8).

91. Cf. Fitzmyer, *Luke*, p. 1131.

92. The verb ἐσθίω occurs 33 times in Luke and seven times in Acts; cf. 26 times in Mark and 23 times in Matthew. Perhaps most surprising is Lk. 22.15, which with its use of ἐπιθυμέω + infinitive is remarkably close to Lk. 15.16 and 16.21, except that in 22.15 Luke uses ἐσθίω.

93. Again, Goulder, *New Paradigm*, II, pp. 800-809, lists only ἀφαιρέω as 'Lucan'.

94. Though Matthew does add it in his redaction of Mk 10.18 (Mt. 19.17; cf. Lk. 18.19).

95. Lk. 6.45; cf. Mt. 12.35.

96. It is listed as pre-Lukan by Rehkopf, *Die lukanische Sonderquelle*, p. 91.

97. Lk. 1.25; cf. Gen. 30.23.

98. It is listed as pre-Lukan by both Easton, 'Linguistic Evidence', p. 151; and Rehkopf, *Die lukanische Sonderquelle*, p. 92.

The Story of Jesus according to L

noun ἐπιμέλεια does occur once at Acts 27.3.[99]

4. ὑποδέχομαι (Lk. 10.38; 19.6). This verb occurs elsewhere in Luke–Acts only at Acts 17.7.[100]

2.3. *Vocabulary in L Material: Summary*

Having sifted through the vocabulary of L material, we have found a total of 24 words, groups of words, or phrases that seem most probably to be pre-Lukan rather than Lukan additions, and which may therefore show pre-Lukan linguistic connections between L pericopae. Which L pericopae are possibly connected by these words are shown in Table 3.

Table 3: *Shared Pre-Lukan Vocabulary in L Material*

Pericope	a	b	c	d	e	f	g	h	i	j	k	l	m	n	o	p	q	r	s	t	u	v	w
a) 3.10-14																							1
b) 4.25-27														1				1					
c) 7.11b-15					1									1									
d) 7.36-47					1				1					1			2		1				
e) 10.30-37a		1	1			1				1						2	2	1					
f) 11.5b-8																					1		
g) [12.16b-20]						1				1						2	1	2					
h) 12.35-38												1											
i) 13.1b-5					1					1			1				1		1				
j) 13.10-17b									1		1	1					1						
k) 14.2-5					1	1				1						1	1	1					
l) 14.8-10, 12-14							1			1					1	1	1						
m) 14.28-32									1							1				1			
n) [15.4-6]										1				1						1			
o) 15.8-9										1				1									
p) 15.11-32	1	1	1		2		2			1			1				2		3				
q) 16.1b-8a			1		2		2		1	1	1	1			2		1						
r) 16.19-31					1		2			1						3	1		1		1		
s) 17.7-10				1					1								1						
t) 17.12-18	1											1	1				1						
u) 18.2-8a					1																		
v) 18.10-14a																		1					
w) 19.2-10	1																						

99. Neither the adverb nor the noun occur anywhere else in the New Testament; the verb occurs elsewhere in the New Testament only at 1 Tim. 3.5.

100. It occurs elsewhere in the New Testament only at Jas 2.25 and is listed as possibly pre-Lukan by Easton, 'Linguistic Evidence', p. 166.

The pericopae are listed with a letter in the first column; by reading across, one finds the letters of the pericopae with which that pericope shares vocabulary, and how many of these words they share.

Twenty-three of the L pericopae still under consideration share some of the un-Lukan vocabulary determined above. Because all of these words were determined to be *probably* pre-Lukan, the occurrence of two or more of these words in seventeen of the pericopae is particularly significant: e.g. supposing there is still a one in three chance that any occurrence of one of these words is in fact due to Luke himself, there is then only a one in nine chance that he added two of these words to one pericope. If these pericopae also share un-Lukan elements of style or usage in addition to their un-Lukan vocabulary, this will further increase the probability that these pericopae are from a pre-Lukan source.[101]

3. *Stylometry: The Study of Common Vocabulary and Syntax*

At the other extreme of stylistic study from the study of *hapax legomena* is stylometry. The basic contours of the method are as follows.[102] The endeavor stems from a desire to define the amorphous concept of 'style' into something that can be quantified and studied. Arguments over exactly how this is to be done still dominate the field, but all the suggested methods seem to share one common, and, on the face of it, plausible, assumption: an author's style is most clearly shown by his or her use of the most common and frequently occurring words or constructions—particles, the verb 'to be', the tenses and moods of verbs, prepositions, and so on—rather than by the occasional occurrences of unusual terms found in the writing. This seems plausible because if an author's style is his or her natural, instinctive, unconscious use of language, then one would expect to find it exhibited most clearly in the unthinking use of empty, stock words; for example, an author would probably stop and weigh his or her choices (and thereby might alter his or her style) before penning a significant word such as 'faith' or

---

101. The overlap between pre-Lukan vocabulary and style will be given in the conclusion to this chapter, section 5.

102. For a good synopsis of the history of the field, see D.S. Williams, *Stylometric Authorship Studies in Flavius Josephus and Related Literature* (Lewiston, NY: Edwin Mellen, 1992), pp. 1-22.

'righteousness', but would not pause before writing down another 'and' or 'but'. This method also has the notable advantage that by studying the most common characteristics of style, a much smaller sample is required.[103]

The analysis of language as though it were in large part an unconscious phenomenon that could be analyzed statistically treats it in a way that is virtually the opposite of works such as Cadbury's or subsequent redaction criticism, which treat writing as one of the more deliberate of enterprises.[104] But interestingly, the work of stylometry arrives at many of the conclusions familiar to us from Cadbury's work: Luke, for instance, is more sparing than Mark in his use of καί,[105] and he uses ἵνα much more seldom than most New Testament writers.[106] Because they ignore any knowledge of Luke's use of Mark, the merely statistical methods of stylometry may have missed some Lukan preferences, such as Luke's aversion to the historical present; but on the other hand they may have uncovered some subtleties, such as Luke's use of negation less frequently than other New Testament authors.[107] I will treat below those constructions in L material that show the most difference from standard Lukan usage.

3.1. *Conjunctions and Particles*

1. καί. Luke is much more sparing in his use of καί than is Mark.[108] This results both from his elimination of parataxis in

103. See S. Hockey, *A Guide to Computer Applications in the Humanities* (Baltimore: The Johns Hopkins University Press, 1980), p. 136.

104. The theoretical problems raised by the fact that language is never truly random and therefore may not be an appropriate subject for statistical analysis is discussed by Kenny, *Computation of Style*, pp. 161-68; cf. the discussion of method in A.Q. Morton, *Literary Detection. How to Prove Authorship and Fraud in Literature and Documents* (New York: Charles Scribner's Sons, 1978), pp. 75-92.

105. Cadbury, *Style and Literary Method*, pp. 142-43; Kenny, *Stylometric Study*, pp. 26-30.

106. Cadbury, *Stlye and Literary Method*, pp. 137-38; Kenny, *Stylometric Study*, pp. 39-40.

107. Kenny, *Stylometric Study*, pp. 38-39.

108. Mark uses the conjunction the most among the Gospels: 9.72 per cent of his total words, second only to Revelation (11.43 per cent) in the New Testament; on the other hand, the frequency of the conjunction in Acts is less than in any of the Synoptics (6.12 per cent). See Kenny, *Stylometric Study*, pp. 26-27; see also Hawkins, *Horae Synopticae*, pp. 120-22.

his redaction of Mark and Q,[109] and from his substitution of
δέ or τε for καί.[110] With this in mind, several of the L pericopae under consideration should be noted as containing an
unusually high number of occurrences of the conjunction.[111]
This should be considered as further mitigating against pure
Lukan composition of these pericopae, as well as perhaps indi-
cating the remains of a source's preference for the conjunction
that Luke's redaction has not completely obscured.

2. ἵνα (Lk. 7.36; 10.40; 12.36; 14.10, 29; 15.29; 16.4, 9, 24, 27,
    28; 18.5; 19.4). The conjunction ἵνα occurs thirteen times in
    the L material under consideration, while Luke uses it only fif-
    teen times in all of Acts, less proportionately than any other
    New Testament writing.[112] Luke lacks parallels to eleven of the
    occurrences of ἵνα in Mark;[113] when he does have a parallel
    to Mark, he omits or makes a substitution for the conjunction
    35 times.[114] Luke agrees with Matthew on three occurrences

109. See Fitzmyer, *Luke*, p. 108.

110. See Cadbury, *Style and Literary Method*, pp. 142-43; Fitzmyer, *Luke*, p. 108.
It should also be noted that τε, of which Luke is very fond (nine times in Luke and
134-158 times in Acts; cf. three times in Matthew, none in Mark), does not occur in
any of the L material under consideration. Goulder, *New Paradigm*, II, p. 808, lists
τε as 'Lucan'. (The wide disparity in the figures for Acts is due to the high number of
variants: see Clark, *Acts of the Apostles*, pp. 396-97; Boismard and Lamouille, *Texte
occidental*, II, pp. 207-208; Neirynck and Van Segbroeck, 'Le texte des Actes', p. 329;
Dawsey, 'Literary Unity', pp. 59-60).

111. Lk. 3.10-14 (8x); 7.11b-15 (12x); 8.2-3 (5x); 10.30-37a (13x, 12 of these in
vv. 30-35); 12.35-38 (8x); 13.6b-9 (7x); 13.10-17b (12x, 7 of these in vv. 11-13);
13.31b-32 (5x, 4 of these in v. 32); 14.2-5 (7x, 6 of these in vv. 3-5); 15.4-6 (5x); 15.8-
9 (4x); 15.11-32 (36x); 16.19-31 (18x, 12 of these in vv. 19-24); 19.2-10 (13x, 5 of
these in vv. 2-3); 19.41-44 (8x, 6 of these in vv. 43-44). Cf. these with the number of
occurrences when Luke is following a Markan passage with a high incidence of καί:
e.g. Mk 2.23-28 (12x)//Lk. 6.1-5 (7x); Mk 10.17-31 (18x)//Lk. 18.18-30 (7x).

112. Acts 2.25 (quoting LXX, Ps. 15.8); 4.17; 5.15; 8.19; 9.21; 16.30, 36; 17.15;
19.4; 21.24; 22.5, 24; 23.24; 24.4; 27.42. Cf. Clark, *Acts of the Apostles*, p. 402; Kenny,
Stylometric Study, pp. 39-40.

113. Mk 6.25, 56; 7.26, 32, 36; 8.6, 22; 9.12; 10.35, 37; 11.25.

114. Lk. 4.43 (cf. Mk 1.38); 6.12-19 (cf. Mk 3.9-14); 8.16-18 (cf. Mk 4.21, 22);
8.38 (cf. Mk 5.18); 8.40-56 (cf. Mk 5.23, 43); 9.1-6 (cf. Mk 6.8, 12); 9.16 (cf. Mk
6.41); 9.21 (cf. Mk 8.30); 9.37 (cf. Mk 9.9); 9.38-40 (cf. Mk 9.22, 30); 11.41 (cf. Mk
7.9); 18.18 (cf. Mk 10.17); 19.12 (cf. Mk 13.34); 19.45 (cf. Mk 11.16); 20.2 (cf. Mk
11.28); 20.23 (cf. Mk 12.15); 21.23 (cf. Mk 13.18); 22.4 (cf. Mk 14.10); 22.41 (cf. Mk
14.35); 22.52 (cf. Mk 14.49); 23.18 (cf. Mk 15.11); 23.25 (cf. Mk 15.15); 23.26 (cf.

in Q.[115] It occurs seven other times in Q material in Luke,[116] some of which may be original to Q, since Matthew also seems averse to the construction.[117] Luke does add ἵνα to his Markan material six times,[118] and it occurs twice in his infancy narrative.[119] Overall, his numerous omissions and extremely infrequent use of the conjunction in Acts would seem to show a general aversion to the construction on Luke's part.[120] It is therefore remarkable that the conjunction occurs almost as many times in eleven L pericopae as it does in all of Acts, which suggests that Luke was influenced by a source in these L pericopae.[121]

3.2. Prepositions

1. παρά (with accusative, comparative) (Lk. 3.13; 13.2, 4; 18.14). The use of παρά with the accusative in the sense of 'more than' or 'beyond' is a Semitism found nowhere else in Luke–Acts.[122] Its peculiar usage in three pericopae that are unrelated in the present plan of Luke's work makes it more likely that it is pre-Lukan and may be a link between these pericopae.[123]

2. Dative (instead of πρός + accusative). The dative after a verb of speaking occurs 40 times in the L material under consideration.[124] This is notable because of Luke's frequent use of πρός

Mk 15.20, 21); 23.35 (cf. Mk 15.32); 23.56 (cf. Mk 16.1). Cf. Cadbury, *Style and Literary Method*, pp. 137-38.

115. Lk. 4.3 (cf. Mt. 4.3); 6.31 (cf. Mt. 7.12); 7.6 (cf. Mt. 8.8).

116. Lk. 6.34; 11.33, 50; 14.23; 17.2; 19.15; 22.30.

117. It occurs 41 times in all of Matthew; cf. 48 times in all of Luke, 65 times in Mark, 145 times in John.

118. Lk. 8.12; 9.45; 20.14; 21.36; 22.30, 32.

119. Lk. 1.4, 43.

120. Cf. the conclusion of Cadbury, *Style and Literary Method*, p. 137.

121. Cf. the similar conclusion of Stanton, *Gospels*, p. 312.

122. See Jeremias, *Parables*, pp. 141-42; Farmer, 'Some of the Synoptic Material', p. 314; Fitzmyer, *Luke*, pp. 124, 1007. Cf. Luke's use of ὑπέρ instead in a similar sense at Lk. 6.40; 16.8; Acts 26.13. Despite its occuring nowhere else in Luke–Acts, Goulder, *New Paradigm*, II, p. 807, lists it as 'Lucan'.

123. Its usage is listed as pre-Lukan by both Easton, 'Linguistic Evidence', p. 149; and Rehkopf, *Die lukanische Sonderquelle*, p. 96.

124. The dative is used at Lk. 3.11, 14; 7.13, 39, 43, 44; 10.40, 41; 11.5; 12.14, 17,

+ accusative after a verb of speaking,[125] and because Luke has
replaced the dative with πρός + accusative 28 times in his
redaction of Mark and Q.[126] Further, an examination of the 202
verses listed in section 2.1 above where Luke is following a
Markan parallel, shows that he has retained the dative only 14
times,[127] and added it only four times.[128] The implications for
the L material can be stated thus: in his redaction of a larger
amount of Markan material Luke has the dative after a verb
of speaking less than half as many times (18 total) as he has it
in the L material under consideration; of these occurrences in
Markan material, the great majority (78 per cent) are original
to the Markan source. It therefore seems likely that most of
the datives in the L material are pre-Lukan as well and
indicate the influence of a source on Luke's language.

3.3. *Numerals*

The numbers 'nine' and 'eighteen' have already been noted as most
likely pre-Lukan, but a more general examination of numbers in the L
material under consideration is more revealing. Of the 38 pericopae,
18 contain cardinal numbers.[129] This frequency in itself is remarkable,
because it is noticeably higher than in Luke's Markan or Q passages.[130]

19, 20; 13.1b, 2, 8, 12, 14, 15, 32; 14.12; 15.6, 12, 18, 21, 27, 29, 31; 16.2, 3, 5, 6, 7
(*bis*), 15, 31; 17.7, 8, 14, 20; 18.4. This does not include any occurrences of the second
person pronoun in the dative, as these are quite common in Luke: see Fitzmyer, *Luke*,
p. 112.

125. πρός + accusative after a verb of speaking is found 99 times in Luke, 52 times
in Acts; see Hawkins, *Horae Synopticae*, pp. 18, 36-37.

126. See Cadbury, *Style and Literary Method*, p. 203; Farmer, 'Some of the
Synoptic Material', p. 314.

127. Lk. 4.35//Mk 1.25; Lk. 5.24, 27//Mk 2.10, 14; Lk. 6.5//Mk 2.27; Lk. 6.8,
10//Mk 3.3, 5; Lk. 8.20//Mk 3.32; Lk. 8.25//Mk 4.40; Lk. 8.48, 50//Mk 5.34, 36; Lk.
9.48//Mk 9.36; Lk. 18.19, 22, 42//Mk 10.18, 21, 52.

128. Lk. 9.12//Mk 6.35; Lk. 9.20//Mk 8.29; Lk. 18.29, 37//Mk 10.29, 47.

129. Lk. 3.10-14 (2); 4.25-27 (3, 6); 7.36-47 (2); 8.2-3 (7); 10.30-37a (2); 10.39-
42 (1); 11.5b-8 (3); 13.1b-5 (18); 13.6b-9 (3); 13.10-17b (18, 6); 14.28-32 (10,000,
20,000); 15.4-6 (100, 99, 1); 15.8-9 (10, 1); 15.11-32 (2); 16.1b-8 (100, 50, 80);
16.19-31 (fi5); 17.12-18 (10, 9); 18.10-14a (2).

130. Of the 36 Markan pericopae in Luke listed in section 2.1 above, only nine
contain cardinal numbers (Lk. 5.12-16//Mk 1.40-45; Lk. 5.17-26//Mk 2.1-12; Lk.
6.12-16//Mk 3.13-19; Lk. 8.22-25//Mk 4.35-41; Lk. 8.40-56//Mk 5.21-43; Lk. 9.1-
6//Mk 6.7-13; Lk. 9.10-17//Mk 6.32-44; Lk. 9.28-36//Mk 9.2-8; Lk. 18.18-23//Mk

Further, Luke even tends to omit numbers in his redaction of Mark and Q.[131] Finally, and perhaps most importantly, 11 of these pericopae contain the numeral before the noun, which is not Luke's preferred word order.[132] Of the pericopae that share this un-Lukan word order, the numbers 'two', 'three', and 'one hundred' are common to more than one pericope.[133] The high incidence of numerals in L material is notable, especially given Luke's treatment of material from his other sources; the un-Lukan word order common to many of these pericopae increases the likelihood that they are from some pre-Lukan source or tradition; and the sharing of three specific numerals in eight of the pericopae further reinforces this impression.

3.4. *Verbs*

1. Historical Present (Lk. 7.40; 13.8; 16.7, 23, 29). Luke omits the overwhelming majority of occurrences of the historical present that he has inherited from Mark: of 151 occurrences in Mark, Luke has retained only one.[134] Its appearance five times in L pericopae is therefore remarkable. Given Luke's avoidance of the historical present, it is most likely pre-Lukan in these pericopae and may show a stylistic link between them.[135]

10.17-22. Of the 57 Q pericopae in Luke listed in section 2.1 above, only 11 contain cardinal numbers (Lk. 4.1-13; 7.18-23; 11.24-26; 12.4-7; 13.20-21; 15.4-7; 16.13; 17.3-4; 17.34; 19.11-27; 22.28-30).

131. Luke omits numbers at Lk. 5.18//Mk 2.3; Lk. 8.8, 15//Mk 4.8, 20; Lk. 8.33//Mk 5.13; Lk. 9.13, 14//Mk 6.37, 40; Lk. 18.30//Mk 10.30; Lk. 22.1, 34, 61//Mk 14.1, 30, 72; Lk. 17.4//Mt. 18.22. See Cadbury, *Style and Literary Method*, pp. 128-29; see also below, Chapter 5, section 2.1.

132. Lk. 3.10; 7.41; 10.35; 11.5; 13.7, 14, 16; 15.4, 11; 16.6, 7, 28; 17.12. On Luke's preference for the numeral following the noun, see Cadbury, *Style and Literary Method*, pp. 153-54; Farmer, 'Some of the Synoptic Material', p. 303.

133. 'Two': Lk. 3.10; 7.41; 10.35; 15.11; 'three': Lk. 11.5; 13.7; '100': Lk. 15.4; 16.6, 7.

134. Lk. 8.49//Mk 5.35; see Hawkins, *Horae Synopticae*, pp. 113-19; Cadbury, *Style and Literary Method*, pp. 158-59. Luke lacks parallels for many of the Markan passages; he has omitted 89 of the 90 occurrences where he does have a parallel: see Jeremias, *Parables*, pp. 182-83.

135. Cf. Jeremias, *Parables*, p. 183, who believes it is 'clear evidence of the existence of an underlying pre-Lucan tradition'; and Farmer, 'Some of the Synoptic Material', p. 315.

2.　Optative Mood. There is only one occurrence of a verb in the optative mood in all of the L material under consideration–Lk. 15.26, a verse that has already been noted as redacted by Luke. The lack of optatives is notable because Luke does use the mood frequently, especially in comparison to the other evangelists, or in comparison to the rest of New Testament except Paul.[136] However, although the mood is more frequent in Luke–Acts relative to the rest of the New Testament, it is still quite rare in his work, accounting for only 0.3 per cent of his total verbs.[137] If the mood were frequent in L material, this would surely increase the probability in favor of Lukan composition; the lack of optatives in L material should therefore be noted as another piece of evidence against pure Lukan composition of all the material, but cannot be used as an argument in favor of a single source behind it.

3.5. *Comparison with Passages of Probable Lukan Composition*

It may be useful here to analyze several passages from Luke–Acts that are most probably Lukan composition in order to see how many of the above un-Lukan stylistic elements occur in them; this will show whether Luke avoids in his own composition the same stylistic elements that he omits in his redaction of Mark and Q. For this purpose I have chosen the summaries from Luke and Acts,[138] Peter's healing of a lame man,[139]

---

136. Matthew never uses the optative; it occurs once each in Mark and John; cf. 11 times in Luke (Lk. 1.29, 38, 62; 3.15; 6.11; 8.9; 9.46; 15.26; 18.36; 20.16; 22.23); 17 times in Acts (Acts 5.24; 8.20, 31; 10.17; 17.11, 18, 27 (*bis*); 20.16; 21.33; 24.19; 25.16 (*bis*), 20; 26.29; 27.12, 39); 32 times in Paul (although 14 of these are occurrences of the formula μὴ γένοιτο); 68 times total in the New Testament. On the optative in Luke–Acts, see Plummer, *Luke*, p. 22; Clark, *Acts of the Apostles*, p. 402; Fitzmyer, *Luke*, p. 108; Kenny, *Stylometric Study*, pp. 68-69, 74; Bruce, *The Acts of the Apostles*, p. 67.

137. See Kenny, *Stylometric Study*, p. 69; it accounts for 0.2 per cent of the total verbs in the Gospel, 0.4 per cent in Acts.

138. Lk. 4.14-15, 31-32, 40; 6.17-19; 8.1; 21.37-38; Acts 2.42-47; 4.32-35; 5.12-16; 6.7; 9.31; 12.24; 16.5; 19.20; 28.30-31; on these, see G.E. Sterling, '"Athletes of Virtue": An Analysis of the Summaries in Acts (2:41-47; 4:32-35; 5.12-16)', *JBL* 113 (1994), pp. 679-96.

139. Acts 3.1-10. If not pure Lukan composition, the story is one of the more heavily redacted that I could find: E. Haenchen, *The Acts of the Apostles. A Commentary* (trans. R. McL. Wilson; Philadelphia: Westminster Press, 1971), pp. 201-202, reckons only vv. 2, 3, and 7 as possibly pre-Lukan.

and Peter's speech in Cornelius' house.[140]

Three of the Lukan summaries do include a high incidence of καί,[141] while one other contains the preposition ἵνα.[142] None of the summaries contain any of the other non-Lukan stylistic elements, and no one summary contains more than one such element. The characteristics of the two pericopae from Acts are also consistent with the previous examination: neither contains any of the un-Lukan stylistic elements. While such a brief survey cannot be considered conclusive, it does offer some confirmation that in general we probably have not been 'fooled' in the L material by Luke composing passages that stylistically run contrary to his observed style elsewhere.

3.6. *Style in L Material: Summary*
I have determined six stylistic elements that distinguish some of the L material from Lukan usage, and which may show pre-Lukan stylistic links between the pericopae: abundant use of καί; use of ἵνα; use of παρά with the accusative in the sense of 'more than'; the use of the dative after a verb of speaking; the position of the numeral before the noun; and the use of the historical present. The L pericopae that contain these stylistic elements are shown in Table 4.

Table 4: *Pre-Lukan Style and Syntax in L Material*

Pericope	καί	ἵνα	παρά	Dative	# Position	Hist. Present
3.10-14	•		•	•	•	
7.11b-15	•			•		
7.36-47		•		•	•	•
8.2-3	•					
10.30-37a	•				•	
10.39-42		•		•		
11.5b-8				•	•	
[12,13b-14]				•		
[12.16b-20]				•		
12.35-38	•	•				
13.1b-5			•	•		
13.6b-9	•			•	•	•

---

140. Acts 10.34-43. Haenchen, *Acts of the Apostles*, p. 360, states simply that this section 'clearly derives from Luke himself'.
141. Lk. 6.17-19; 8.1; Acts 9.31.
142. Acts 5.15.

13.10-17b	•			•	•	
13.31b-32	•			•		
14.2-5	•					
14.8-10, 12-14		•		•		
14.28-32		•				
[15.4-6]	•			•	•	
15.8-9	•					
15.11-32	•	•		•	•	
16.1b-8a		•		•	•	•
[16.8b-12]		•				
16.15				•		
16.19-31	•	•		•	•	•
17.7-10				•		
17.12-18				•	•	
17.20-21				•		
18.2-8a		•		•		
18.10-14a			•			
19.2-10	•	•				
19.41-44	•					

As was noted above in the case of pre-Lukan vocabulary, these stylistic elements are corroborative of one another, where the presence of two or more of these elements in one pericope is especially significant. Moreover, our comparison with several passages of probable Lukan composition makes it seem even more unlikely that we would find two or more of these un-Lukan stylistic elements in a single pericope that had in fact been composed by Luke himself. The coincidence between these stylistic elements and the pre-Lukan vocabulary of Table 3 is also significant and will be summarized below.

4. *Other Stylometric Criteria*

As noted at the beginning of the discussion of stylometry, there is still great disagreement over which characteristics should be counted. Some mention should be made here of what has been left out.

It may have been noticed that all of the above discussion has dealt with the forms and uses of words and constructions, but not with the sentence. The sentence as indicative of style has been championed by Andrew Q. Morton in several works.[143] He has considered sentence

---

143. See A.Q. Morton and J. McLeman, *Paul, the Man and the Myth: A Study in the Authorship of Greek Prose* (London: Hodder & Stoughton, 1966), esp. pp. 52-64.

length,[144] as well as the relative position of words within the sentence,[145] in an attempt to prove that these are indicative of an author's style. However, Morton's work on the sentence has been attacked on numerous points. The most obvious objection to it is that in ancient texts, the sentence divisions are ambiguous and have been inserted by later editors.[146] Even setting this aside, there is the further problem that in stylometric studies of English texts, sentence length has been found to be inconclusive or even misleading.[147] Finally, Morton has been justly criticized for his tendency to concentrate exclusively on one criterion,[148] and his data have been found to be inconsistently reported,[149] or to lead to bizarre conclusions.[150] The sum of these criticisms has led me to neglect further consideration of his work here.

5. *Conclusions: The Evidence from Vocabulary and Style*

My investigation of the vocabulary and style of the L material under consideration has begun to show which pericopae have the highest and which the lowest probability of being from a single pre-Lukan source. The L pericopae have exhibited pre-Lukan vocabulary and style to varying degrees, and may be divided in the following way: a) pericopae that contain both shared pre-Lukan vocabulary and style;[151] b) pericopae that contain either two or more pre-Lukan words, or two or more

---

144. Morton and McLeman, *Paul*, pp. 52-64.

145. He has championed this to the point where it is now a recognized sub-field, 'positional stylometry'. See Morton and McLeman, *Paul*, pp. 80-84; S. Michaelson and A.Q. Morton, 'Last Words: A Test of Authorship for Greek Writers', *NTS* 18 (1971–72), pp. 192-208; Morton, *Literary Detection*, pp. 109-29.

146. See Kenny, *Stylometric Study*, p. 101; Williams, *Stylometric Authorship Studies*, p. 8.

147. See Williams, *Stylometric Authorship Studies*, p. 4.

148. As in S. Michaelson and A.Q. Morton, 'The New Stylometry: A One-Word Test of Authorship in Greek Writers', *Classical Quarterly* 22 (1972), pp. 89-102. See the criticism in Hockey, *Computer Applications*, p. 139.

149. As pointed out by Kenny, *Stylometric Study*, pp. 108-109.

150. Such as that Paul could have written 1 Corinthians or Romans, but not both: see P.F. Johnson, 'The Use of Statistics in the Analysis of the Characteristics of Pauline Writings', *NTS* 20 (1973–74), pp. 92-100.

151. Lk. 3.10-14; 7.11b-15, 36-47; 10.30-37a; 11.5b-8; [12.16b-20]; 12.35-38; 13.1b-5, 10-17b; 14.2-5, 8-10, 12-14, 28-32; [15.4-6]; 15.8-9, 11-32; 16.1b-8, 19-31; 17.7-10, 12-18; 18.2-8a, 10-14a; 19.2-10.

elements of pre-Lukan style, but not both;[152] c) pericopae that contain no pre-Lukan vocabulary and only one of the five elements of pre-Lukan style;[153] d) pericopae that contain neither shared pre-Lukan vocabulary nor style.[154] These four groups are listed in descending order of their dissimilarity to Lukan usage, as well as descending order of the number of pre-Lukan characteristics they share with one another. The 22 pericopae in the first category show several elements of dissimilarity to Lukan usage, and several links with each other. They have the highest probability of being from a single pre-Lukan source. Those in the second group also have some un-Lukan elements in common, though fewer than those of the first group. Pericopae in the final two groups show very little identifiable dissimilarity to Lukan usage and almost no stylistic connection with other L pericopae. They stand very little chance of being from a single pre-Lukan source with other L material, and will therefore not be considered further.[155] Of the 197 verses with which we began this chapter, another 33 have been eliminated because of their lack of dissimilarity to Lukan style, and their lack of similarity to other L material.[156]

152. Lk. 4.25-27; 10.39-42; 13.6b-9, 31b-32.

153. Lk. 8.2-3; [12.13b-14]; [16.8b-12]; 16.15; 17.20-21; 19.41-44. There would be an equivalent group that contained no pre-Lukan style and only one shared pre-Lukan word, but no pericopae happened to fall into such a category.

154. Lk. 5.4-9; 9.52-53a, 54-55; [11.27b-28]; 17.28-29, [31-32]; [19.39-40].

155. Further, five of the twelve pericopae in these two groups were bracketed in our consideration, and therefore stood under suspicion from the start.

156. Those that will continue to be considered are Lk. 3.10-14; 4.25-27; 7.11b-15, 36-47; 10.30-37a, 39-42; 11.5b-8; [12.16b-20]; 12.35-38; 13.1b-5, 6b-9, 10-17b, 31b-32; 14.2-5, 8-10, 12-14, 28-32; [15.4-6]; 15.8-9, 11-32; 16.1b-8a, 19-31; 17.7-10, 12-18; 18.2-8a, 10-14a; 19.2-7, [8], 9, [10].

Chapter 4

FORMAL CHARACTERISTICS

The legends, the parables, the dramas, are among the choicest treasures of
mankind.

—G.B. Shaw[1]

1. *Introduction: The Forms Found in L Material*

For purposes of analysis, the form and the content of the L material will
be examined separately. This is often difficult, however, as the two are
always interrelated.[2] It is also complicated by the composite nature of
some of the pericopae.[3]

As in the previous chapter on style and vocabulary, this formal examination of the L material is concerned with determining two related
qualities of the material: 1) the extent to which the material is formally
dissimilar to other material in Luke–Acts; and 2) the extent to which the
L pericopae exhibit formal similarities to each other. As with style and
vocabulary, the greater the material's formal *dis*similarities to other
Lukan material and the greater its internal similarities, the greater the
likelihood that it came to Luke in a source with characteristics dis-
cernible from Luke's own. However, unlike style and vocabulary, the

---

1.   G.B. Shaw, 'Back to Methuselah: A Metabiological Pentateuch', in D.H.
Laurence (ed.), *Bernard Shaw: Collected Plays with their Prefaces* (7 vols.; New
York: Dodd, Mead, & Co., 1972), V, p. 329.
2.   E.g. I will consider below stories of purity violation, which could just as easily
be considered part of the content or subject of the stories; however, since the violation
usually leads to the story being redacted into a controversy or pronouncement story (a
formal category) I have included them in this chapter. Similarly, the sections below on
dialogue and questions could have been included in the previous chapter on style; however, dialogue and questions are intrinsic to some formal categories (controversy
stories) and rare in others (parables) and therefore are treated in this chapter.
3.   E.g. healings redacted into pronouncement or controversy stories; see below,
sections 3.2 and 3.5.

dissimilarity to other Lukan material cannot be expected to be as sharply defined. This is for two reasons: 1) there are few formal categories in which a source would be unique from others;[4] and 2) there are few formal characteristics to which Luke can be shown to have an aversion.[5] The goal of this chapter will therefore be to determine how different the forms of the L pericopae are from pericopae elswewhere in Luke. Those unusual characteristics that are shared by several L pericopae will be the more important to this examination, as they may show formal coherence and homogeneity within the material.

The two formal types of parables and healings account for the great majority of L pericopae still being considered. These will be examine*d* first.

2. *L Parables*

Of the 26 pericopae still being considered, the majority are parables.[6] From a form critical point of view, these are different from the parables of Mark and Matthew in several ways. The L parables in general do not draw their analogies from nature or agriculture, but rather from the interrelations between people.[7] None of the L parables is explicitly a

---

4.   E.g. Mark and Q both include miracles and parables. The distinction therefore is not as simple as distinguishing a 'parable source' from a 'miracle source' along strictly formal lines.

5.   E.g. although Luke omits several Markan miracles (Mk 7.24-30, 31-37; 8.22-26) this would not lead one to the conclusion that Luke dislikes miracles stories *per se*.

6.   There are 14 L parables considered here: Lk. 7.40-43; 10.30-37a; 11.5b-8; [12.16b-20]; 13.6b-9; 14.28-32; [15.4-6]; 15.8-9, 11-32; 16.1b-8a, 19-31; 17.7-10; 18.2-8a, 10-14a. Luke himself labels the sayings in Lk. 14.8-10, 12-14 as a 'parable', but this does not seem an accurate formal categorization: see Bultmann, *Synoptic Tradition*, pp. 103-104, 179; Fitzmyer, *Luke*, pp. 1044-45; and Koester, *Ancient Christian Gospels*, p. 338. Some consider that behind Lk. 12.35-38 there is also a parable: thus Jeremias, *Parables*, pp. 53-55; Schneider, *Lukas*, II, p. 289; B.B. Scott, *Hear Then the Parable: A Commentary on the Parables of Jesus* (Minneapolis: Fortress Press, 1989), pp. 212-13. Although it contains a comparison, in its present form Lk. 12.35-38 does not seem parabolic: see Bultmann, *Synoptic Tradition*, p. 118; Fitzmyer, *Luke*, p. 985. On the 'deparabolization' of some parables, see also R. Bauckham, 'Synoptic Parousia Parables and the Apocalypse', *NTS* 23 (1977), pp. 162-76.

7.   See Stanton, *Gospels*, p. 231; and more recently, J. Drury, *The Parables in the Gospels: History and Allegory* (New York: Crossroad, 1985), pp. 114-15. In this respect L parables are most different from Luke's Markan ones, which are almost all based on non-human analogies: Mk 4.2-9, 26-29, 30-32; 13.28-31. The special

Kingdom parable.[8] Finally, the lack of allegorization in L parables has been noted,[9] most often as an indication of their authenticity as parables of the historical Jesus.[10]

The fourteen L parables are therefore formally dissimilar from the parables Luke has taken over from Mark and Q in these three important ways. We will now see to what extent they are formally similar to one another; these formal similarities among the L parables will be particularly significant if they are formal characteristics that are avoided or minimized by Luke in his redaction of Mark and Q.

2.1. *Dialogue and/or Monologue*

All the L parables except the first (Lk. 7.40-43) contain dialogue and/or monologue between characters within the parable itself.[11] The presence of monologue has been noted as a peculiarity of Lukan parables,[12] although it has often been attributed to Luke himself.[13] It appears,

Matthean parables also contain several analogies to inanimate objects: Mt. 13.24-30, 44, 45-46, 47-50. In this respect, the L parables are similar to those in Q, which only contain one non-human analogy: Lk. 13.20-21//Mt. 13.33.

8.   See Stanton, *Gospels*, p. 231; Bartlet, 'The Sources', p. 349.

9.   See Jeremias, *Parables*, p. 87; Drury, *Parables*, p. 116. Goulder, *New Paradigm*, I, pp. 99-100, takes this as indicative of Luke himself, but his examples are primarily from these L parables, and even he must admit that on several occasions Luke's version is more allegorical than Matthew's (Q's).

10.   On the rejection of allegory as a part of authentic parables of the historical Jesus, see C.H. Dodd, *The Parables of the Kingdom* (New York: Charles Scribner's Sons, 1961), pp. 4-12; Jeremias, *Parables*, pp. 66-89, esp. p. 89; Via, *Parables*, pp. 3-10; Drury, *Parables*, p. 116. The exclusion of allegory from Jesus' parables has been criticized, however: see C.L. Blomberg, *Interpreting the Parables* (Downers Grove, IL: Inter-Varsity Press, 1990), pp. 29-69. Although I am not interested here in the historical Jesus, I note the lack of allegory as another way in which L parables are formally dissimilar from others in Luke.

11.   Lk. 10.30-37a; 11.5b-8; 13.6b-9; 14.28-32; [15.4-6], 8-9; 16.19-31; 17.7-10 all contain dialogue. Lk. 18.2-8a, 18.10-14a contain monologue. Lk. [12.16b-20]; 15.11-32; 16.1b-8a contain both dialogue and monologue. Throughout this chapter, I use 'dialogue' to designate a verbal exchange between characters written in direct discourse; this is more narrow than simple speech, which would include all sayings material.

12.   Monologue as a feature of L parables has been noted by Drury, *Parables*, p. 115; Evans, *Luke*, p. 28; Parrott, 'Luke's Special Parable Collection', pp. 509-10.

13.   This conclusion is based primarily on Luke's expansion of the monologue at Mk 12.6 // Lk. 20.13 and on the presence of monologue in these L parables: see Fitzmyer, *Luke*, p. 1284; Goulder, *New Paradigm*, I, pp. 94-95. There is monologue in

however, that both types of discourse are rare in parables from other sources:[14] dialogue and/or monologue occur in only one Markan parable,[15] and in only five Q parables,[16] while it occurs in 13 of the 14 L parables.

The frequency of dialogue or monologue in the L parables is all the more remarkable when one notes that Luke has often omitted or shortened dialogue in his redaction of Mark.[17] This makes it less likely that Luke has added dialogue to nearly all of the L parables.

The L parables under consideration therefore show themselves formally similar by their frequent inclusion of dialogue and/or monologue in the parable proper, while this formal characteristic is rare in parables taken by Luke from his other sources. Further, judging by Luke's redaction of Mark, this characteristic is not likely to be from Luke himself, and may therefore show the influence of a source where such a form was common to parables.

2.2. *Questions*

Eleven of the L parables contain one or more questions.[18] Leaving aside the special Matthean parables,[19] there are only two Markan and four Q

Q only at Lk. 12.45//Mt. 24.48. But Luke himself is equally likely to omit a monologue: cf. Lk. 8.44//Mk 5.28; see also below. Luke can nowhere be shown to have introduced a monologue into his narrative, unless it is assumed that he himself wrote these L parables. See also P. Sellew, 'Interior Monologue as a Narrative Device in the Parables of Luke', *JBL* 111 (1992), pp. 239-53, esp. pp. 249-51, who admits that the attribution of these monologues to Luke himself is problematic.

14.   I owe this observation to Patton, *Sources*, p. 193; cf. Bultmann, *Synoptic Tradition*, pp. 190-91.

15.   Mk 12.1-12//Lk. 20.9-19; see above n.13.

16.   Lk. 7.31-35//Mt. 11.16-19; Lk. 12.42-46//Mt. 24.45-51; Lk. 13.22-27//Mt. 7.13-14, 22-23; Lk. 14.16-24//Mt. 22.1-10; Lk. 19.11-27//Mt. 25.14-30.

17.   See Cadbury, *Style and Literary Method*, pp. 79-81. Luke has omitted or shortened dialogue at Lk. 4.42//Mk 1.37; Lk. 5.14//Mk 1.44; Lk. 8.24//Mk 4.39; Lk. 8.29, 30, 32, 42, 44//Mk 5.8, 9, 12, 23, 28; Lk. 9.10, 13//Mk 6.31, 37-38; Lk. 9.37, 42-43, 46//Mk 9.16, 21-29, 33; Lk. 18.24, 40//Mk 10.24, 49; Lk. 20.7//Mk 11.33; Lk. 21.5//Mk 13.1; Lk. 22.2, 23, 47//Mk 14.2, 19, 45; Lk. 23.23//Mk 15.14. Again, Goulder, *New Paradigm*, I, pp. 94-95, does not deal with these omissions. It should also be noted that the tendency in oral transmission is also to omit direct discourse: see Taylor, *Formation of the Gospel*, p. 208: 'Direct speech is replaced by indirect.'

18.   Lk. 7.40-43; 10.30-37a; 11.5b-8; [12.16b-20]; 13.6b-9; 14.28-32; [15.4-6]; 15.8-9; 16.1b-8a; 17.7-10; 18.2-8a.

19.   Several of these do contain questions: Mt. 13.27, 28; 18.33; 20.6, 13,

parables that include questions,[20] while 11 of the 14 L parables contain them.

As with dialogue in general, Luke has particularly omitted questions in his redaction of Mark;[21] because of this, the Q passages where Matthew has a question while Luke lacks one are also more likely to be omissions by Luke.[22] This makes it less likely that Luke has added questions to the majority of L parables.

The frequent occurrence of questions in the L parables is therefore another shared formal similarity that is rare in parables from other sources. Luke's redaction of Mark and Q shows that this characteristic is probably not due to Luke himself. Like the frequency of dialogue and monologue in L parables, it may show the remnants of a source's preference for this form of parable, or indeed for the question form in general.[23]

2.3. *Contrasting or Antithetical Characters*

Five of the L parables are of the type that contrasts two or more characters with one another,[24] a device labelled 'antithesis' by both Bultmann and Dibelius.[25] Again, it should be noted that this formal type is not common in parables elsewhere in Luke and occurs predominantly in the

---

15; 21.28, 31; 22.12; 25.37, 38, 39, 44.

    20.   In Mark: Mk 4.30//Lk. 13.18; Mk 12.9, 11//Lk. 20.15, 17. In Q: Lk. 7.31//Mt. 11.16; Lk. 12.42//Mt. 24.45; Lk. 19.23//Mt. 25.26; and possibly at Lk. 13.20 (cf. Mt. 13.33).

    21.   See A. Harnack, *The Sayings of Jesus: The Second Source of St Matthew and St Luke* (trans. J.R. Wilkinson; London: Williams and Norgate; New York: G.P. Putnam's Sons, 1908), p. 6, 69; Cadbury, *Style and Literary Method*, pp. 81-82; Farmer, 'Some of the Synoptic Material', p. 313. Luke has omitted a question or condensed two questions into one at Lk. 5.33//Mk 2.19; Lk. 8.11, 25//Mk 4.13, 40; Lk. 8.21//Mk 3.33; Lk. 9.25//Mk 8.37; Lk. 9.41//Mk 9.19; Lk. 20.6//Mk 11.32; Lk. 20.22, 34//Mk 12.15, 24; Lk. 22.46, 71//Mk 14.37, 64; Lk. 23.20//Mk 15.12; Lk. 24.1//Mk 16.3.

    22.   See Harnack, *Sayings of Jesus*, pp. 26, 86; Cadbury, *Style and Literary Method*, pp. 82-83. Matthew has a question where Luke lacks one at Lk. 6.32, 33//Mt. 5.46, 47; Lk. 6.44//Mt. 7.16; Lk. 12.23, 28, 29//Mt. 6.25, 30, 31; Lk. 17.4//Mt. 18.21. (These would all be definite omissions if we follow Goulder's hypothesis that Luke has Matthew and not Q in front of him.)

    23.   See below on questions in L material of other formal types.

    24.   Lk. 7.40-43; 10.30-37a; 15.11-32; 16.19-31; 18.10-14a.

    25.   See M. Dibelius, *From Tradition to Gospsel* (trans. B.L. Woolf; New York: Charles Scribner's Sons, 1965), pp. 251-52; Bultmann, *Synoptic Tradition*, p. 192.

L parables:[26] the only other examples of it in the Gospels are three occurrences in Q and two in the special Matthean parables.[27]

Unlike the above observations on dialogue and questions, we have no example of Luke omitting stories that include antithetical characters in his redaction of Mark or Q. Therefore there is still some possibility that Luke himself has a preference for parables of this type. That five L parables include the narrative device of antithetical characters must, however, be counted as another formal similarity between them, and one that is not demonstrably Lukan.

2.4. *Example Stories*

Four of the L parables are generally accepted as example (or exemplary) stories,[28] without a figurative interpretation necessary.[29] However, attempts have been made recently to see even these stories as similitudes.[30] Because these attempts have proven unconvincing to the majority of scholars,[31] I will take it as most likely that these parables are indeed example stories and that they are formally different from other parables in the Gospels.

26.   Dibelius, *From Tradition to Gospel*, pp. 250-52, and Parrott, 'Luke's Special Parable Collection', p. 510, treat antithetical characters as a distinctive feature of the L parables.

27.   Lk. 6.47-49//Mt. 7.24-27; Lk. 12.42-46//Mt. 24.45-51; Lk. 19.11-27//Mt. 25.14-30; Mt. 21.28-31; 25.1-13.

28.   Lk. 10.30-37a; [12.16b-20]; 16.19-31; 18.10-14a.

29.   On example stories and their differences from parables proper, see Bultmann, *Synoptic Tradition*, pp. 177-79; Linnemann, *Jesus of the Parables*, pp. 4-5; Via, *Parables*, pp. 12-13.

30.   This is done especially in the case of the good Samaritan: see J. D. Crossan, 'Parable and Example in the Teaching of Jesus', *NTS* 18 (1972), pp. 285-307; *idem*, *In Parables*, pp. 57-66; R.W. Funk, 'The Good Samaritan as Metaphor', *Semeia* 2 (1974), pp. 74-81, reprinted in *Parables and Presence: Forms of the New Testament Tradition* (Philadephia: Fortress Press, 1982), pp. 29-34; Scott, *Hear Then the Parable*, pp. 29-30, 189-202. On the other hand, for an allegorical interpretation of the good Samaritan, see J. Daniélou, 'Le bon Samaritain', in *Mélanges bibliques rédigés en l'honneur de André Robert* (Paris: Bloud et Gay, 1957), pp. 457-65; B. Gerhardsson, 'The Good Samaritan—The Good Shepherd?', *ConNT* 16 (1958), pp. 1-31; H. Binder, 'Das Gleichnis vom barmherzigen Samariter', *TZ* 15 (1959), pp. 176-94; H. Gollwitzer, *Das Gleichnis vom Barmherzigen Samariter* (BS, 34; Neukirchen–Vluyn: Neukirchener, 1962), esp. pp. 68-75.

31.   For critiques of these attempts, see Marshall, *Luke*, pp. 444-45; Nolland, *Luke*, p. 591; W.C. Linss, 'Example Stories?', *CurTM* 17 (1990), pp. 447-53.

Because there are no other example stories preserved in the Gospels, we have no instance of Luke omitting them or redacting them into another form. Therefore we cannot say that this form is specifically un-Lukan.[32] But the form of example story is a characteristic that these four L parables share; it is not a demonstrably Lukan form, and it therefore increases the likelihood of some pre-Lukan connection between them.

2.5. *Reasoning* a minori ad maius

Five of the L parables explicitly or implicitly contain an argument reasoning from lesser to greater (*a minori ad maius*).[33] Such reasoning, quite common in Jewish literature, is present elsewhere in the Gospels only once in Q.[34] In particular, these five L parables all ask the hearer to draw a conclusion about God's actions based on their knowledge of human actions in analogous situations.[35]

This type of reasoning is explicit in the parable of the unjust judge.[36] Although not explicit, the reasoning in the parable of the importunate friend (Lk. 11.5b-8) is also widely recognized as *a minori ad maius*.[37] The reasoning is also implicit in the parables of the lost sheep and lost coin, even without their secondary endings.[38] The parable of the barren

---

32.   However, it should be taken as significant that Luke feels it necessary to append further applications to two of the four example stories (Lk. 10.37b; 18.14b). In the case of the good Samaritan, Luke's framing results in some confusion over the definition of 'neighbor' (object of love or subject of love). On this shift, see esp. L.P. Trudinger, 'Once Again, Now "Who Is My Neighbour?"' *EvQ* 48 (1976), pp. 160-63; N.H. Young, 'Once Again, Now "Who Is My Neighbour?": A Comment', *EvQ* 49 (1977), pp. 178-79. On this as an example of Lukan 'muddle', see Goulder, *New Paradigm*, II, pp. 487-91.

33.   Lk. 11.5b-8; 13.6b-9; [15.4-6]; 15.8-9; 18.2-8a.

34.   Lk. 11.9-13//Mt. 7.7-11; on Jewish parallels, see Bultmann, *Synoptic Tradition*, p. 185.

35.   Of course, this sometimes results (Lk. 11.5b-8; 18.2-8a) in an unflattering depiction of God. It has led some to treat these, along with the parable of the unjust steward, as a separate category of 'unedifying' stories: see Creed, *Luke*, p. lxix.

36.   Lk. 18.2-8a; see Hendrickx, *Parables*, p. 223; Donahue, *Gospel in Parable*, pp. 183-84.

37.   See Bultmann, *Synoptic Tradition*, p. 185; Jeremias, *Parables*, p. 159; Blomberg, *Interpreting the Parables*, p. 275. Luke makes it more explicit in this case by appending to it the only Q passage that also includes a conclusion *a minori ad maius*, again showing that he is not completely satisfied with this material as he found it.

38.   Verses 7 and 10; see Jeremias, *Parables*, pp. 135-36.

fig tree ends abruptly without any explicit application,[39] but it seems accurate to say that like the other four, its implied reasoning is from human to divine actions, *a minori ad maius*.[40]

These five L parables share the rhetorical device of asking their audience to reason *a minori ad maius*, from known human behavior to expected divine behavior. This reasoning is rare in parables elswhere in Luke, and is not demonstrably Lukan in character.

2.6. *Crisis Near the Beginning*

Drury concluded that all the L parables share the formal characteristic of having the crisis near the middle or beginning of the parable rather than near the end.[41] His analysis is particularly forced in the case of the rich fool (Lk. 12.16b-20) where the crisis clearly comes at the very end of the parable (v. 20), but it may be allowed in most of the other L parables.[42] Although Drury's observation is an interesting one, it does not appear as significant as he claims, particularly because there are so few counter-examples of parables with the crisis near the end.[43] I include it here as a similarity shared by most of the L parables, but do not consider it as important as the other formal characteristics, which show formal dissimilarities to parables elsewhere in Luke, and/or dissimilarities to Luke's own redactional habits.

2.7. *L Parables: Summary*

Even setting aside Drury's observation that the crises occur nearer the middles of L parables, there are still five formal characteristics that these 14 parables do share with one another to varying degrees. The

39. See Bultmann, *Synoptic Tradition*, p. 175; Jeremias, *Parables*, p. 105.

40. Cf. Parrott, 'Luke's Special Parable Collection', p. 511.

41. See Drury, *Parables*, pp. 112-14. His attempt to make all the L parables fit this formal pattern is sometimes forced, and the connection with Luke's concept of 'the middle of time' seems tenuous. On this aspect of Luke's theology, see H. Conzelmann, *The Theology of St Luke* (trans. G. Buswell; New York: Harper & Row, 1961), esp. pp. 170-206.

42. Although I can find no trace of such a pattern in Lk. 7.40-43; [12.16b-20]; 17.7-10; 18.10-14a.

43. Drury, *Parables*, p. 112, claims that the pattern of having the crisis at the end is common to the Matthean parables, but he gives no examles. I can find only three parables in which the crisis (when there is one) occurs noticeably nearer the end than in the L parables: Mk 12.1-11//Lk. 20.9-19; Lk. 19.11-27//Mt. 25.14-30; Mt. 20.1-16 (no parallel).

form of example story, the use of contrasting characters, and reasoning *a minori ad maius* occur in several of the L parables and are notable because these characteristics are not common in parables found elsewhere in Luke. The inclusion of dialogue, monologue, and questions are more notable because these characteristics are not only uncommon in parables from Luke's other sources, but are also avoided by Luke in his redaction of Mark and Q. Furthermore, one or more of these unusual formal characteristics occurs in all of the L parables. The results of this examination are summarized in Table 5.

Table 5: *L Parables*

	Dialogue/ monologue	Questions	Contrasting characters	Example stories	Lesser/ greater	Crisis in middle
7.40-43		•	•			
10.30-37a	•	•	•	•		•
11.5b-8	•	•			•	•
[12.16b-20]	•	•		•		
13.6b-9	•	•			•	•
14.28-32	•	•				•
[15.4-6]	•	•			•	•
15.8-9	•	•			•	•
15.11-32	•		•			•
16.1b-8a	•	•				•
16.19-31	•		•	•		•
17.7-10	•	•				
18.2-8a	•	•			•	•
18.10-14a	•		•	•		

3. L Miracles: Healings

As with the parables, I will first note how the miracle stories in the L material are dissimilar from those in other traditions, in this case especially the miracle stories taken over by Luke from Mark.

It is remarkable that all the L miracles are healings; there are no other formal types.[44] The lack of exorcisms, the formal type closest to healings and one so common to Mark, is particularly notable.[45] These

44.   The four healings considered here are Lk. 7.11b-15; 13.10-17b; 14.2-5; 17.12-18. On the hybrid nature of the last three, see below.
45.   On the formal differences between exorcisms and healings, see T.A. Burkill, 'The Notion of Miracle with Special Reference to St Mark's Gospel', *ZNW* 50 (1959), pp. 33-48, esp. pp. 43-44; G. Theissen, *The Miracle Stories of the Early Christian*

four healings also lack any mention of the patients' faith.[46] This is significant from the point of view of Lukan interests, as Luke could be expected to accentuate or supply a reference to 'faith' in these healings if they were composed or heavily redacted by him.[47] It is also worth noting that the L miracles are different from many of those in Acts, which include some aspects of magic.[48] These healings show themselves formally dissimilar to Luke's Markan stories and to Lukan interests in these ways; we will now see to what extent they are formally similar to one another.

3.1. *No Request for Healing*

Besides lacking any mention of the patients' faith, the L healings also lack any specific request for healing from the patient to the miracle worker.[49] The only possible exception to this is the lepers' cry at Lk. 17.13; but as has often been noted, this could just as well be a request for alms as for a healing.[50] The verb ἐλεέω has no specific connection with healing, but only with kindness or mercy in general.[51] The lack of the patient's request for healing is a striking formal similarity shared by

Tradition (trans. F. McDonagh; Edinburgh: T. & T. Clark; Philadelphia: Fortress Press, 1983), pp. 85-90; R. Latourelle, *The Miracles of Jesus and the Theology of Miracles* (trans. M.J. O'Connell; New York: Paulist Press, 1988), pp. 243-45. This is a formal distinction, and does not deny the connection between demonic forces and disease in L material (see Lk. 13.16) as well as throughout the New Testament and the ancient world.

46. This is perhaps most remarkable in Lk. 7.11b-15, where the story has not been redacted into a pronouncement or controversy story, and therefore the focus is on the healing: see R.H. Fuller, *Interpreting the Miracles* (Philadelphia: Westminster Press, 1963), p. 64. On 'faith' in miracle traditions, see Theissen, *Miracle Stories*, pp. 129-40.

47. The discontinuity with Lukan interests is noted in reference to Lk. 7.11b-15 by Latourelle, *Miracles of Jesus*, p. 193. Luke does append πίστις to one of the L healings (Lk. 17.19). Luke also shows his preference for 'faith' language in his redaction of the parable of the sower (Lk. 8.12-13//Mk 4.15-17): see Marshall, *Luke*, p. 325. On 'faith' in Luke, see also Fitzmyer, *Luke*, pp. 235-37.

48. See H.C. Kee, *Miracle in the Early Christian World. A Study in Socio-historical Method* (New Haven: Yale University Press, 1983), p. 211.

49. On the different forms the patients' requests can take, see Theissen, *Miracle Stories*, pp. 53-55.

50. See Fitzmyer, *Luke*, p. 1154; Nolland, *Luke*, p. 846.

51. See R. Bultmann, 'ἐλεέω', *TDNT* II, pp. 477-87. Note esp. Lk. 16.24, where the verb obviously cannot refer to healing.

these four healings, especially because such a request is considered a key element of healings and miracle stories in general.[52]

3.2. *Questions*

One formal characteristic that is common between L material of different formal types is the presence of questions in three of the four L healings.[53] This is of course related to the fact that two of the miracles (Lk. 13.10-17b; 14.2-5) have been redacted at some point into controversy or pronouncement stories, where questions are nearly ubiquitous.[54] However, the cleansing of the ten lepers (Lk. 17.12-18) is clearly not a controversy story, but a composite of a miracle story and apothegm,[55] and in apothegms questions are much less common than they are in the specific form of controversy stories.[56]

More importantly for distinguishing these pericopae from Luke's own interests, one should again note that Luke tends to omit questions in his redaction of Mark and Q,[57] and this is particularly the case in

52.   See Latourelle, *Miracles of Jesus*, p. 242. This peculiarity is noted by Fuller, *Interpreting the Miracles*, p. 64, in relation to Lk. 7.11-17; and Fitzmyer, *Luke*, p. 1011, notes the absence of a request in Lk. 13.10-17.

53.   Lk. 13.10-17b; 14.2-5; 17.12-18. Moreover, these pericopae contain not one, but two (Lk. 13.15, 16; 14.2, 5) and even three (Lk. 17.17, 18) questions. (I have not included in the examination of these healings the presence of dialogue in general, as this is extremely common in healing stories.)

54.   Questions are included in nearly all the controversy or pronouncement stories preserved in the Gospels: Mk 2.1-12, 15-17, 18-22//Lk. 5.17-26, 29-32, 33-39; Mk 2.23-28//Lk. 6.1-5; Mk 3.1-6//Lk. 6.6-11; Mk 3.22-30//Lk. 11.14-23; Mk 7.1-23 (Luke omits); Mk 10.1-12 (Luke omits); Mk 10.17-31//Lk. 18.18-30; Mk 10.35-45//Lk. 22.24-27; Mk 11.27-33//Lk. 20.1-8; Mk 12.13-17, 18-27//Lk. 20.20-26, 27-40; Mk 12.28-34//Lk. 10.25-28; Mt. 11.7-19//Lk. 7.24-35; only Mk 9.38-41//Lk. 9.49-50 lacks a question. See Bultmann, *Synoptic Tradition*, pp. 12-27; Taylor, *Formation*, pp. 63-71.

55.   See Bultmann, *Synoptic Tradition*, p. 33; Taylor, *Formation*, pp. 153-55; Betz, 'The Cleansing', pp. 322-23; Fitzmyer, *Luke*, p. 1150.

56.   Of the twenty biographical apothegms listed by Bultmann, *Synoptic Tradition*, pp. 28-37 (cf. Taylor, *Formation*, pp. 71-77) only eight contain questions: Mk 3.31-35//Lk. 8.19-21; Mk 6.1-6a//Lk. 4.16, 22, 24; Mk 11.15-19//Lk. 19.45-48; Mk 13.1-2//Lk. 21.5-7; Mk 14.3-9 (Luke omits); Lk. 10.38-42; 17.11-19; 23.27-31.

57.   See above, section 2.2; see also Harnack, *Sayings of Jesus*, pp. 6, 26, 69, 86; Cadbury, *Style and Literary Method*, pp. 81-83; Farmer, 'Some of the Synoptic Material', p. 313.

apothegms such as Lk. 17.12-18.[58] Although the form of Lk. 13.10-17b
and 14.2-5 may have necessitated the inclusion of at least one question,
this is certainly not the case with Lk. 17.12-18; and given Luke's treatment of questions in his other sources, one would not have expected him
to include multiple questions in these pericopae if they were composed
or heavily redacted by him. It is another un-Lukan formal similarity
shared by these healings, and one which they share with L material of
other formal types.

3.3. *Jesus Touches the Patient*

Perhaps most remarkable in that it is most discontinuous with Lukan
interests is Jesus' touching of the patient in three of the four L healings.[59] As has been noted, Luke is averse to depicting Jesus' emotions or
his physicality in general. In his redaction of Markan miracles he has
several times omitted references to Jesus touching the patient,[60] although
this is a common feature in healing miracles.[61] The discontinuity with
Lukan interests is particularly striking in Lk. 7.11b-15, where Jesus'
emotions are also depicted.[62] Further, it should be noted that two of
these healings involve healing by word as well as by touching, a combination that is infrequent in the Gospels,[63] while the third includes only

---

58.   Of the five Markan apothegms that include questions, Luke has omitted one
entirely (Mk 14.3-9) and omitted the questions from the other four: Mk 3.31-35//Lk.
8.19-21; Mk 6.1-6a//Lk. 4.16, 22, 24 (Luke omits two of the three Markan questions
here); Mk 11.15-19//Lk. 19.45-48; Mk 13.1-2//Lk. 21.5-7.

59.   Lk. 7.14; 13.13; 14.4.

60.   Luke omits the detail of touching at Lk. 4.39//Mk 1.31 and Lk. 9.42//Mk 9.27,
while he has completely omitted the grossly physical miracle stories of Mk 7.31-37 and
8.22-26; see Cadbury, *Style and Literary Method*, pp. 91-92, and Fitzmyer, *Luke*,
pp. 94-95.

61.   See Bultmann, *Synoptic Tradition*, p. 222; Theissen, *Miracle Stories*, pp. 62-
63.

62.   Lk. 7.13. The peculiarity of this in Luke's work is noted by B. Rigaux,
Témoignage de l'évangile de Luc (Paris: Desclée de Brouwer, 1970), p. 404; A.
George, 'Le miracle dans l'oeuvre de Luc', in X. Léon-Dufour (ed.), *Les miracles
des Jésus selon le Nouveau Testament* (Paris: Editions du Seuil, 1977), pp. 249-68,
esp. p. 254; and Latourelle, *Miracles of Jesus*, p. 193.

63.   Lk. 7.11b-15; 13.10-17b. Although uncommon, accounts of healings that
include both techniques are not unknown in Luke's Markan miracles: Mk 1.40-45//Lk.
5.12-16; Mk 5.21-24, 35-43//Lk. 8.40-42, 49-56. Again, Luke lacks any parallel to Mk
7.31-37, which also includes healing by both word and touch. See Bultmann, *Synoptic*

touching.[64] In Lk. 13.13 the combination appears particularly awkward, in that the touching *follows* the healing word (v. 12), while in the other Gospel examples in which the two techniques are combined, the touching always *precedes* the word.[65]

These three L miracles are formally similar in their inclusion of Jesus' touching of the patient, a detail unlikely to be from Luke himself. The first two of these miracles also combine healing by word as well as by touch, an unusual characteristic in Luke or the other Gospels. These similarities are therefore probably not due to Luke himself, nor to influence from other traditions with which he was familiar; thus they may indicate a pre-Lukan connection between these pericopae.

3.4. *Stories of Law Violation*

Three of the four healings involve Jesus' violation of some Jewish law: the raising of the widow's son involves Jesus in the impurity of a corpse,[66] while both the healing of the crippled woman and the man with dropsy are violations of the sanctity of the Sabbath.[67] The latter two lead to a controversy story, although the first does not.

Although law violation as part of a healing story is not unknown in Mark,[68] the L healings of the crippled woman and the man with dropsy are further distinguished by the fact that they are both violations of the

---

Tradition, p. 222, for lists of Christian and non-Christian healing accounts that include touching and/or speaking.

64.   Lk. 14.2-5; cf. Lk. 4.39//Mk 1.31, where Luke has redacted a healing story that includes *only* touching into one that includes *only* the healing word.

65.   Mk 1.40-45//Lk. 5.12-16; Mk 5.21-24, 35-43//Lk. 8.40-42, 49-56; Mk 7.31-37.

66.   Lk. 7.14. On the uncleanness of a corpse in Jewish law, see Num. 19.11, 16; see also *m. Ohol.*, esp. 1.1-4. Cf. Marshall, *Luke*, p. 286.

67.   Lk. 13.14-16; 14.3-5. On the Sabbath, see esp. Exod. 20.9-10; Deut. 5.13-14.

68.   See Mk 2.1-12//Lk. 5.17-26; Mk 3.1-6//Lk. 6.6-11. In the first case the accusation is blasphemy, which originally would have been confined to misuse of the tetragrammaton (see Lev. 24.14-16), but here is conceived more broadly as disrespect towards God: see H.W. Beyer, 'βλασφημέω', *TDNT* I, pp. 621-25. The second case is another example of violation of the Sabbath (see above). All may be seen as examples of the general element of 'Criticism from Opponents' in miracle accounts: see Theissen, *Miracle Stories*, pp. 56-57. There are also some stories, like Lk. 7.11b-15, where the purity violation does not draw any objection: Mk 1.40-45//Lk. 5.12-16; Mk 5.35-43//Lk. 8.49-56; Mk 7.32-37 (Luke omits); Mk 8.22-26 (Luke omits).

Sabbath, and could even be considered doublets of Mk 3.1-6.[69] Because Luke often avoids doublets, their inclusion in his Gospel is all the more remarkable, and further lessens the possibility that they were composed by him.[70]

Finally, it may be noted that the other L healing, the cleansing of the ten lepers, also presupposes Jewish law, although in this case it depicts both Jesus and the lepers conforming to it rather than violating it.[71]

Thus the L healings show similarities with regard to Jewish law in the following ways: 1) the first three L healings all depict Jesus violating Jewish law; 2) the second and third L healings are both violations of the Sabbath and are similar enough to Mk 3.1-6 that one might have expected Luke to omit them; 3) all four L healings presuppose Jewish law.

3.5. *Controversy or Pronouncement Central*

Besides including questions, the latter three L healings are also similar in that their formal type is unclear and composite in nature. However one evaluates the relative importance of speech and narrative in these pericopae, it must be admitted that in all three stories the narrative is at least rivalled by if not indeed subordinated to Jesus' sayings.[72] These three pericopae are therefore hybrd in form, somewhere between miracle stories and apothegms proper.

Although such a composite form of healing and apothegm is already

---

69.   Although Lk. 13.10-17b and 14.2-5 can be seen as a male–female pair in which Luke has composed one or both of the pericopae: see M.R. D'Angelo, 'Women in Luke–Acts: A Redactional View', *JBL* 109 (1990), pp. 441-61. This will be discussed more thoroughly in the next chapter, but we may note here that the likelihood of Lukan composition is diminished by the intervening Q material, and more importantly by the fact that almost all other male-female pairs in Luke–Acts include the male story first.

70.   On Luke's avoidance of doublets, see Schürmann, *Traditionsgeschichtliche Untersuchungen*, pp. 272-89; and Fitzmyer, *Luke*, pp. 79-82.

71.   The lepers keep a distance from Jesus (Lk. 17.12), thus not contaminating him (see Lev. 13.45-46); Jesus commands them to show themelves to the priests in conformity to the ritual described in Lev. 14.2-32. On the Jewish background of this and other L material, cf. Easton, *Luke*, p. xxvii; W. Manson, *The Gospel of Luke* (MNTC, 3; New York: Harper & Brothers, 1927), p. xx; and below, Chapter 6.

72.   Cf. the different attempts at classification by Dibelius, *From Tradition to Gospel*, pp. 55, 97-98, 120; Bultmann, *Synoptic Tradition*, pp. 12-13, 33, 209; Taylor, *Formation*, pp. 65, 69, 153.

present in Mark and Q,[73] it is not frequent in the material that Luke took from those sources. Further, there is no example of Luke himself composing such a hybrid on his own from Markan or Q material.[74] The composite formal nature of these three L healings should therefore be noted as a shared similarity that is not common in healings elsewhere in Luke, and is not demonstrably Lukan.

3.6. *Contrasting Characters*
Another formal characteristic that transcends formal categories is the use of contrasting characters in the cleansing of the ten lepers.[75] Although this is the only example in the L healings, it should be noted because it is a device that has been observed above in the L parables and shows some formal similarity between this healing and other L material.[76]

3.7 *L. Healings: Summary*
The above examination of the L healings has uncovered six formal characteristics in them that are uncommon in healing stories elsewhere in Luke and are not demonstrably Lukan. In particular, two of the characteristics (Jesus touching the patient and the inclusion of multiple questions in the narrative) seem to be positively un-Lukan, judging by Luke's redaction of his Markan and Q material. All of the L healings share at least three of these six formal characteristics; also, all of them include at least one of the two demonstrably un-Lukan characteristics. Further, two of these formal characteristics (the inclusion of questions and the use of contrasting characters) are found in L material of other formal types. The L healings do exhibit noticeable formal similarities to one another as well as to other L material, and are also different from what one might have expected from Luke himself. The results are summarized in Table 6.

---

73. Mk 2.1-12//Lk. 5.17-26; Mk 3.1-6//Lk. 6.6-11; Mk 7.24-31 (Luke omits); Mt. 8.5-13//Lk. 7.1-10. Also cf. Mk 9.14-29//Lk. 9.37-43a, which contains some sayings of Jesus, though remains more clearly a miracle story than the others.

74. Although at Lk. 9.43a//Mk 9.28-29, Luke omits the final verbal exchange in the healing story, and thereby diminishes its composite nature.

75. Lk. 17.12-18; the Samaritan is contrasted with the others in vv. 17-18.

76. See section 2.3 above; see below on contrasting characters in L material of other formal types.

Table 6: *L healings*

	No request	Question	Touching	Law violation	Controversy or saying	Contrasting characters
7.11b-15	•		•	•		
13.10-17b	•	•	•	•	•	
14.2-5	•	•	•	•	•	
17.12-18	•	•			•	•

4. Other Forms in L Material

The remaining nine L pericopae are from a variety of formal types.[77] As above, we will examine them to see whether they show any formal similarities to each other, or to the L parables and healings already examined.

4.1. *Biographical Apothegms or Stories about Jesus*

Two of the L pericopae include fairly extensive narrative material leading up to a saying of Jesus and have therefore been classified as biographical apothegms or stories about Jesus.[78] Whether the narrative material is subordinate to the saying, or the saying merely provides the appropriate conclusion to the narrative is debatable,[79] though it is clear that the two elements are not separable and do form some unity in the tradition. Whatever the relative importance of the saying and narrative material in these two stories, they are formally similar.

Both of these stories, like most of the L parables,[80] contain dialogue,

---

77. The following L pericopae are neither parables nor healings: Lk. 3.10-14; 4.25-27; 7.36-39, 44-47; 10.39-42; 12.35-38; 13.1b-5, 31b-32; 14.8-10, 12-14; 19.2-10. Some of the synoptic apothegms have recently been reclassified as chreiai: see G.W. Buchanan, *Jesus: The King and His Kingdom* (Mercer, GA: Mercer University Press, 1984), pp. 91-93, 227-30; J.R. Butts, 'The Chreia in the Synoptic Gospels', *BTB* 16 (1986), pp. 132-38; B.L. Mack, 'The Anointing of Jesus: Elaboration within a Chreia', in B.L. Mack and V.K. Robbins (eds.), *Patterns of Persuasion in the Gospels* (Foundations and Facets: Literary Facets; Sonoma, CA: Polebridge Press, 1989), pp. 85-106. Few of the L pericopae have been thus reclassified, however, and the category seems to be the functional equivalent of apothegm anyway; it should not affect our search for un-Lukan characteristics in this material.

78. Lk. 10.39-42; 19.2-10. Thus they are quite closely related to the healing of the ten lepers (Lk. 17.12-18); see above.

79. Thus, Bultmann, *Synoptic Tradition*, pp. 33-34, categorizes them as biographical apothegms, while Taylor, *Formation*, p. 153, considers them stories about Jesus.

80. See above, section 2.1.

in this case between Jesus and the other characters in the stories.[81] Lk. 10.40, like most of the L parables and healings,[82] also contains a question. This question is more remarkable in that it is something of an accusation of apathy against Jesus very similar to Mk 4.38, which Luke has redacted to exclude both the question and the accusation.[83] Further, both stories include contrasting characters (Martha and Mary, Zacchaeus and the crowd) a device found in several of the L parables and one of the L healings.[84]

A further characteristic of these L pericopae that has not yet been observed in L material is that the minor characters (i.e. those other than Jesus) are given more prominence and detail than we might have expected in such stories.[85] Besides their speech, the characters are even named, and we are given other details about them—the mundane problems of entertaining guests, the difficulties of being short–affording us a rare glimpse at their lives and motivations.[86] Such detailed accounts are not typical of the other Gospels or of Luke's own tendencies.[87]

81.   Lk. 10.40 (Martha), 41-42 (Jesus); 19.5 (Jesus), 7 (crowd), 8 (Zacchaeus), 9-10 (Jesus). Dialogue is not particularly common in apothegms, especially not in Luke: of the seven apothegms he has taken over from Mark (Lk. 4.16-30//Mk 6.1-6; Lk. 8.19-21//Mk 3.31-35; Lk. 9.49-50//Mk 9.38-40; Lk. 18.15-17//Mk 10.13-16; Lk. 19.45-48//Mk 11.15-19; Lk. 21.1-4//Mk 12.41-44; Lk. 21.5-6//Mk 13.1-2), only three contain dialogue in their Lukan form (Lk. 4.16-30//Mk 6.1-6; Lk. 8.19-21 // Mk 3.31-35; Lk. 9.49-50//Mk 9.38-40). Luke has shortened the dialogue in one (Lk. 8.21//Mk 3.33-34) and omitted it in another (Lk. 21.5//Mk 13.1).

82.   On questions in L parables and healings, see above, sections 2.2 and 3.2; on the relative infrequency of questions in apothegms, see above, section 3.2.

83.   Mk 4.38 // Lk. 8.24; the wording is even partially identical: οὐ μέλει σοι ὅτι is in both Mk 4.38 and Lk. 10.40. On Luke's redaction of Mk 4.38, see Cadbury, *Style and Literary Method*, p. 95; Fitzmyer, *Luke*, p. 730.

84.   See above, section 2.3 and 3.6.

85.   Cf. the analysis of minor characters in Mark in D. Rhoads and D. Michie, *Mark as Story: An Introduction to the Narrative of a Gospel* (Philadelphia: Fortress Press, 1982), p. 130; and also W.H. Kelber, *The Oral and the Written Gospel: The Hermeneutics of Speaking and Writing in the Synoptic Tradition, Mark, Paul, and Q* (Philadephia: Fortress Press, 1983), p. 51.

86.   This is part of what has made the L material so endearing: cf. Evans, *Luke*, p. 28; Creed, *Luke*, pp. lxviii-lxix.

87.   On the general tendency to omit details, see Taylor, *Formation*, p. 208. On the tendency of Luke in particular to omit details, especially proper names, see Cadbury, *Style and Literary Method*, pp. 127-28, 156. Goulder, *New Paradigm*, I, pp. 93-97, lists such details as 'Lucan', but he does not account for the omissions and his examples are exclusively from L material.

The inclusion of dialogue, questions, and the use of contrasting characters are formal characteristics that have been observed in other L material and that these pericopae also share. These two pericopae are also similar to one another in their depiction of minor characters as more prominent and detailed than in material found elsewhere in Luke.

4.2. *Controversy or Pronouncement Stories*

Three of the remaining L pericopae are generally acknowledged as controversy or pronouncement stories.[88] These pericopae are more concerned with the sayings and include less narrative material than do the biographical apothegms treated above, and can therefore be formally distinguished from them.

These three pericopae show some of the formal characteristics observed in other L material. Although two of the three pronouncement stories include dialogue between Jesus and the other characters,[89] and two of them also include questions,[90] this should not be taken as particularly significant, as both dialogue and questions are almost always included in pronouncement stories.[91] More significant is the inclusion of monologue in the first of these, a peculiarity observed in several L parables.[92] Two include the device of contrasting characters.[93] Finally, as observed in the biographical apothegms, the first pronouncement story features the minor characters more prominently than in other stories.[94] The L pronouncement stories, especially the first, therefore display some formal similarities to each other and to other L material.

---

88. Lk. 7.36-39, 44-47; 13.1b-5, 31b-32. On the form-critical classification of these, see Bultmann, *Synoptic Tradition*, pp. 20-21, 23, 35; Taylor, *Formation*, pp. 69, 75, 153; and Fitzmyer, *Luke*, 684, 1004, 1028. Also, see above on the L healings/pronouncement stories, esp. Lk. 17.12-18.

89. Lk. 7.44-47; 13.31b-32; see also section 2.1 above.

90. See Lk. 7.44; 13.2, 4; see also sections 2.2 and 3.2 above.

91. See section 3.2 above on the inclusion of these in pronouncement stories.

92. Lk. 7.39; see section 2.1 above.

93. See Lk. 7.36-39, 44-47 (Simon and the woman); 13.1b-5 (vv. 1b-3: murdered Galileans and other Galileans; vv. 4-5: those who died and others in Jerusalem).

94. The host's name is given in both the enclosed parable and in v. 44; the woman's actions are described in detail twice, first in narrative (vv. 37-38) and then by Jesus (vv. 44-46).

4.3. *Other Sayings Material*

The remaining four L pericopae are sayings of various types.[95] They have been categorized differently, partly because some of them are included in larger units in Luke's redaction.[96] Whatever sub-category of sayings material one might decide for each pericope, they are clearly not apothegms, as the narrative element is almost non-existent, and they also do not appear to be either parables or pronouncement stories.[97]

Two of these pericopae contain dialogue,[98] and the first also contains several questions.[99] Two of them include a contrast between characters or groups.[100] Finally, the first pericope includes more details about the minor characters than elsewhere in the Gospels.[101]

Of these four pericopae, Lk. 12.35-38 displays no noticeable formal similarities to other L material. However, the other three, especially Lk. 3.10-14, do include formal characteristics observed in other L material.

4.4. *Other Forms in L Material: Summary*

Despite the miscellaneous character of the last nine L pericopae examined, most of them do display some formal similarities to each other and to other L material. Other than Lk. 12.35-38, all of them have at least one formal characteristic observed in other L material: they include either dialogue, monologue, questions, and/or a contrast between characters. Further, four of the nine pericopae are similar to one another by their more prominent and more detailed treatment of minor characters;

95.   Lk. 3.10-14; 4.25-27; 12.35-38; 14.8-10, 12-14. On the form-critical classification of these, see Bultmann, *Synoptic Tradition*, 103-104, 116, 118, 179, 245-47; Fitzmyer, *Luke*, 464, 527, 985, 1044.

96.   Thus Lk. 3.10-14 is part of the larger account of John's ministry (Lk. 3.1-18), and Lk. 4.25-27 is part of Jesus' inaugural sermon (Lk. 4.16-30).

97.   See section 2 above on the possibility that the latter two pericopae are parables or the remnants of parables.

98.   Lk. 3.10-14 is almost entirely dialogue between John and his interlocutors. Lk. 14.9-10 includes Jesus attributing dialogue to the hypothetical host, and in this respect is especially similar to the form of L parables; see section 2.1 above.

99.   A total of three: Lk. 3.10, 12, 14.

100.   Lk. 4.25-27 (Israelites and gentiles); Lk. 14.8-10 (less honorable and more honorable guests), 12-14 (rich and poor guests).

101.   Although the first question is asked by the generic 'crowds' so common in the Gospels (ὄχλος: 38 times in Mark, 49 times in Matthew, 41 times in Luke; also 22 times in Acts), the latter two groups of questioners are more specific.

this treatment distinguishes these pericopae from similar stories found elsewhere in Luke or the other Gospels. The results of this analysis are summarized in Table 7.

Table 7: *Other forms in L Material*

	Dialogue/ monologue	Questions	Contrasting characters	Minor characters prominent
3.10-14	•	•		•
4.25-27			•	
7.36-39, 44-47	•	•	•	•
10.39-42	•	•	•	•
13.1b-5		•	•	
13.31b-32	•			
14.8-10, 12-14	•		•	
19.2-10	•		•	•

5. Conclusions

Within the formal categories examined above, the L pericopae have in most cases displayed noticeable formal similarities to each other. All of the L parables contain dialogue, monologue, and/or questions; characteristics which are uncommon in parables elsewhere in Luke and which are also omitted by Luke in his redaction of Mark and Q. The L healings are remarkably similar to one another in their lack of a request for healing, a formal characteristic almost ubiquitous in all other healing stories. The L healings also include Jesus' touching of the patient and the asking of questions, characteristics that are more notable because they seem particularly un-Lukan. Finally, the other L pericopae of various types of sayings are most similar to one another in their inclusion of dialogue and their use of contrasting characters.

Between pericopae of different formal types, three formal characteristics stand out as possibly indicative of pre-Lukan formal similarities between the disparate material:[102] 1) 19 of the 26 L pericopae, regardless of their formal type, include dialogue and/or monologue;[103] 2) 17

102. Only Lk. 12.35-38 does not include one of these three characteristics; this pericope will continue to be considered to determine whether it contains any similarities of content to other L material.

103. Lk. 3.10-14; 7.36-47; 10.30-37a, 39-42; 11.5b-8; [12.16b-20]; 13.6b-9, 31b-32; 14.8-10, 12-14, 28-32; [15.4-6]; 15.8-9, 11-32; 16.1b-8a, 19-31; 17.7-10; 18.2-8a, 10-14a; 19.2-10.

of the pericopae include questions;[104] and 3) 11 of the pericopae contain some contrast between characters.[105]

Both within formal categories and across formal lines, the L material shows several points of formal similarity. For the most part, these similarities are also dissimilar to forms found elsewhere in Luke, as well as dissimilar to Luke's own redactional habits.

---

104. Lk. 3.10-14; 7.36-47; 10.30-37a, 39-42; 11.5b-8; [12.16b-20]; 13.1b-5, 6b-9, 10-17b; 14.2-5, 28-32; [15.4-6]; 15.8-9; 16.1b-8a; 17.7-10, 12-18; 18.2-8a.
105. Lk. 4.25-27; 7.36-47; 10.30-37a, 39-42; 13.1b-5; 14.8-10, 12-14; 15.11-32; 16.19-31; 17.12-18; 18.10-14a; 19.2-10.

Chapter 5

CONTENT

That strange and morbid world into which the Gospels lead us—a world
like the plot of a Russian novel, in which the scum of society, neurosis, and
childish imbecility are brought together—must inevitably have coarsened
the legend of Jesus.

—Nietzsche[1]

1. Introduction: The Content of L Material

This chapter will examine the L pericopae isolated thus far, regardless
of their formal types, to determine the topical or thematic similarities
among them. If this L material in fact represents the remnants of a
coherent tradition conveying an identifiable message through different
formal types, then one would expect noticeable content similarities
among the pericopae. Such content similarities will be even more
indicative of a pre-Lukan source if such similarities (like the formal
characteristics examined in the previous chapter) are noticeably different from the content of Luke's Markan and Q sections, and are distinguishable from themes in which Luke has shown a particular interest.
Content similarities will also be more significant if the pericopae in
question are proximate to one another in the L material,[2] as this may
show pre-Lukan groupings by subject or content in L.[3]

The content of the L material will be examined under three headings:
details found in the L pericopae, general content similarities shared with
other sources, and more specific thematic groupings in the L material.

1.   F. Nietzsche, *The Antichrist* (trans. E. Haldmean-Julius; New York: Arno
Press, 1972), p. xxxi.
2.   I.e. little or no intervening L material as isolated thus far, regardless of how
much Markan or Q material now intervenes in Luke: e.g. Lk. 7.36-47 and 10.30-37a are
proximate among the L pericopae isolated, although they are now separated by a sizeable amount of material in Luke.
3.   Such groupings will be considered more fully in Chapter 6, on the structure
and order of L.

2. Details in L Pericopae

Almost all the L pericopae still under consideration contain a number of details in their accounts.[4] 'Details' is here taken to mean specific references which are not intrinsic to the story.[5] Such details are of four types: numerical references, personal names, place names, and embellishments or 'colorful' details. The presence of these details is more remarkable when it is noted that their inclusion runs contrary to both Luke's observed redactional habits,[6] and also to oral transmission.[7] It should therefore be taken as another indication diminishing the likelihood that this material stems from either Luke's use of oral tradition or his own free composition; it is another point in favor of the material being from a pre-Lukan written source.

2.1. *Numerical References*
The most prevalent detail found in L pericopae is the inclusion of numerical references.[8] We have already noted the un-Lukan word placement of the cardinal number before the noun in 11 of these pericopae.[9] The presence of so many numerical references is again noted

---

4.   Only five of the 26 pericopae lack one or more such details: Lk. [12.16b-20]; 14.2-5, 8-10, 12-14; 17.7-10; 18.2-8a.

5.   E.g. the description of the woman's illness in Lk. 13.11 is not a detail, as such a description is intrinsic to the form of a healing story. Zacchaeus' height (Lk. 19.3) is not a detail, because it furthers the plot of the story, but his climbing a 'sycamore' tree (Lk. 19.4) is a gratuitous detail, because any tree or building would have functioned equally well.

6.   See Cadbury, *Style and Literary Method*, p. 127; also E.F.F. Bishop, 'Local Colour in Proto-Luke', *ExpTim* 45 (1933-34), pp. 151-56. Again, cf. Goulder, *New Paradigm*, I, pp. 93-97, who believes such details are 'Lucan'.

7.   This has long been observed in oral traditions: see A. Olrik, 'Epische Gesetze der Volksdichtung', *Zeitschrift für deutsches Altertum* 51 (1909), pp. 1-12; Cadbury, *Making of Luke–Acts*, p. 34; Taylor, *Formation*, p. 208; E.L. Abel, 'The Psychology of Memory and Rumor Transmission and Their Bearing on Theories of Oral Transmission in Early Christianity', *JR* 51 (1971), pp. 270-81.

8.   Twenty of the 26 pericopae (77 per cent) contain some numerical detail: Lk. 3.10-14; 4.25-27; 7.36-47; 10.30-37a, 39-42; 11.5b-8; 12.35-38; 13.1b-5, 6b-9, 10-17b, 31b-32; 14.28-32; [15.4-6], 8-9, 11-32; 16.1b-8a, 19-31; 17.12-18; 18.10-14a; 19.2-10. Three of these (Lk. 12.35-38; 13.31b-32; 19.2-10) are not cardinal numbers, and therefore were not noted above.

9.   See above, Chapter 3, section 3.3.

here because such a high incidence of them is characteristic of neither Luke's Markan nor Q material;[10] moreover, Luke tends to omit such references in his redaction of Mark and Q.[11] It is therefore an unusual characteristic of the L material, distinguishable from either of Luke's known sources and from his own redactional habits observed elsewhere in his work.

2.2. *Personal Names*

Eight of the L pericopae contain personal names.[12] 'Lazarus' is perhaps the most remarkable of these, in that it is the only occurrence of a character in a parable being named.[13]

Luke has frequently omitted personal names in his redaction of Mark and Q.[14] Moreover, on the only occasions when he has added personal names to Mark, it has been to specify the names of disciples.[15] This points to another way in which the content of the L material is unusual: none of the disciples are named in it. In fact, the disciples are hardly mentioned in it at all.[16] The inclusion of personal names in these L pericopae runs contrary to Lukan redactional habits; the lack of any mention of the names of the disciples—the one group whose names one might have expected them to include, or which Luke might have been inclined to add—is also remarkable.

---

10.   As noted in Chapter 3, section 3.3, cardinal numbers are included in only 25 per cent of the listed Markan pericopae in Luke, and only 19 per cent of the listed Q pericopae.

11.   See Cadbury, *Style and Literary Method*, pp. 128-29; and above, Chapter 3, section 3.3.

12.   Lk. 4.25-27 (Elijah, Zarephath, Elisha, Naaman); 7.36-47 (Simon); 10.39-42 (Martha, Mary); 13.1b-5 (Pilate), 10-17b (Abraham), 31b-32 (Herod); 16.19-31 (Lazarus, Abraham, Moses); 19.2-10 (Zacchaeus, Abraham).

13.   Lk. 16.20, 23, 24, 25. Cf. Marshall, *Luke*, p. 635; Fitzmyer, *Luke*, p. 1129; D.L. Tiede, *Luke* (Augsburg Commentary on the New Testament; Minneapolis: Augsburg, 1988), p. 290.

14.   Luke has omitted personal names at Lk. 3.19//Mk 6.17; Lk. 4.38//Mk 1.29; Lk. 5.27//Mk 2.14; Lk. 6.14//Mk 3.17; Lk. 8.51//Mk 5.37; Lk. 11.51//Mt. 23.35; Lk. 18.35//Mk 10.46; Lk. 21.7//Mk 13.3; Lk. 22.40, 46//Mk 14.33, 37; Lk. 23.26, 55//Mk 15.21, 47. See Cadbury, *Style and Literary Method*, p. 128.

15.   Lk. 8.45//Mk 5.31; Lk. 22.8//Mk 14.13.

16.   They are only mentioned once at Lk. 7.11b. Luke's special designation for the Twelve (ἀπόστολος: six times in Luke, 30 times in Acts) is completely missing from the L material.

2.3. *Place Names*

Four of the L pericopae contain references to specific geographical locations.[17] Although most of these names are not unusual, the name Ναΐν (Lk. 7.11) is unique to this story, appearing nowhere else in the New Testament, nor anywhere in the LXX.[18] The incident at Σιλωάμ (Lk. 13.4) is also unusual, in that the place is elsewhere always associated with a fountain or reservoir;[19] this is the only story to mention a 'tower' at the location. Also, as with the other details noted, Luke frequently omits specific geographical references in his redaction of Mark.[20] Although not as prevalent as the other details noted, the inclusion of place names in these L pericopae and the unusual character of two of these names further enhances the likelihood that they are pre-Lukan.

2.4. *'Colorful' Details*

At least five of the L pericopae deserve some notice for the vividness with which their stories are told.[21] I include here only those in which the details are the most concrete and seem gratuitous, not intrinsic to the story.

The story of the good Samaritan (Lk. 10.30-37a) details both the extent of the man's wounds (v. 30) as well as the Samaritan's improvised treatment of them (v. 34).[22] The details of the barren fig tree needing 'manure' (Lk. 13.8) and the prodigal son hungering for 'carob pods'

17.   Lk. 4.25-27 (Sidon, Syria); 7.11b-15 (Nain); 10.30-37a (Jerusalem, Jericho); 13.1b-5 (Galilee, Siloam, Jerusalem). On geographical locations in the Gospels, see G. Theissen, *The Gospels in Context: Social and Political History in the Synoptic Tradition* (trans. L.M. Maloney; Minneapolis: Fortress Press, 1991), pp. 236-58.
18.   Cf. Fitzmyer, *Luke*, p. 656.
19.   See Isa. 8.6; Neh. 3.15; Jn 9.7, 11. See also Josephus, *BJ*, V, 4,2 §145; and J. Finegan, *The Archeology of the New Testament: The Life of Jesus and the Beginning of the Early Church* (rev. edn; Princeton, NJ: Princeton University Press, 1992), pp. 190-92.
20.   Luke has omitted place names at Lk. 3.21//Mk 1.9; Lk. 4.37//Mk 1.28; Lk. 5.17, 27//Mk 2.1, 13; Lk. 6.17//Mk 3.7-8; Lk. 8.4//Mk 4.1; Lk. 8.39, 40//Mk 5.20, 21; Lk. 9.18//Mk 8.27; Lk. 9.43, 46//Mk 9.30, 33; Lk. 18.31//Mk 10.32; Lk. 19.45//Mk 11.15; Lk. 20.1//Mk 11.27; Lk. 22.39, 40//Mk 14.28, 32; Lk. 23.33, 49//Mk 15.22, 41. Cf. Cadbury, *Style and Literary Method*, pp. 127-28, 156.
21.   Lk. 10.30-37a; 13.6b-9; 15.11-32; 16.19-31; 19.2-10.
22.   The Samaritan pours on 'oil and wine'. It should be noted that Luke elsewhere (Lk. 9.6//Mk 6.13) does not consider the use of oil as an appropriate treatment; see Chapter 3, section 2.1, on ἔλαιον.

(Lk. 15.16) are both details of a rural or agricultural nature similar to details Luke has omitted or altered in his redaction of Mark.[23] The suffering of the prodigal son and Lazarus, as well as the opulence of the banquet at the prodigal's return and the feasting of the rich man, are vividly described, sometimes even in the same terms.[24] Finally, Zacchaeus climbing a 'sycamore tree' (Lk. 19.4) is a gratuitous detail,[25] and one that raises problems with the story's urban setting.[26] None of these seem to be the type of details we would expect from Luke himself, and they reinforce the impression that these pericopae are pre-Lukan.

3. *General Themes in L Material*

It may be observed here that the content or subject of almost all the L pericopae still under consideration can be subsumed under three broad categories:[27] money or possessions,[28] women,[29] and servants.[30] Of course, these categories are admittedly broad, and are not unique to L material. We may note then that the L material is fairly uniform in its subject matter, although this subject matter is not noticeably different from that found in the rest of the Gospels.[31]

Since there is a superabundance of work on Luke's attitudes towards

23.   See Cadbury, *Style and Literary Method*, pp. 130-31, for such examples of Luke's 'loss of Palestinian color' in his redaction of Mark: e.g. his substitution of a tile roof for the thatch roof of the Markan story of the paralytic (Lk. 5.19//Mk 2.4).

24.   Both the prodigal son and Lazarus 'desire' (ἐπιθυμέω) 'to be fed' (χορτασθῆναι—aorist passive infinitive in both pericopae): Lk. 15.16; 16.21. Both the father of the prodigal son and the rich man 'rejoice' (εὐφραίνω): Lk. 15.23, 24, 29, 32; 16.19. See above, Chapter 3, section 2.2 on these verbs. Both the elder son and the rich man are referred to as τέκνον (Lk. 15.31; 16.25). Other details in these stories are the gifts to be given to the prodigal son (Lk. 15.22), the clothing of the rich man (Lk. 16.19), and the dogs licking Lazarus' sores (Lk. 16.21).

25.   συκομορέα is found nowhere else in the New Testament, nor anywhere in the LXX.

26.   See Fitzmyer, *Luke*, p. 1224; Finegan, *Archeology*, pp. 150-52.

27.   There are only four pericopae not included in one or more of these categories: Lk. 13.1b-5, 31b-32; 14.2-5; 17.12-18.

28.   Lk. 3.10-14; 7.36-47; 10.30-37a; 11.5b-8; [12.16b-20]; 14.8-10, 12-14, 28-32; [15.4-6]; 15.8-9, 11-32; 16.1b-8a, 19-31; 18.10-14a; 19.2-10.

29.   Lk. 4.25-27; 7.11b-15, 36-47; 10.39-42; 13.10-17b; 15.8-9; 18.2-8a.

30.   Lk. 10.39-42; 12.35-38; 13.6b-9; 15.11-32; 16.1b-8a; 17.7-10.

31.   Although some of the subject matter missing from L material is noticeable: e.g. no mention of the Kingdom; see above, Chapter 4, section 2.

women and money, I will examine more closely the treatment of these subjects in the L material to determine to what extent the attitude exhibited in the L material differs from Luke's own. Although less well developed, some note will also be made here of the characteristics of the L pericopae on servants.[32]

3.1. *L's Attitude towards Wealth*

The attitude towards money and material possessions in the L material seems distinguishable from Lukan interests.[33] In several instances, Luke has made the teachings on wealth found in his sources more radical or harsh and in general shows a more radical and negative attitude towards wealth than his sources.[34] In particular, Luke often writes of the necessity of giving up 'all' wealth or 'everything' (πᾶς) as alms in order to follow Jesus or be a part of the (ideal) Christian community: this is shown in his redaction of Markan material,[35] Q material,[36] and in Acts.[37] Luke also accentuates or adds specific negative comments against

---

32.   The secondary literature on these is minimal compared with the other two subjects. It is also primarily concerned with the historical Jesus and therefore less relevant for our present work: see A. Weiser, *Die Knechtsgleichnesse der synoptischen Evangelien* (SANT, 29; Munich: Kösel–Verlag, 1971), esp. pp. 105-20, 161-77; J.D. Crossan, 'The Servant Parables of Jesus', *Semeia* 1 (1974), pp. 192-221; Scott, *Hear Then the Parable*, pp. 205-15.

33.   On the treatment of possessions in Luke–Acts overall, see L.T. Johnson, *The Literary Function of Possessions in Luke–Acts* (SBLDS, 39; Missoula, MT: Scholars Press, 1977), esp. pp. 170-71; *idem*, *Sharing Possessions: Mandate and Symbol of Faith* (Overtures to Biblical Theology, 9; Philadelphia: Fortress Press, 1981); P.F. Esler, *Community and Gospel in Luke–Acts: The Social and Political Motivations of Lucan Theology* (SNTSMS, 57; Cambridge: Cambridge University Press, 1987), pp. 164-200; J. Donahue, 'Two Decades of Research on the Rich and the Poor in Luke–Acts', in A. Knight and P.J. Paris (eds.), *Justice and the Holy: Essays in Honor of Walter Harrelson* (Atlanta: Scholars Press, 1989), pp. 129-44, esp. pp. 133-34; Ireland, *Stewardship and the Kingdom of God*, pp. 161-97.

34.   On Luke's radicalizing tendency, see H.J. Cadbury, *The Making of Luke–Acts* (New York: Macmillan, 1927; repr. London: SPCK, 1958), pp. 260-63; Fitzmyer, *Luke*, pp. 247-51; W.E. Pilgrim, *Good News to the Poor: Wealth and Poverty in Luke–Acts* (Minneapolis: Augsburg, 1981), esp. pp. 87-122.

35.   See Lk. 5.11//Mk 1.20; Lk. 5.28//Mk 2.14; Lk. 18.22//Mk 10.21. Cf. Esler, *Community and Gospel*, p. 166.

36.   See Lk. 6.30//Mt. 5.42; Lk. 6.34-35//Mt. 5.46-47; Lk. 12.33//Mt. 6.20. See also Lk. 14.33 for a similar addition. Cf. Esler, *Community and Gospel*, pp. 167-68; Donahue, 'Rich and Poor', pp. 132-33.

37.   See Acts 2.44-47; 4.32-37; 5.1-11.

wealthy people in his redaction of Markan material,[38] Q material,[39] and in other additions.[40]

Compared with this Lukan attitude, the attitude towards wealth portrayed in these L pericopae is quite lax indeed. John the Baptist tells the tax-collectors and soldiers only to refrain from getting their money through fraud or violence (Lk. 3.10-14), not to give up any of their gains. Zacchaeus does indeed give half of his possessions to the poor (Lk. 19.8), but the dissonance between this pericope and that of the rich ruler who has just been rejected by Jesus because he could not give 'all' (Lk. 18.22) is noticeable, especially given their proximity. In some of these pericopae, it is implicit that one should be glad to have enough money and should even rejoice at this fact.[41] Some of the acts of kindness praised in these stories even require that one have a sizeable amount of wealth in order to exercise generosity.[42] In the parable of the unjust steward (Lk. 16.1b-8a) the prudent (or even cunning) handling of money to help one's personal position seems to be held up for praise; it is at least not discredited.[43]

The possession of wealth is depicted negatively in the L pericopae only when it has obscured or overridden the character's other concerns, becoming the most important thing in his or her life (Lk. [12.16b-20]; 16.19-31). This is illustrated by excessive concern over financial as opposed to spiritual well-being (Lk. [12.16b-20]). The incorrect ordering of priorities can also be manifested by a lack of kindness or generosity towards others (Lk. 16.19-31), or in an opposite way by a boastful feeling of pride over one's own generosity (Lk. 18.10-14a). In all of the L pericopae, the proper attitude towards wealth is depicted as one of appreciation and generosity, but never renunciation. Given Luke's preference elsewhere in his double work for complete renunciation of wealth or possessions and his criticisms of the rich, the attitude found in L material seems distinguishable from Luke's own predilections.

---

38. See Lk. 8.14//Mk 4.19; Lk. 9.3//Mk 6.8; Lk. 21.1//Mk 12.41. Cf. Esler, *Community and Gospel*, p. 165.

39. See Lk. 6.24-26 (the Woes, absent in Matthew's version); Lk. 7.25//Mt. 11.8.

40. See esp. Lk. 1.53; 12.15; 16.14.

41. Lk. 14.28-32; [15.4-6]; 15.8-9, 11-32.

42. Lk. 7.36-47; 10.30-37a; 14.8-10, 12-14; 15.11-32; 19.2-10.

43. Hence the embarrassment felt by interpreters of this parable: see the excellent summary of exegesis in Ireland, *Stewardship and the Kingdom of God*, pp. 5-47.

3.2. *L's Attitude towards Women*

First, it should be noted that Luke's own attitude towards women remains problematic. Until recently, it was more or less taken for granted that Luke is the evangelist most sympathetic to the plight of women,[44] or even that the author of Luke–Acts might have been a woman.[45] This view of Luke's attitude towards women as positive has recently come under attack, however.[46] It seems unclear whether the older consensus will be overthrown, but it certainly has come under suspicion.[47]

Regardless of how one resolves this issue, it is more important for our redactional and source-critical investigation to observe and specify the literary character of the stories about women in Luke, rather than the context or authorial intention that might have given rise to their inclusion in Luke or his sources. On a purely literary level, the inclusion of the stories is much less ambiguous: it is clear that Luke has (for whatever reasons) included more stories about women than the other evangelists, and that he is particularly fond of pairing stories about

44.	This is still a mainstream view: see L. Swidler, *Biblical Affirmations of Women* (Philadelphia: Westminster Press, 1979), pp. 163-216, 254-81; B. Witherington, III, *Women in the Earliest Churches* (SNTSMS, 58; Cambridge: Cambridge University Press, 1988), pp. 128-57. For a summary of the debate, see A. Black, 'Women in the Gospel of Luke', in C.D. Osburn (ed.), *Essays on Women in Earliest Christianity* (Joplin, MO: College Press Publishing Co., 1993), pp. 445-69.

45.	Swidler, *Biblical Affirmations*, pp. 261-62, 271, 280-81, believes that L was possibly written by a woman. E.J. Via, 'Women in the Gospel of Luke', in U. King (ed.), *Women in the World's Religions* (New York: Paragon House, 1987), pp. 38-55, believes that Luke–Acts itself may have been written by a woman. See the critiques of her position by S. Davies, 'Women in the Third Gospel and the New Testament Apocrypha', in A.-J. Levine (ed.), *'Women Like This': New Perspectives on Jewish Women in the Greco–Roman World* (SBL Early Judaism and Its Literature, 1; Atlanta: Scholars Press, 1991), pp. 185-97; D'Angelo, 'Women in Luke–Acts', p. 443; and Black, 'Women in the Gospel of Luke', pp. 452-53. Cf. also A. Brenner, 'Female Social Behaviour: Two Descriptive Patterns within the "Birth of the Hero" Paradigm', *VT* 36 (1986), pp. 257-73.

46.	See esp. E. Tetlow, *Women and Ministry in the New Testament* (New York: Paulist Press, 1980), pp. 101-108; E. Schüssler Fiorenza, *In Memory of Her*, p. 161; *idem*, 'A Feminist Critical Interpretation for Liberation. Martha and Mary. Luke 10:38-42', *Religion and Intellectual Life* 3 (1986), pp. 21-36.

47.	Cf. the conclusion of M.A. Powell, *What Are They Saying about Luke?* (New York: Paulist Press, 1989), pp. 95-96.

women with similar stories about men.[48] To what extent do the L stories about women fit this Lukan pattern?

Before addressing this question, it should be noted that Luke is neither the only nor even the first to adopt this literary pattern: it is used in both of his known sources,[49] and sometimes he has not made a male–female pair as clear as it could be.[50] Therefore, even if the L material fell into male–female pairs, this would not disprove Luke's use of a source for this material.

The L material fits the Lukan pattern only partially. First, in the vast majority of Luke's male–female pairs (whether taken over from his known sources or added to them) the male story or reference is first.[51] Nowhere has Luke reversed the order of the pair as found in his source; nowhere has he added a female reference before a male reference, or a male reference after a female reference.[52] Of the only eight pairs of female–male stories in Luke–Acts that include the woman first, three of them are pairs internal to L,[53] while two are taken over from Mark.[54]

48.   A frequently observed Lukan technique: see Cadbury, *Making of Luke–Acts*, pp. 233-34; Witherington, *Women in the Earliest Church*, pp. 143-45; D'Angelo, 'Women in Luke–Acts', pp. 443-48; Black, 'Women in the Gospel of Luke', pp. 446-50.

49.   From Mark: Lk. 4.31-39//Mk 1.21-31; Lk. 8.26-56//Mk 5.1-43; Lk. 20.45-21.4//Mk 12.37-44; Lk. 24.1-11//Mk 16.1-8; from Q: Lk. 11.29-32//Mt. 12.38-42; Lk. 12.53//Mt. 10.35; Lk. 13.18-21//Mt. 13.31-33; Lk. 14.26//Mt. 10.37; Lk. 17.34-35//Mt. 24.40-41. Cf. D'Angelo, 'Women in Luke–Acts', pp. 443, 447; Black, 'Women in the Gospel of Luke', p. 448.

50.   Thus Lk. 17.34-35 is not as clearly a male–female pair as Mt. 24.40-41; see also Black, 'Women in the Gospel of Luke', p. 448.

51.   This is the case in 17 of the pairs in the Gospel and 15 of the pairs in Acts: Lk. 1.5-23, 26-38; 2.25-38; 4.31-39; 5.17-26, 7.36-50; 6.12-16, 8.1-3; 7.1-10, 11-17; 8.26-56; 10.25-37, 38-42; 11.29-32; 12.53; 13.18-21; 14.26; 15.1-10; 17.34-35; 20.45-21.4; 23.27; 23.49; Acts 1.13-14; 2.17-18; 5.1-11; 5.14; 8.3; 8.12; 9.2; 9.32-43; 14.8-20, 16.16-40; 17.4; 17.34; 18.1-4; 22.4; 24.24; 25.13, 23. This is 32 out of 40 occurrences, or 80 per cent. Cf. Cadbury, *Making of Luke–Acts*, p. 234.

52.   Although he has made the pairing tighter in his redaction of Mk 14.66-71: Mark has a maid and then a crowd (grammatically masculine—οἱ παρεστῶτες—but of mixed gender?) accuse Peter; Luke has changed this to a maid, a man, and another man (Lk. 22.56-60). He has added the female reference after the male at Lk. 23.27 (cf. Mk 15.21), and the male reference before the female at Lk. 23.49 (cf. Mk 15.40-41). He also makes the female story follow the male when he pairs a story from Mark or Q with a story from elsewhere: Lk. 6.12-16//Mk 3.13-19, Lk. 8.1-3; Lk. 7.1-10//Mt. 8.5-13, Lk. 7.11-17; Lk. 5.17-26//Mk 2.1-12, Lk. 7.36-50.

53.   That is they are not paired by Luke with stories from Mark or Q: Lk. 4.25-

Judging by his pairing of male–female stories in both the Gospel
and Acts, the order found in these L pericopae appears to be un-
Lukan, as well as different from that usually found in Luke's Markan
or Q material.

Of the four remaining L stories about women, two should be noted as
not being as clearly paired with male stories as the other pairs observed
in Luke–Acts.[55] Their pairing is debatable, or is partially due to Lukan
redaction.

Two further peculiarities of the L stories of women may be observed
here. First, three of the stories are about widows. Each of these is about
an individual widow as a character in the story, a rarity elsewhere in
Luke–Acts.[56] More generally, it is remarkable that none of the women
in the L pericopae are attached to any man, neither father nor husband.
This runs contrary to what we would have expected in a work from the
patriarchal culture of the first century, in which a woman's identity is
tied to her male protector.[57]

Thus, the L stories of women are consonant with Luke's general tendency to multiply stories of women. Several of them differ, however,
from Luke's pattern of placing the male story first in his male–female
pairs. Two of the L stories are not as tightly paired as the other male–
female stories in Luke–Acts. Several of the L stories are specifically
about individual widows. Finally, none of the L stories mention any
men connected with these women, an unusual characteristic in both
Luke's work and his society in general.

27; 13.10-17b, 14.2-5; 18.2-8a, 10-14a.

54.   Lk. 22.56-60//Mk 14.66-71; Lk. 24.1-11//Mk 16.1-8; thus, in all of Luke–
Acts there are only three other pairs that are in the order female–male: Lk. 1.46-56, 67-
79 (possibly a chiasmus with the preceding male–female pair, Lk. 1.5-23, 26-38); Acts
13.50; 17.12.

55.   Lk. 7.36-47; 10.30-37a. Both of these pairings are more debatable than others
in Luke–Acts: see D'Angelo, 'Women in Luke–Acts', pp. 444-45; Black, 'Women in
the Gospel of Luke', p. 447.

56.   See below, section 4.1.

57.   See B.J. Malina and J.H. Neyrey, 'Honor and Shame in Luke–Acts: Pivotal
Values of the Mediterranean World', in J.H. Neyrey (ed.), *The Social World of Luke–
Acts: Models for Interpretation* (Peabody, MA: Hendrickson Publishers, 1991),
pp. 25-65, esp. p. 61. Cf. Lk. 1.5, 27; 3.19; 8.3; Acts 5.1; 18.2; 24.24; 25.13, 23.

3.3. *The L Pericopae on Servants*

Six of the L pericopae mention servants or serving.[58] The last four of these are all parables and are therefore formally similar.[59] Lk. 12.35-38 and 17.7-10 are probably the most noticeably similar to one another in content: they both use the unusual verb περιζώννυμαι, 'to gird oneself';[60] also, they are both in the form of departure and return stories.[61] Lk. 12.25-38 is also similar to Lk. 13.6b-9 in that both are warnings about watchfulness and imminent judgment.[62] The last three of these six pericopae all explicitly mention honor and shame.[63] Finally, it may be noted that the ecclesiastical overtones of 'ministry' that are often associated with the words διακονέω/διακονία in Acts seem completely lacking in these stories;[64] in all of these L pericopae the words have their general and secular meaning of 'service', especially serving at table.[65] This is hardly unique to these pericopae, as the general meaning of the words is the more common; I only note here that a meaning of διακονέω/διακονία found frequently in Acts is absent in these L pericopae.

The L pericopae on servants show some similarities of content, especially in their treatment of watchfulness and honor/shame; these will be examined more fully in the following sections.

4. *Groupings by Theme or Content in L Material*

The following are nine groupings by theme or content found among the L pericopae which may indicate pre-Lukan connections among them.[66]

---

58.   Lk. 10.39-42; 12.35-38; 13.6b-9; 15.11-32; 16.1b-8a; 17.7-10.

59.   Lk. 12.35-38 may also be considered a parable; see above, Chapter 4, section 2.

60.   Though in the case of Lk. 12.35, this may be due to Luke assimilating the verse to the LXX (Exod. 12.11): see above, Chapter 3, section 2.1.

61.   See Scott, *Hear Then the Parable*, pp. 208-13.

62.   See below, section 4.6.

63.   See below, section 4.8.

64.   See H.W. Beyer, 'διακονέω', *TDNT* II, pp. 81-93; cf. Acts 1.17, 25; 12.25; 20.24; 21.19.

65.   Though this has been debated in the case of Lk. 10.39-42: see Schüssler Fiorenza, 'Martha and Mary', p. 30; see also below, section 4.3.

66.   Since in most of the cases there is intervening Markan or Q material, these groupings could not very well be Lukan constructs.

They are treated in the order in which the first member of the group is found in Luke.

4.1. *Tax Collectors, Widows, and Lepers*

The accounts of the inaugural sermons of John the Baptist and Jesus in the L material make mention of 'tax collectors' (Lk. 3.12-13), 'widows' (Lk. 4.25-26), and 'lepers' (Lk. 4.27). These same three groups, in the opposite order, are the subject of the last four L pericopae: the cleansing of the ten lepers (Lk. 17.12-18), the parable of the importunate widow (Lk. 18.2-8a), the parable of the Pharisee and the publican (Lk. 18.10-14a), and the story of Zacchaeus (Lk. 19.2-10).[67] 'Widow' may also provide a link between Lk. 4.25-27 and the following L pericope, the raising of the widow's son (Lk. 7.11b-15).

The content similarities in these pericopae go beyond the bare mention of the three groups. John advises the crowds to give *some* of what they have to the poor: 'He who has two coats, let him share with him who has none.'[68] Zacchaeus is depicted as acting in a way that is consonant with this advice: 'Behold, Lord, the half of my goods I give to the poor (Lk. 19.8).' John advises the soldiers not to 'defraud' anyone (Lk. 3.14), while Zacchaeus avoids 'defrauding' anyone and makes restitution if he has done so (Lk. 19.8).[69] Both the praying publican and Zacchaeus provide concrete examples of correct behavior, in contrast to the other characters in their stories,[70] even though each is called a 'sinner'.[71] Although the mention of 'widows' as a group is found in both Luke and Acts,[72] stories of specific widows such as we have in these three L pericopae are much less common.[73] Both of the first two L

---

67.   Zacchaeus being an ἀρχιτελώνης. Further, although the 'soldiers' of Lk. 3.14 do not reappear at the end of the L material, John's advice to them does: see below.

68.   Lk. 3.11. Again, cf. the harsher advice of Q, where one is to give *all* that one has, even more than what is requested (Lk. 6.29).

69.   The same verb—συκοφαντέω—is used in both pericopae; it occurs nowhere else in the New Testament. See above, Chapter 3, section 2.1, on συκοφαντέω; see also Manson, 'John the Baptist', p. 412; Schweizer, *Luke*, p. 290.

70.   Again, it should be noted that parables used as example stories are found only in the L material: see above, Chapter 4, section 2.4. Contrasting characters are also common in L material: see above, Chapter 4, sections 2.3, 3.6, and 4.1-4.3.

71.   Lk. 18.13; 19.7. Both the publican and Zacchaeus also 'come down'—καταβαίνω (Lk. 18.14; 19.5, 6).

72.   See Lk. 20.47//Mk 12.40; Acts 6.1; 9.39, 41.

73.   There are no such stories in Acts; 'widows' are always spoken of as a group

stories of widows (Lk. 4.25-26; 7.11b-15) allude to the story of Elijah's raising of the widow's son (1 Kgs 17.8-24).[74] Finally, both Naaman the Syrian (Lk. 4.27) and the grateful Samaritan (Lk. 17.16-18) are non-Jewish foreigners who are cleansed of leprosy; Naaman, like the Samaritan, also returns to give thanks for his cleansing (2 Kgs 5.15).

The first three and the last four L pericopae show similarities of content in general by their inclusion and affirmation of these three marginalized or despised groups—tax collectors, widows, and lepers. As shown, the stories also share several more specific points of similarity in their content.

4.2. *Love or Compassion*
Four of the L pericopae refer specifically to love or compassion.[75] The first three of these are adjacent among the L pericopae isolated thus far. All of them depict love as the motivation behind concrete acts of kindness:[76] Jesus' raising the widow's son is motivated by his love or compassion (Lk. 7.13),[77] the sinful woman shows her love for Jesus by her actions (Lk. 7.37-38, 44-47), the Samaritan is motivated by compassion (Lk. 10.33), and the prodigal son's father is filled with love at his son's return and feels compelled to show it (Lk. 15.20-24).

On several more specific points, these four pericopae show similarities in their content. The first and second both depict the women as weeping.[78] The second and third both mention the use of oil.[79] The

---

in Acts. Luke follows Mark's story of the widow's offering (Lk. 21.1-4//Mk 12.41-44). Luke designates Anna the prophetess as a widow (Lk. 2.37), although in this story the emphasis seems to be on Anna's ascetic and holy lifestyle, as opposed to the material destitution and helplessness associated with widowhood in the other stories.

74. See esp. Lk. 4.26 (cf. 1 Kgs 17.9); Lk. 7.15 (cf. 1 Kgs 17.23).

75. Lk. 7.11b-15, 36-47; 10.30-37a; 15.11-32. The verb used is σπλαγχνίζομαι in Lk. 7.11b-15; 10.30-37a; and 15.11-32; ἀγαπάω is used in Lk. 7.36-47. See above, Chapter 3, section 2.1, on σπλαγχνίζομαι.

76. They are therefore also similar to the following group of stories about hospitality, although these latter lack specific references to love as the motivation; see below.

77. Particularly unusual in Luke: see above, Chapter 4, section 3.3.

78. Lk. 7.13, 38, 44. The woman's weeping is missing from both the Markan (Mk 14.3-9) as well as the Johannine (Jn 12.1-8) versions of the anointing, though there are some contacts between the Lukan and Johannine versions: anointing of the feet instead of the head, wiping with the hair; see Creed, *Luke*, pp. 109-10; Brown, *John*, pp. 449-52.

79. Lk. 7.46; 10.34; see Chapter 3, section 2.1, on ἔλαιον.

second and fourth both involve kissing the beloved person.[80] Finally, the first, third, and fourth of these pericopae all involve the resuscitation of someone who is literally or figuratively dead: in the first pericope the person is literally dead (Lk. 7.12); in the third he is 'half-dead' (Lk. 10.30); in the fourth he is either on the verge of death (Lk. 15.17), or has been considered as good as dead by his family (Lk. 15.24, 31).

In their general theme, these four pericopae represent a unified message on love: love manifests itself in concrete acts towards the beloved person. Even in their specific imagery, they are similar: love is shown by anointing with oil (Lk. 7.38, 46; 10.34), or kissing (Lk. 7.38, 45; 15.20), and the result of these acts of love is to make alive again one who was dead.[81]

4.3. *Hospitality*

Five L pericopae share the subject of hospitality towards guests.[82] Three of these are nearly adjacent in the L material.[83] In general, all five are similar in their depiction of hospitality as material generosity towards guests.[84]

The five pericopae are similar in some of their specific points as well. Four of the stories are specifically about meals for guests, and the fifth may be as well.[85] The first two are about women.[86] Two also refer to the guests as 'friends'.[87] These five pericopae are similar in both their

---

80.   Lk. 7.38, 45; 15.20; it is another detail unique to this version of the anointing. 'Kiss' is found elsewhere in Luke–Acts only at Lk. 22.47 (//Mk 14.45) where Luke uses φιλέω; and Acts 20.37, where the verb is καταφιλέω, as in these L pericopae.

81.   Lk. 7.12; 10.30; 15.17, 24, 31. Such imagery, like that of losing and finding (see below) is not typical of Luke, from whom we would have expected 'salvation' language: words from the σώζω group occur 27 times in Luke and 23 times in Acts; cf. 15 times in Mark and 16 times in Matthew.

82.   Lk. 7.36-47; 10.39-42; 11.5b-8; 14.8-10, 12-14; 19.2-10.

83.   Lk. 7.36-47; 10.39-42; 11.5b-8; they are separated only by the good Samaritan story, which is certainly cognate in its depiction of acts of kindness.

84.   Although in the second this is nuanced somewhat to become a debate over what kind of attention one should show the guest. The fourth of these pericopae is phrased as warnings about the proper showing of this generosity.

85.   Lk. 7.36-47; 10.39-42; 11.5b-8; 14.8-10, 12-14. Cf. Schüssler Fiorenza, 'Martha and Mary', p. 30; Malina and Neyrey, 'Honor and Shame', p. 62. A meal is probably also implied in Lk. 19.2-10, though not mentioned specifically.

86.   Lk. 7.36-47; 10.39-42; see above, section 3.2.

87.   Lk. 11.5, 5, 6, 8; 14.10, 12. It is, moreover, in the vocative in both of these

general subject of hospitality and in some more specific details; this is especially so in the first three of these stories.[88]

4.4. *Setting at Night*

Three adjacent L pericopae are stories that are said specifically to occur at night.[89] The first and third even specify the time of night: 'midnight' (Lk. 11.5b), 'second or third watch' (Lk. 12.38).[90] Like the details treated above, Luke sometimes omits or condenses references to time in his redaction of Mark.[91] That three adjacent L pericopae would share the same temporal setting is an odd coincidence, and one that Luke is unlikely to have supplied himself.[92]

4.5. *Prayer*

Three of the L pericopae are about prayer.[93] All three are parables. The last two of these are adjacent in the L material isolated.[94] The first two, although separated, are formally quite similar.[95] They also share the same point that persistence in prayer is efficacious,[96] while the third is

---

pericopae (Lk. 11.5; 14.10), a seldom used case in the New Testament: see Kenney, *Stylometric Study*, p. 57. φίλος is also found in all three of the 'lost' parables (Lk. 15.6, 9, 29). 'Friend' is uncommon elsewhere in Luke–Acts (six other times in Luke; three times in Acts).

88. The first three include several of the observed connections: all three are proximate to one another in the L material (see above); the first two are formally related (biographical apothegm or pronouncement story: see Chapter 4, sections 4.1 and 4.2); the first two are about women; and all three share the detail of a meal for a guest.

89. Lk. 11.5b-8; [12.16b-20]; 12.35-38.

90. Cf. the related saying, Mk 13.35, where the time designations are different.

91. See Cadbury, *Style and Literary Method*, pp. 130, 152. On Luke's special time expressions, see Cadbury, 'Some Lukan Expressions of Time', pp. 272-78.

92. This is especially so since the three pericopae are not now adjacent in Luke. All three pericopae are, moreover, sayings of Jesus. Such coincidences may indicate a pre-Lukan link by catchword between the pericopae, as will be argued in the next chapter.

93. Lk. 11.5b-8; 18.2-8a, 10-14a.

94. And may be a female–male pair; see above, section 3.2.

95. Thus both begin with the petitioned, not the petitioner (Lk. 11.5; 18.2); both then have the petitioned refuse (Lk. 11.7; 18.4); and both end with the petitioned giving in because of frustration or weariness with the petitioner (Lk. 11.8; 18.5). Cf. Hendrickx, *Parables*, pp. 217-18; Blomberg, 'Midrash, Chiasmus', pp. 240-41. On the expression παρέχειν κόπον in both pericopae (Lk. 11.7; 18.5), see above, Chapter 3, section 2.1.

96. They also share a seemingly unflattering portrayal of God: see Creed, *Luke*, p. lxix; and above, Chapter 4, section 2.5.

about the content or attitude of prayer.

Luke does show an interest in the theme of prayer;[97] these parables would clearly fit his theme in their general content. But, as in the case of stories of women, Luke's more specific attitude towards prayer is less clear. On the one hand, Lk. 18.1-8 has been used as the linchpin for understanding Luke's theology of prayer;[98] as might be expected, this analysis has been widely attacked as overlooking or slighting the other material in Luke–Acts.[99] On the other hand, analyses that attempt to synthesize more of the prayer material in Luke–Acts tend to minimize the place of these three parables.[100] Luke's distinctive attitude towards prayer is usually found in his Q material,[101] or in his portrayal of the prayers of Jesus and the apostles.[102] It is this final category that seems to be Luke's own particular emphasis in his work.[103]

However, paraenetic material on prayer such as these three L parables, although not incompatible with Luke's theology of prayer, does not further the Lukan interest of depicting prayer as part of salvation history; it therefore seems less likely that Luke has composed these stories purely for his own peculiar purposes and interests. The potentially unflattering portrayal of God in the first two seems unlikely to have come from Luke himself; the theme of persistence in these parables is also in some tension with other Lukan material.[104] If the last two

97.   See Plummer, *Luke*, pp. xlv-xlvi; Fitzmyer, *Luke*, pp. 244-47.

98.   See W. Ott, *Gebet und Heil: Die Bedeutung der Gebetsparänese in der lukanischen Theologie* (Munich: Küsel, 1965).

99.   E.g. P.T. O'Brien, 'Prayer in Luke–Acts', *TynBul* 24 (1973), pp. 111-27; A.A. Trites, 'The Prayer Motif in Luke–Acts', in C.H. Talbert (ed.), *Perspectives on Luke–Acts* (Danville, VA: Association of Baptist Professors of Religion, 1978), pp. 168-86.

100.   Thus they are barely mentioned in two recent monographs on prayer in Luke–Acts: S.F. Plymale, *The Prayer Texts of Luke–Acts* (New York: Peter Lang, 1991), pp. 56-58, 109; D.M. Crump, *Jesus the Intercessor: Prayer and Christology in Luke–Acts* (WUNT, 2/49; Tübingen: Mohr [Paul Siebeck], 1992), pp. 131-34.

101.   Thus P. Edmonds, 'The Lucan Our Father: A Summary of Luke's Teaching on Prayer?', *ExpTim* 91 (1979-80), pp. 140-43; and simizlarly, S. Smalley, 'Spirit, Kingdom and Prayer in Luke–Acts', *NovT* 15 (1973), pp. 59-71.

102.   E.g. L.O. Harris, 'Prayer in the Gospel of Luke', *Southwestern Journal of Theology* 10 (1967), pp. 59-69; H.M. Conn, 'Luke's Theology of Prayer', *Christianity Today* 17 (1972), pp. 290-92.

103.   Cf. Trites, 'Prayer Motif', p. 169.

104.   Thus the idea of persistence in Lk. 11.5b-8 is somewhat blunted by Luke's linking it to Q 11.9-13. Also cf. Acts 4.24-31, where the believers' prayer is answered

of these parables are intended as a male–female pair, then their order is un-Lukan.[105] Finally, the third portrays individual prayer, a rarity in Luke–Acts;[106] it is also one of the formally anomalous example stories that are found only in L material.[107]

These parables on prayer are not perfectly fitted to Luke's own theme of prayer, although they fit well enough for him to have decided to include them. The first two are quite close in form and content, while the second two are adjacent in the L material, as well as making a female–male pair on prayer. All of this serves to increase the likelihood that they are from a pre-Lukan source.

4.6. *Watchfulness*

Four adjacent L pericopae all include the idea of watchfulness in the face of imminent judgment or accountability, although none of them include an explicit mention of the coming of the Kingdom or the parousia.[108] Such crisis parables were previously judged as authentic parables of the historical Jesus,[109] although they have more recently been rejected as such.[110] Regardless of whether or not one attributes them to the historical Jesus, their difference from Lukan eschatology is noticeable: their expectation of the nearness and suddenness of judgment represents an eschatology considerably more imminent than Luke's own.[111]

immediately.

105. See above, section 3.2.

106. Thus in the Gospel, only Jesus is said to pray alone (Lk. 3.21; 5.16; 6.12; 9.18, 28, 29; 22.41). In Acts, Paul (Acts 9.11; 22.17; 28.8), Cornelius (Acts 10.2, 30), and Peter (Acts 9.40; 10.9; 11.5) also pray alone, although the vast majority of references to prayer are in a group or community setting (Acts 1.14, 24; 2.42; 3.1; 6.4, 6; 8.15; 12.5, 12; 13.3; 14.23; 16.13, 16, 25; 20.36; 21.5). Cf. Bailey, *Through Peasant Eyes*, pp. 145-47.

107. See above, Chapter 4, section 2.4.

108. Lk. [12.16b-20]; 12.35-38; 13.1b-5, 6b-9; all four are also sayings of Jesus.

109. See Dodd, *Parables*, pp. 122-39; Jeremias, *Parables*, pp. 160-80. Related crisis parables include Mk 13.33-37; Lk. 6.47-49//Mt. 7.24-27; Lk. 12.39-40, 42-46//Mt. 24.43-44, 45-51; Mt. 25.1-13.

110. Thus Crossan, *Historical Jesus*, pp. 250-51, 253-55.

111. On Luke's delayed eschatology, see Conzelmann, *Theology*, p. 135; Fitzmyer, *Luke*, p. 235; J.T. Carroll, *Response to the End of History: Eschatology and Situation in Luke–Acts* (SBLDS, 92; Atlanta: Scholars Press, 1988), p. 166. See also E.E. Ellis, *Eschatology in Luke* (Facet Books, Biblical Series, 30; Philadephia: Fortress Press, 1972); E. Franklin, *Christ the Lord: A Study in the Purpose and Theology of*

Besides their general similarity in expecting an imminent judgment, the first, third, and fourth of these pericopae are also alike in their expectation that the judgment will be unfavorable; all three use the specific image that the result will be death (Lk. 12.20; 13.3, 5, 9). Only the second pericope considers the possibility that the judgment will be favorable (Lk. 12.38).

It is suggestive of a pre-Lukan connection between these pericopae that they are generally similar in their theme of watchfulness while being adjacent among the L pericopae. That their eschatology is more imminent than Luke's own renders this suggestion even more likely.

4.7. *Children of Abraham*

Three of the L pericopae are each about a 'child of Abraham'.[112] In the singular, this expression is found nowhere else in Luke–Acts.[113] All three occur in the second half of L material, though they are not adjacent. All three are similar in their general concept of what it means to be a 'child of Abraham'. In all three it is an honorific that entitles one to benefits: these can be experienced as healing (Lk. 13.16), comfort and 'good things' (Lk. 16.25), or Jesus' praise and presence (Lk. 19.9).[114] The enjoyment of these benefits may be postponed (Lk. 13.16; 16.25), or the entitlements may even be exhausted (Lk. 16.25), though the title itself still remains valid.[115]

All three have similar main characters and plots. Each of the three has as its main character someone who is doubly handicapped in his or her standing in the community. Each of the main characters belongs first to a generally marginalized group: a woman (Lk. 13.11), a poor man (Lk. 16.20), or a tax-collector (Lk. 19.2). Each is further encumbered by

---

as realized rather than delayed, see J.B. Chance, *Jerusalem, the Temple, and the New Age in Luke–Acts* (Macon, GA: Mercer University Press, 1988).

112. Lk. 13.10-17b; 16.19-31; 19.2-10. The term used is different in each: 'daughter' (θυγάτηρ—Lk. 13.16), 'child' (τέκνον—Lk. 16.25), 'son' (υἱός—Lk. 19.9).

113. Abraham 'our father' is found at Lk. 1.55, 73; 3.8; Acts 3.13, 25; 7.2; see also 'sons of the family of Abraham' (Acts 13.26).

114. Although in the last of these, the specific language of 'salvation' is probably due to Luke; see above, section 4.2.

115. Thus Abraham still refers to the rich man as 'child' (Lk. 16.25), and notes that the benefits he can expect from the title have simply been used up, while Lazarus's rewards have begun after a lifelong delay. Cf. W. Hendriksen, *New Testament Commentary: Exposition of the Gospel according to Luke* (Grand Rapids: Baker Book House, 1978), p. 786; Marshall, *Luke*, p. 638; Fitzmyer, *Luke*, p. 1133.

some physical impairment: a crippling disease (Lk. 13.11), hunger and sores (Lk. 16.20-21), or being extremely short (Lk. 19.3).[116] All three stories affirm these people despite their impairments. Each story shows the physical impairment being eliminated or overcome and the character's lower status being reversed as she or he regains the status and reaps the benefits of again being a 'child of Abraham'.

These three stories are similar in their use of the title 'child of Abraham,' which is not used in this way elsewhere in Luke–Acts. They depict 'children of Abraham' in the same way, as people who are doubly excluded from the group, but who are ultimately vindicated and rewarded.

4.8. *Honor and Shame*
Six of the L pericopae specifically mention honor or shame.[117] All of these are near each other in the L material isolated. Three of these use one of the words from the αἰσχύνη group,[118] two use the language of worthy and unworthy,[119] and the other speaks of mockery.[120]

Besides Lk. 13.10-17b, which may be connected to the other pericopae only by its use of the same vocabulary,[121] these stories are similar in

---

116. Such an impairment would obviously be necessary in a healing story such as Lk. 13.10-17b, but not in the other two stories. On such gratuitous details in L material, see above, section 2.4. Such a depiction of marginalized groups is also similar to those treated in section 4.1 above.

117. Lk. 13.10-17b; 14.8-10, 12-14, 28-32; 15.11-32; 16.1b-8a; 17.7-10. On the variety of terms that can indicate honor and shame, see Malina and Neyrey, 'Honor and Shame', pp. 46-47.

118. Lk. 14.9 (αἰσχύνη); 16.3 (αἰσχύνομαι); 13.17 (καταισχύνω); see above, Chapter 3, section 2.2, on these words. See also R. Bultmann, 'αἰσχύνω', *TDNT* I, pp. 189-91.

119. Lk. 15.19, 21 (ἄξιος); Lk. 17.10 (ἀχρεῖος). ἄξιος occurs twice in Q (Lk. 3.8//Mt. 3.8; Lk. 10.7//Mt. 10.11), four times elsewhere in the Gospel (Lk. 7.4; 12.48; 23.15, 41), and seven times in Acts; see G. Bertram, 'ἄξιος', *TDNT* I, pp. 379-80. ἀχρεῖος occurs nowhere else in Luke–Acts, and only once elsewhere in the New Testament (Mt. 25.30). Cf. Malina and Neyrey, 'Honor and Shame', p. 26.

120. Lk. 14.29 (ἐμπαίζω); the only other occurrences of the verb in Luke–Acts are in the third Passion prediction (Lk. 18.32//Mk 10.34) and in the Passion itself (Lk. 22.63; 23.11, 36; cf. Mk 15.20, 31); see W. Foerster, 'ἐμπαίζω', *TDNT* , pp. 630-35.

121. It is, moreover, formally different from the others in this group, being the only healing/controversy story. It therefore falls into the typical 'challenge–riposte' category of stories of acquired honor: see Malina and Neyrey, 'Honor and Shame', pp. 29-32, 49-50.

their treatment of honor and shame. Three of them are about servants;[122] in two of these, servanthood is specifically equated with a less
honorable status.[123] Two of the pericopae include a reversal, in which
abasing oneself results in being raised to a more honorable status.[124]
Finally, three of the pericopae depict shame as being either brought
upon oneself or avoided based on prudent management of funds.[125]

These pericopae are similar in their general subject matter of honor
and shame. More importantly and distinctively, they are also similar on
several more specific points in their treatment of honor and shame: to be
a servant is less honorable; ironically, dishonor can be avoided and
honor gained by abasing oneself; and honor can be obtained or lost
based on one's use of money.

4.9. *Joy at Finding the Lost*

Four of the L pericopae are about something 'lost' being 'found'.[126] The
first three of these are adjacent and are all parables; their grouping has
often been considered as pre-Lukan.[127] All four stories also share the
idea of the 'joy' that is experienced when the 'lost' are 'found'.[128] Three
of the stories also state that the 'lost' are actively 'sought'.[129] The first
two stories are about lost objects, while the second two are about lost
persons; in both the last two stories the lost person is welcomed despite
being hated by the other characters in the story.[130]

122. Lk. 15.11-32; 16.1b-8a; 17.7-10.

123. Lk. 15.11-32; 17.7-10.

124. Lk. 14.8-10, 12-14; 15.11-32. On the honoring of the prodigal son, see Malina
and Neyrey, 'Honor and Shame', p. 55.

125. Lk. 14.28-32; 15.11-32; 16.1b-8a.

126. Lk. [15.4-6]; 15.8-9, 11-32; 19.2-10. The verb is 'wandered off' rather than
'lost' in the Matthean version of the lost sheep (πλανάω—Mt. 18.12, 13).

127. See Blomberg, 'Midrash, Chiasmus', p. 242; Nolland, *Luke*, p. 769. On the
pre-Lukan elements of the Zacchaeus story, see Drury, *Tradition and Design*, pp. 72-
75; J. O'Hanlon, 'The Story of Zacchaeus and the Lukan Ethic', *JSNT* 12 (1981),
pp. 2-26, esp. pp. 6-9.

128. See above, Chapter 3, section 2.2, on εὐφραίνω in Lk. 15.11-32. 'Joy' is
found in the story of Zacchaeus (Lk. 19.6), though in this case it is the lost person's
joy, and it is Luke's preferred verb, χαίρω.

129. Lk. 15.4, 8; 19.10. In the third, the prodigal son does return on his own,
although his father rushes out to meet him before he himself can close the distance (Lk.
15.20).

130. The Zacchaeus story is also similar to that of the sinful woman (Lk. 7.36-47):
see D.A.S. Ravens, 'Zacchaeus: The Final Part of a Lucan Triptych?', *JSNT* 41 (1991),

That the idea of losing and finding is not Luke's preferred language is seen by his redaction of these stories. He has appended his preferred language of sin and repentance to the first two (Lk. 15.7, 10), while in the fourth he has reworked the ending to include salvation language.[131] The three parables of Luke 15 all end in exactly the same way in the language of 'lost' and 'found' that Luke has not considered adequate or explicit enough.[132]

That Luke felt it necessary to augment or alter the language of these stories shows that they are not purely his own creation. The four stories present a consistent message: the lost are actively sought; and when they are found, there is great (even gratuitous) joy, despite whatever they may have done.

5. *The Content of L Material: Summary*

From the point of view of content, the L material has displayed noticeable dissimilarities from Luke's own interests. It also has some internal content similarities of its own which will now be summarized.

The content of the L material is considerably more detailed than one would have expected if it were pure Lukan composition, since Luke tends to omit details in his redaction of Mark. Such detailed accounts are also anomalous if one postulates that the L material is Lukan reworking of one or more oral traditions, because such details also tend to be eliminated in oral transmission. The L material is particularly rich in numerical details, although several pericopae also include personal names, place names, or other seemingly superfluous 'colorful' details.

In its general content, the L material is not noticeably different from the rest of the Gospels in its inclusion of stories about money, women, and servants. In its specific attitudes towards these subjects, however,

---

pp. 19-32, esp. pp. 29-30; and P. Kariamadam, *The Zacchaeus Story (Lk. 19, 1-10): A Redactional–Critical Investigation* (Kerala, India: Pontifical Institute Publications, 1985), pp. 32-33.

131. Lk. 19.9, 10. The resulting awkwardness is most clear in v. 10, where the verbs used are lose/seek/save instead of lose/seek/find. Cf. the similar addition at Lk. 7.50.

132. Lk. 15.6, 9, 24, 32.

the L material does exhibit some differences from the attitudes of Luke himself.

The attitude towards wealth in the L material has been shown to be much more lax and accomodating than Luke's own. The L pericopae nowhere encourage complete renunciation of possessions as found elsewhere in Luke–Acts. The primary attitudes they encourage are generosity and prudent use of money, always presupposing that one still has appreciable funds with which to exercise such generosity.

The treatment of women in the L material is also somewhat different from Lukan interests. Whatever his attitude towards women in the real world, in his literary world Luke has included more stories about women than the other evangelists, and has usually made these part of male–female pairs. The L stories of women are sometimes not as closely paired as others in Luke–Acts. When they are paired, the female stories come first in several instances; this order is almost never found elsewhere in Luke–Acts. Several of the L stories are also about widows. None of the women in L stories are linked to a male companion or protector, an anomaly in either Luke's work or elsewhere.

Nine specific thematic groupings have been examined in the L material. The L material begins and ends with stories about tax collectors, widows, and lepers. The first half of the L material seems to be concerned with stories of love, hospitality, and finally, watchfulness. This final group is the most noticeably different from Lukan theology, in that its eschatology is more imminent than Luke's own. The second half of the L material, while also echoing some of the same themes, includes many specific references to honor and shame in its stories; it also contains several stories about children of Abraham and the finding of the lost.

The differences in content between the L material and Lukan interests are enough to decrease further the idea that this material is purely or primarily Lukan composition. The internal similarities are further indications that the material may have originated from the same pre-Lukan source. The next chapter will elaborate these links and postulate what such a source might have been like.

Chapter 6

CONCLUSIONS

Probability. Anyone can add to it, no one can take away.
—Pascal[1]

1. *The Evidence Favoring a Pre-Lukan Source*

The preceding three chapters have all been concerned with determining two qualities of the L material in Luke 3–19: 1) the extent to which this material differs from what we might have expected if Luke had composed it himself; and 2) the extent to which this material shows internal similarities among its pericopae. The analysis has utilized several different criteria—stylistic, formal, and thematic—for determining similarity. It has also employed several different methodologies—vocabulary studies, stylometry, form criticism, and redaction criticism—for analyzing the data. The evidence will now be summarized briefly.

Chapter 3 isolated 26 pericopae (164 verses) in Luke 3–19 as un-Lukan based on their dissimilarity to Lukan style and vocabulary. All 26 of these pericopae exhibit two or more un-Lukan characteristics of style and/or vocabulary. It may be noted that the great majority of these in fact include three or more un-Lukan characteristics.[2] The corroboration of two or more stylistic and/or vocabulary criteria was necessary, as each such criterion was deemed probably (and not definitively) un-Lukan in each individual case.

1.   Pascal, *Pensées*, p. 240.
2.   Twenty of the 26: Lk. 3.10-14; 7.11b-15, 36-47; 10.30-37a; 11.5b-8; [12.16b-20]; 12.35-38; 13.1b-5, 6b-9, 10-17b; 14.2-5, 8-10, 12-14, 28-32; [15.4-6], 11-32; 16.1b-8, 19-31; 17.12-18; 18.2-8a; 19.2-7, [8], 9, [10]. Not surprisingly, the longer pericopae tend to have more un-Lukan characteristics: the longest pericope, Lk. 15.11-32, has the most such characteristics (12) and the second longest pericope, Lk. 16.19-31, has the second most (10).

Based on the stylistic evidence, it seems unlikely that Luke composed the L material purely on his own. Further, although there is no one stylistic element present in all of the L material, several are found in many or most of the L pericopae: the dative after a verb of speaking occurs in 18 of the pericopae, a high incidence of καί is found in 13 of the pericopae, the numeral is placed before the noun in 11 of the pericopae, and the conjunction ἵνα occurs in ten of the pericopae.[3] Since these stylistic elements were shown to be most probably un-Lukan, their presence in a large number of scattered pericopae cannot be explained as being due to the final redactor; their repeated inclusion in the L material when they are excluded by Luke elsewhere therefore requires some further explanation. Such a frequency of un-Lukan stylistic elements could be explained if this L material originated in a common source, a source that preferred these stylistic elements and which Luke's redaction has not completely obscured; but it does not seem that the style of these pericopae is homogenous enough to prove the existence of such a source, even though it may support the hypothesis of such a source.

We may sum up the stylistic evidence in the following way. It functioned to exclude several pericopae by showing that they exhibited little or no difference from Lukan usage.[4] It further made the wholesale composition of the remaining L pericopae by Luke appear unlikely, as their style is demonstrably different from Luke's own. Finally, although the stylistic data supports the possible existence of a single source behind this material, it does not demand the postulation of such a source. Although the style of the L material is distinct from Luke's own, it is not homogenous enough among the L pericopae to prove the existence of a source on purely stylistic grounds.[5]

It was in Chapter 4 that similarities among the L pericopae began to appear more strongly. Both within formal types and across formal lines, the L pericopae show noticeable formal similarities; most of these similarities are also dissimilar to Lukan usage elsewhere.

All of the L parables examined include dialogue, monologue, and/or questions. These formal characteristics are not only rare in parables in Luke's Markan and Q sections, they are also avoided or diminished by

3.   See above, Chapter 3, section 3.6, for the table listing the pericopae exhibiting each characteristic.

4.   See above, Chapter 3, section 5, for a list of the pericopae thus excluded.

5.   Cf. Kenny, *Stylometric Study*, pp. 72-79; Williams, *Stylometric Authorship Studies*, pp. 1-22.

Luke in his redaction of these sources.[6] All four L healings are formally similar to one another by their lack of a request for healing from the sick person(s), a formal characteristic usually thought intrinsic to the form of a healing story.[7] Three of the L healings report Jesus' touching of the patient, an un-Lukan characteristic.[8] Three of the L healings, like most of the L parables, also include questions, another formal characteristic avoided by Luke elsewhere.[9] Finally, the miscellaneous L pericopae of various sayings material frequently include dialogue and/or contrasting characters,[10] characteristics also observed frequently in the L parables.

Three of the formal similarities observed among L pericopae of the same formal type are also frequently found between L pericopae of different formal types: 1) dialogue and/or monologue; 2) questions; and 3) contrasting characters.[11] Almost all of the L pericopae contain one or more of these three formal characteristics. Again, the first two of these are characteristics Luke omits or minimizes elsewhere in his work.

In summary, the L material has been found to be formally distinct in several ways when compared with Luke's Markan or Q material of the same formal type. These formal peculiarities are unlikely to be from Luke himself, as they are contrary to his observed redactional habits. Finally, several of these formal characteristics of the L material are shared by the majority of the L pericopae, even though they are of different formal types. The L material is formally different from Luke's own formal preferences as shown by his redactional habits: this is further evidence against Lukan composition of the material. There are also several points of formal similarity among the L pericopae, both among pericopae of the same formal type and among those of different formal types: this is evidence in favor of the material being from a common source.

In Chapter 5 the content of the L material was examined. As with the formal characteristics examined, several points of content similarity were found within the L material; these points are also often dissimilar to Lukan interests.

---

6. See above, Chapter 4, sections 2.1 and 2.2.
7. See above, Chapter 4, section 3.1.
8. Lk. 7.11b-15; 13.10-17b; 14.2-5; see above, Chapter 4, section 3.3.
9. Lk. 13.10-17b; 14.2-5; 17.12-18; see above, Chapter 4, section 3.2.
10. See above, Chapter 4, sections 4.1-4.4.
11. See above, Chapter 4, section 5.

The most prevalent content similarity in the L pericopae is the inclusion of a number of details in the accounts.[12] Such detailed accounts are not typical of oral transmission; further, Luke tends to omit such details in his redaction of Mark. Numerical details are the most common detail in the L material, occuring in the great majority of the L pericopae, while numerical references are quite rare in Luke's Markan and Q sections. The un-Lukan aspect of these details is accentuated by the fact that in many of the L pericopae the number placement is un-Lukan. Many of the L pericopae also include personal names, place names, or 'colorful' details, all of which are the types of details frequently omitted by Luke in his redaction of Mark. That almost all the L pericopae contain the types of details that Luke omits elsewhere in his work is further evidence against Lukan composition of this material. Further, since such details are also often omitted in oral transmission and are rare in Luke's other sources, this is further evidence in favor of a common source for the L material.

In terms of general themes, the L material was found to be amenable to Luke's purposes, but not with the kind of perfect fit that we might have expected had Luke composed it himself or thoroughly redacted it. The attitudes towards money and towards women found in the L pericopae are somewhat different from Luke's own. The L material's attitude towards wealth is less radical than Luke's attitude elsewhere.[13] The material's treatment of women is peculiar in its placement of female stories before male stories when the two are paired, and also in its lack of any mention of men attached to the women in its stories.[14] The material's similarity to Lukan interests clearly accounts for his inclusion of it in his work; but its dissimilarities show that he was neither working from whole cloth, nor redacting the material so perfectly that it would be indistinguishable from his own hand.

In terms of more specific themes, nine thematic groups were found in proximate L material.[15] Stories of tax collectors, widows, and lepers are found at the beginning and the end of the L material. Love, hospitality towards guests, and a night-time setting occur in the earlier L pericopae. Four of the L pericopae are about watchfulness, and display an eschatology noticeably different from Luke's own. Finally, the latter L

12. See above, Chapter 5, sections 2.1–2.4.
13. See above, Chapter 5, section 3.1.
14. See above, Chapter 5, section 3.2.
15. See above, Chapter 5, sections 4.1-4.9.

pericopae are about 'children of Abraham', honor and shame, and the finding of the 'lost'. These thematic groupings may show the remnants of a source's organization, as will be examined below.

The L material does seem to have enough dissimilarities from Lukan style, form, and content to make it probable that this material is pre-Lukan. It also displays several internal consistencies of style, form, and content, enough to make it seem unlikely that the material originated in a number of sources and traditions that accidentally overlapped in these unusual and un-Lukan ways. We must now examine the recovered material to see what sort of whole it constituted. Four questions need to be answered in this context: 1) Does the material as recovered show any internal organization or structure? 2) Is this order predominantly oral, or are there signs of literary structures? 3) Are there any analogous works to which we can appeal for confirmation on the grounds of a shared genre? 4) What was the probable date and place of composition of such a source?

2. *The Probable Order and Structure of L*

It must be admitted at the beginning that, unlike Q, we have no outside evidence for checking Luke's arrangement of the L material. However, we may repeat here that throughout our various examinations, we have assumed that Luke has treated the L material, whatever its origin, in a way similar to the treatment of his Markan and Q material. If we can continue in this assumption as we examine the order of the L material, then we find that there is some reason to believe that Luke has preserved the order of the source that lies behind this material. This is because it is widely accepted that Luke has preserved the order of both Mark and Q with considerable consistency, and has indeed let the order of his sources shape his final work rather than rearrange material on a large scale.[16] It is not unreasonable to assume then that the present order of

16.. On Luke's preservation of the Markan order, see F. Neirynck, 'The Argument from Order and St Luke's Transpositions', *ETL* 49 (1973), pp. 784-815; Fitzmyer, *Luke*, pp. 66-72. On Luke's preservation of the order of Q, see B.H. Streeter, 'On the Original Order of Q', in W. Sanday (ed.), *Oxford Studies in the Synoptic Problem* (Oxford: Clarendon Press, 1911), pp. 141-64; Manson, *Sayings*, p. 15; V. Taylor, 'The Order of Q', *JTS* 4 (1953), pp. 27-31; *idem*, 'The Original Order of Q', in A.J.B. Higgins (ed.), *New Testament Essays: Studies in Memory of T.W. Manson* (Manchester: Manchester University Press, 1959), pp. 246-69; Kloppenborg, *Formation*, pp. 64-80; Nolland, *Luke*, p. xxxi.

the L pericopae in Luke largely represents their original order in the putative source.

Does the present order of the L pericopae show any signs of organization? Without rearranging the pericopae, can the material be outlined in a way that is coherent and convincing? Some organization by theme or looser catchword association has already been hinted at in Chapter 5. The L material begins and ends with stories of tax-collectors, widows, and lepers, forming an *inclusio*. After the sermons of Jesus and John, there are three sections that begin with healings and then relate Jesus' teachings. The first of these sections begins with a healing motivated by Jesus' love and moves on to teachings on love; it ends with a series of warnings on watchfulness and imminent judgment. The second section begins with the healing of 'a child of Abraham', a title that reappears twice more in the later L pericopae. This second section is primarily Jesus' teaching on honor, especially the ironic reversal of gaining honor through abasement. The section also includes several stories about the joy experienced at the finding of the lost. These two themes of honor through abasement and joy at the lost being found are brought together in the longest of the L parables, the parable of the prodigal son (Lk. 15.11-32). The final L pericope, the story of Zacchaeus (Lk. 19.2-10), provides a sort of multiple *inclusio*, reiterating the theme of tax collectors with which L began, as well as providing a final story about 'a child of Abraham' and the joy of finding the lost, repeating themes from the second section of L. The L material may be outlined then in the following way, in which larger themes and sections are the headings, and catchword or looser associations between pericopae are in brackets.[17]

An Outline of L

Introduction: Preaching to the Outcasts—Tax Collectors, Widows, and Lepers

Lk. 3.10-14	[tax collectors]
Lk. 4.25-27	[widow]
	[lepers]

---

17. Cf. the similar outline in F.C. Grant, *The Growth of the Gospels* (New York: Abingdon Press, 1933), pp. 92-93; his outline is abbreviated, with topic headings removed, in the later revised edition (Grant, *Gospels*, pp. 61-62). Both of Grant's versions, however, assume that L contained Passion and resurrection narratives, and also contain some Q material.

Part I: Love and Warnings

A) Jesus heals—a demonstration of love

    Lk. 7.11b-15   [love, widow, weeping]

B) Jesus teaches

1) On love and receiving guests

    Lk. 7.36-47   [love, oil, woman, weeping, hospitality]s
    Lk. 10.30-37a   [love, oil]
    Lk. 10.39-42   [woman, hospitality]
    Lk. 11.5b-8   [night, hospitality]

2) Warnings/Watchfulness

    Lk. [12.16b-20]   [night, death]
    Lk. 12.35-38   [night]
    Lk. 13.1b-5   [death, 18]
    Lk. 13.6b-9   [death]

Part II: Honor and Children of Abraham

A) Jesus heals

    Lk. 13.10-17b   [daughter of Abraham, 18, honor, Sabbath]
    Lk. 13.31b-32 ('I perform cures')
    Lk. 14.2-5   [Sabbath]

B) Jesus teaches on honor and joy

    Lk. 14.8-10, 12-14   [honor, money]
    Lk. 14.28-32   [honor, money]
    Lk. [15.4-6]   [joy, lost]
    Lk. 15.8-9   [joy, lost]
    Lk. 15.11-32   [joy, lost, servants, honor, money]
    Lk. 16.1b-8   [servants, honor, money]
    Lk. 16.19-31   [a child of Abraham, money]
    Lk. 17.7-10   [servants, honor]

Part III: The Vindication of the Outcasts—Lepers,
Widows, and Tax Collectors

A) Jesus heals

    Lk. 17.12-18   [lepers]

B) Jesus teaches

    Lk. 18.2-8a   [widow, prayer]
    Lk. 18.10-14a   [tax collector, prayer]
    Lk. 19.2-10   [tax collector, son of Abraham]

There does seem to be a degree of order and organization among the L pericopae in their present Lukan order. The order of the L material presents us with an identifiable structure: introductory sermons, followed by three cycles of healings and teachings, the third of which forms an *inclusio* that repeats the themes of the introductory sermons, as well as repeating the two major themes of the preceding cycle. The two central cycles of healings and teachings also show some thematic coherence: a healing motivated by Jesus' love or compassion (Lk. 7.11b-15) is followed by teaching on love and compassion (Lk. 7.36-47; 10.30-37a); a healing of a 'child of Abraham' that puts Jesus' opponents to 'shame' (Lk. 13.10-17b) is followed by teaching on 'children of Abraham' (Lk. 16.19-31; 19.2-10) and on honor and shame (Lk. 14.8-10, 12-14, 28-32; 15.11-32; 16.1b-8; 17.7-10). This order seems more pronounced than one would have expected if the material were, in fact, drawn from a variety of sources and traditions and any order ascribed to it was merely accident or coincidence; such order is further evidence of the material's origin in a common source. Since there is most often intervening Markan or Q material between these pericopae in Luke's final work, this order would hardly seem to be from Luke himself.

L appears to be a source with an identifiable structure and not a miscellaneous collection of material from a number of sources and traditions. It is obvious, however, that this structure is loose and free-flowing. We therefore move on to the question of whether the structure of this source is purely oral.

3. *L: Oral or Written?*

As has been noted, most of the L pericopae are more detailed than one would have expected from an oral tradition. Although stories in oral traditions tend to be vivid, they tend not to be specific, and details such as personal names and place names which are found in many of the L pericopae would have tended to drop out during oral transmission.[18] But one detail that can function in an oral tradition as a mnemonic device is the inclusion of certain numbers in the narrative, especially two and

---

18. See above, Chapter 5, section 2; see also Olrik, 'Epische Gesetze', p. 3; Cadbury, *Making of Luke–Acts*, p. 34; Bultmann, *Synoptic Tradition*, pp. 187-90; Taylor, *Formation of the Gospel*, p. 208; Abel, 'The Psychology of Memory and Rumor Transmission', pp. 275-76.

three.[19] With this in mind, it should be noted that many of the L pericopae in fact contain either the number two or three.[20] Even in other pericopae that do not mention the numbers explicitly, they can be present in the number of narrative features: three men happen upon the injured man (Lk. 10.30-37a), Jesus visits two sisters (Lk. 10.39-42), Jesus recounts two fatal disasters (Lk. 13.1b-8), and two debtors are approached by the unjust steward (Lk. 16.1b-8a). Although many of the details in the L pericopae certainly decrease the probability that it was a purely oral source, the frequency of oral dyads and triads shows that the source did retain a high level of orality, whatever its own final form or means of transmission.[21]

As outlined above, the L pericopae are most often grouped by catchwords or other loose associations of theme, setting, or content. Such loose structure is usually associated with oral traditions, where the catchword functions as a mnemonic device to lead the tradent on to the next pericope.[22] Again, as with the high frequency of the numbers two and three observed above, such catchword association is also found in written documents produced in the pervasively oral culture of

19. See Olrik, 'Epische Gesetze', p. 4; Dibelius, *From Tradition to Gospel*, p. 251; Bultmann, *Synoptic Tradition*, p. 188; Kelber, *Oral and Written Gospel*, p. 59. See also A. Dundes, *Interpreting Folklore* (Bloomington: Indiana University Press, 1980), pp. 134-59.

20. Nine of them: Lk. 3.10-14; 7.36-47; 10.30-37a; 11.5b-8; 12.35-38; 13.6b-9, 31b-32; 15.11-32; 18.10-14a. (I have not included the 'three years and six months' of Lk. 4.25, which is based on the LXX, clearly not an oral source.) Cf. Goulder, *New Paradigm*, I, 114-15, who believes Luke prefers pairs over threes.

21. That oral characteristics often appear in written documents has been widely observed. On such characteristics in Mark, see Kelber, *Oral and Written Gospel*, pp. 44-89. On the co-existence of orality and literacy throughout antiquity, see E.A. Havelock, *The Muse Learns to Write: Reflections on Orality and Literacy from Antiquity to the Present* (New Haven, CT: Yale University Press, 1986); T.M. Lentz, *Orality and Literacy in Hellenic Greece* (Carbondale, IL: Southern Illinois University Press, 1989); P.J. Achtemeier, 'Omne verbum sonat: The New Testament and the Oral Environment of Late Western Antiquity', *JBL* 109 (1990), pp. 3-27.

22. On catchword association in the pre-Gospel oral traditions, see Manson, *Sayings*, pp. 13-14. See also B. Gerhardsson, *Memory and Manuscript: Oral Tradition and Written Transmission in Rabbinic Judaism and Early Christianity* (trans. E.J. Sharpe; Uppsala: Almqvist & Wiksells, 1961), pp. 148-49. For a more general discussion of oral mnemonics, see W.J. Ong, *Orality and Literacy: The Technologizing of the Word* (London: Methuen, 1982), pp. 33-41.

antiquity.[23] If L were a written source, it clearly retained the oral structure and organization found in other written documents, such as Q, *Thomas*, or Mark, that were also based on oral traditions.

There is one final observation that inclines the probability in favor of L being a written and not an oral source. This is that Luke probably would have felt free to reword an oral tradition at least as much as he did Mark.[24] If Luke were the first person to put this material in writing (whether working from oral traditions or freely composing), then his stylistic stamp should be strongly, indeed pervasively, upon it; but since the first criterion used to isolate the L material was its dissimilarity from Lukan style and vocabulary, this does not seem to be the case. Indeed, by its non-Lukan style and its retention of details, it would seem that Luke was perhaps somewhat more conservative with the L material than he was with his Markan material, a fact probably due to L being predominantly sayings material, with which Luke is noticeably more conservative.[25]

Ultimately, in the absence of a second witness, there can be no definitive proof of whether L was an oral or a written source.[26] This is because there is no known characteristic that is found only in written sources, nor any such characteristic found only in oral traditions; the overlap and co-existence of both oral and literary characteristics is found in most of the extant works from antiquity (all of which, of course, have come down to us only in written form). The explanation that best explains the data would seem to be that L was a written source that retained a high level of orality. Its written form would account for the inclusion of so many details in the material and Luke's preservation

23. On the written nature of Q despite its use of catchword association, cf. Kloppenborg, *Formation*, pp. 50-51. On catchword groupings in *Thomas*, see Koester, *Ancient Christian Gospels*, p. 81; also H.E.W. Turner and H. Montefiore, *Thomas and the Evangelists* (Naperville, IL: Alec R. Allenson; Chatham, UK: W. & J. MacKay & Co., 1962), pp. 23-24. On such groupings in the Synoptics, see Bultmann, *History of the Synoptic Tradition*, pp. 325-26. On Paul's use of the technique, see K. Paffenroth, 'Romans 12:9-21—A Brief Summary of the Problems of Translation and Interpretation', *IBS* 14 (1992), pp. 89-99.

24. Cf. Nolland, *Luke*, p. xxxi.

25. This is true in both Luke's Markan and Q material. See T.R. Rosché, 'The Words of Jesus and the Future of the "Q" Hypothesis', *JBL* 79 (1960), pp. 210-20; Carlston and Norlin, 'Statistics and Q', pp. 64-68; Nolland, *Luke*, p. xxxi.

26. Even with a second witness, the issue probably could not be settled, as shown in the case of Q: see the discussion in Kloppenborg, *Formation*, pp. 42-51.

of a number of un-Lukan language characteristics, facts that are more problematic if the source is assumed to have come to Luke in purely oral form. At the same time, the source's high residual orality would account for the frequent dyads and triads in the narrative as well as the material's organization by catchword association.[27] Such residual orality in a written document is hardly remarkable; it is also frequently observed in other literary works from the same time period. We turn now to the question of what kind of literary work L most resembles.

4. *The Genre of L*

I remain wary of questions of genre, because in case after case the evidence has proven too scanty or ambiguous for us to determine what were or were not genres or types in antiquity, or how these were used. In the case of the *theios aner* typology, the result was the 'recovery' of a pre-Markan 'source', based on a genre that has become increasingly elusive and problematic.[28] A genre was postulated, and a 'source' was then culled from the Gospel of Mark to fit it. On the other hand, a known genre can of course be incorrectly applied to a known document, as seems to be the case with the hypothesis that Q is most nearly like the *Lives* of the Cynic philosophers.[29] I have therefore postponed questions of genre until now because it seems that the method is not reliable enough to make it the primary criterion for the reconstruction of a document. However, it must be admitted that if L as reconstructed above bears no generic resemblance to any other work, this will be a serious flaw in the hypothesis. We must therefore now ask whether L is analogous to other ancient works. If it is, this will provide further confirmation that my reconstruction of it is sound.

L as reconstructed above is composed primarily of parables and healings, with a few other sayings types and apothegms also included. It is a source that includes both sayings material and narrative, but in which the sayings material greatly predominates.[30] Further, the

27. Its residual orality also explains some of the genre questions; see below.
28. For a recent critique of the *theios aner* debate, see B. Blackburn, *Theios Aner and the Markan Miracle Traditions* (WUNT, 2.40; Tübingen: Mohr, 1991).
29. See above, Chapter 1 n. 62, for this position and its critics.
30. Twenty of the 26 pericopae (77 per cent) are sayings material: Lk. 3.10-14; 4.25-27; 7.36-47; 10.30-37a; 11.5b-8; [12.16b-20]; 12.35-38; 13.1b-5, 6b-9, 31b-32; 14.8-10, 12-14, 28-32; [15.4-6]; 15.8-9, 11-32; 16.1b-8a, 19-31; 17.7-10; 18.2-8a, 10-14a.

narrative material, and in particular the miracle accounts, seem to be used to frame or structure the teachings material. Finally, the source is distinguished by its lack of an account of Jesus' Passion.[31] In sum, L as reconstructed appears to have been a sayings collection with some biographical material, but without a narrative of its subject's death.

From the above description of L, it is obvious that Q is the closest analogue. Q is also predominantly a sayings collection, though it too contains some small amount of narrative, biographical material: the temptation story (Q 4.1-13), and two miracle stories (Q 7.1-10; 11.14-26).[32] In this respect, L stands closer to Q than does *Thomas*, which lacks these pericopae and has remained purely a sayings collection.[33] As in L, the narrative material in Q seems to provide some structure to the document.[34] The mixing of narrative with sayings is facilitated if the miracle has been 'apothegmatized', redacted into a controversy story or apothegm, as is clearly the case with Q 11.14-26, and to a lesser extent in Q 7.1-10; this mixing of forms is also found in three of the four L healings.[35] Finally, Q is similar in length to L.[36]

The formally mixed nature of L and Q is problematic for the genre classification of either. But, as shown by Kloppenborg for Q,[37] there are other analogous works from antiquity. I give here those that are most similar to L in their mixing of narrative and sayings material; they are treated in chronological order.

Ahikar was an extremely ancient and well-known story in antiquity (*c.* fifth century BCE), combining sayings material with narrative.[38] As

31. Although, as in the case Q, this cannot be proved and remains a question: see above, Chapter 2, section 3.

32. See Kloppenborg, *Formation*, pp. 117-27, 246-62, 317-28.

33. See Kloppenborg, *Formation*, pp. 27-34.

34. Thus, in Koester's outline of Q, the temptation story (Q 4.1-13) is the culmination of the first section of Q, while the healing of the centurion's servant (Q 7.1-10) is the beginning of the third section: see Koester, *Ancient Christian Gospels*, pp. 135-39.

35. Lk. 13.10-17b; 14.2-5; 17.12-18.

36. Obviously, there is quite a range in the estimations of the extent of Q, but the estimate I used in the statistical analysis in Chapter 3 is ca. 232 verses or parts of verses, versus the 164 verses attributed here to L.

37. See Kloppenborg, *Formation*, pp. 263-316.

38. See R.H. Charles (ed.), *The Apocrypha and Pseudepigrapha of the Old Testament* (2 vols.; Oxford: Clarendon Press, 1963), II, pp. 715-84; J.M. Lindberger, 'Ahiqar', in J.H. Charlesworth (ed.), *The Old Testament Pseudepigrapha* (2 vols.;

in the case of L and Q, the sayings material is predominant, though the tradition seems to have included somewhat more biographical material than L or Q.[39] As in L, the narrative material gives some structure to the sayings material.[40] Depending on the version, Ahikar is similar in length to L or Q.[41]

From the Greek world a similar combination of narrative with sayings material is found in the numerous collections that include both Aesop's fables and biographical material about him.[42] In the Aesop traditions, the biography is used as an introductory prologue, though the biographical material can even come to dominate the story.[43] Within the biographical section itself, however, narrative and sayings are woven together, as situations in the life of the sage are used as occasions for his giving a witty remark. The extant Aesop traditions are all longer than Q or L, with the tendency towards accretion continuing throughout later versions.

Another similar story from the Hellenistic world is the *Life of Secundus the Silent Philosopher*.[44] The work is predominantly sayings

Garden City, NY: Doubleday, 1985), II, pp. 479-507; see also the discussion in Kloppenborg, *Formation*, pp. 276-83, 325-26.

39. In the version used by Lindberger, 'Ahiqar', pp. 494-507, 130 of the 209 extant lines (62 per cent) are the sayings of Ahikar. (Since the document breaks off at the end, there may have been much more sayings material).

40. Though the kind of structuring varies in the versions. Earlier versions simply use the narrative as an introduction to the sayings, while later versions have two cycles of narrative followed by sayings: see Lindberger, 'Ahiqar', pp. 480-81.

41. Again, the version used by Lindberger is 209 lines (shorter than L or Q), but there is no telling how long it might have been, and later versions of the story are longer. For discussion and bibliography on the later versions, see Lindberger, 'Ahiqar', pp. 480, 493.

42. See B.E. Perry (ed.), *Aesopica* (Urbana, IL: University of Illinois Press, 1952); L.W. Daly (ed. and trans.), *Aesop without Morals: The Famous Fables, and a Life of Aesop* (New York: Thomas Yoseloff, 1961), pp. 11-26, 31-90; J.E. Keller and L.C. Keating (trans. and eds.), *Aesop's Fables. With a Life of Aesop* (Lexington, KY: University Press of Kentucky, 1993). The dating of the *Life of Aesop* varies: Daly, *Aesop without Morals*, p. 21, dates it as early as the fifth century BCE; Kloppenborg, *Formation*, p. 298, places it as late as ca. first century BCE–first century CE. On the incorporation of the Ahikar into the Aesop traditions, see Charles (ed.), *Apocrypha and Pseudepigrapha*, II, pp. 780-84; Lindberger, 'Ahiqar', pp. 490-91; Kloppenborg, *Formation*, p. 298.

43. Cf. Kloppenborg, *Formation*, p. 298.

44. See B.E. Perry (trans. and ed.), *Secundus the Silent Philosopher* (APA

material despite its being the 'life' of someone who is 'silent'.[45] The bio-graphical material is brief, and is used as a narrative frame at the begin-ning and end of Secundus's teaching. The story overall is quite short and similar in length to L or Q.[46]

Whatever its original extent, the partial 'Gospel' found in *Papyrus Egerton 2* contains both sayings and narrative material.[47] The two ele-ments are approximately equal in the fragments we now have and are woven together rather than standing apart: a controversy story, fol-lowed by a story of an attempt to arrest Jesus, a healing, another con-troversy story, and some sort of miracle.[48] There is no way to know the original extent of the document: there are now fragments of four pages. Like L or Q, *Egerton* combined narrative and sayings material, though probably with a greater preponderance of the former than either L or Q.[49]

Finally, many Greek *Lives* of philosophers are predominantly the sayings of their protagonists, with a minimum of biographical, narra-tive material included.[50] Therefore, even in a *bios*, the sayings material can predominate, as it does in L and Q.

Philological Supplements, 22; Ithaca, NY: Cornell University Press, 1964). On Q's similarities to *Secundus*, see Kloppenborg, *Formation*, pp. 307-309. *Secundus* is dated to the second century CE.

45. Secundus is able to transmit his teaching while maintaining his silence by writ-ing on a tablet. In Perry's Greek version, *Secundus the Silent Philosopher*, pp. 68-91, Secundus's teaching takes up the majority of the document, or about 64 per cent.

46. Two-hundred and twenty lines in Perry's Greek version.

47. See the discussion in Koester, *Ancient Christian Gospels*, pp. 205-16; see also R.J. Miller, *The Complete Gospels: Annotated Scholars Version* (Sonoma, CA: Polebridge, 1992), pp. 406-11. Koester, *Ancient Christian Gospels*, p. 206, dates it to the end of the second century CE; Miller, *Complete Gospels*, p. 407, gives a much ear-lier date of late first century CE.

48. The last lines are extremely fragmentary. Koester, *Ancient Christian Gospels*, p. 206, identifies them as a miracle story, though he does not give them in his recon-struction; Miller, *Complete Gospels*, p. 410, does give a reconstruction of them as some sort of nature miracle in which Jesus causes plants to grow spontaneously.

49. Again, we have no way of knowing what the ratio between the two types of material might have been in the original. Koester, *Ancient Christian Gospels*, pp. 205-16, calls it generically a 'Collection of Narratives about Jesus', though not one of the 'Miracle Catenae'; Miller, *Complete Gospels*, pp. 406-11, avoids any label and calls it simply a 'Fragmentary Gospel'.

50. Cf. Downing, 'Quite Like Q', p. 197. (I make this comparison without pressing the labels 'Cynic' or *bios* on to either L or Q).

It appears that in both the Hellenistic and the Near Eastern worlds, and across a wide span of time in antiquity, the combination of a figure's teaching with biographical information about him can be observed. Moreover, the length of these documents and the predominance of the sayings material in them approximate to those of L and Q. The formally mixed nature of L and Q, although surprising, is therefore not anomalous.

But the inclusion of biographical material in a sayings source leads us to the other problem with the genre classification of either L or Q: the lack of a narrative of Jesus' death.[51] Again, although this evidence may be somewhat surprising in a Gospel tradition, it does not significantly diminish the probability of L's existence. Even in complete biographies from antiquity, the subject's death is frequently not mentioned. This can be shown quickly by a survey of Diogenes Laertius, in which over one third of the *Lives* do not include the philosopher's death.[52] Neither the story of Ahikar nor Secundus, already noted as similar to L in their mixing of narrative and sayings material, includes an account of its subject's death. Although we cannot be sure because of its fragmentary nature, there is no intrinsic reason to believe that the original document behind *Papyrus Egerton 2* contained a Passion narrative. Even in the story of Apollonius, where narrative material has come to dominate the work, there may have been a version that did not include Apollonius' death.[53] All of these examples are further supported by the observation that biographies in antiquity tend to treat events in the subject's life as typical: there is therefore no need to narrate all the events of his or her life, nor those that we might consider important or interesting, such as

51. On Q's possible inclusion of a Passion narrative, see Kloppenborg, *Formation*, pp. 85-87.

52. See Diogenes Laertius, *Lives of Eminent Philosophers* (trans. R.D. Hicks; LCL; 2 vols.; Cambridge: Harvard University Press; London: Heinemann, 1925). Twenty-eight of Diogenes' 82 *Lives* do not narrate the philosopher's death: Archelaus (2.16-17), Aeschines (2.60-64), Aristippus (2.65-104), Phaedo (2.105), Euclides (2.106-12), Crito (2.121), Simon (2.122-24), Glaucon (2.124), Simmias (2.124), Cebes (2.125), Clitomachus (4.67), Demetrius (5.75-85), Antisthenes (6.1-19), Monimus (6.82-83), Onesicritus (6.84), Hipparchia (6.96-98), Menedemus (6.102-105), Herillus (7.165-66), Sphaerus (7.177-78), Archytas (8.79-83), Alcmaeon (8.83), Hippasus (8.84), Xenophanes (9.18-20), Parmenides (9.21-23), Melissus (9.24), Leucippus (9.30-33), Diogenes (9.57), and Pyrrho (9.61-108).

53. See Philostratus, *The Life of Appollonius of Tyana* (trans. F.C. Conybeare; LCL; Cambridge, MA: Harvard University Press, 1912), 8.29.

his or her birth or death.[54] What is true of biographies would probably also be true of sayings collections with biographical tendencies or interests, such as L or Q. The presence of biographical material in L without a complete account of Jesus' life and death is therefore not that surprising, due to the variety and flexibility of the genre.[55]

A further observation is that L's high level of residual orality also helps to explain its departures from or adaptations of the strictures of known genres. It is a characteristic of orality that deeds and words are treated as interchangeable or even equivalent: words explain actions, while actions illustrate or make concrete words.[56] It is also a characteristic of oral narratives that they do not usually include a full account of the subject's life and death; the stories tend to circulate in clusters, not full accounts.[57] L's combination of Jesus' words and deeds and its lack of a narrative of his death can both be explained by that source's residual orality influencing its final form.

All in all, it seems most accurate to say that L is a sayings collection that uses a small number of biographical narratives to structure its sayings material. L has moved slightly further on a trajectory towards including more narrative material than did Q. Further, L's high level of residual orality has probably affected its final form, causing it to mix sayings and narrative material and to stop short of a full account of Jesus' life, giving us only a partial account of his ministry while ignoring his birth, childhood, and death.

---

54. On this point, see C.H. Talbert, *Literary Patterns, Theological Themes, and the Genre of Luke–Acts* (SBLMS; Missoula, MT: Scholars Press, 1974), p. 128; D.L. Barr and J.L. Wentling, 'The Conventions of Classical Biography and the Genre of Luke–Acts: A Preliminary Study', in C.H. Talbert (ed.), *Luke–Acts: New Perspectives from the Society of Biblical Literature* (New York: Crossroad, 1984), pp. 63-88, esp. p. 68. See also the thorough examination of R.A. Burridge, *What are the Gospels? A Comparison with Graeco–Roman Biography* (SNTSMS, 70; Cambridge: Cambridge University Press, 1992), pp. 124-25, 148-49, 182-84, 211-13, 233-34.

55. On the lack of death narratives even in biographies, see Downing, 'Quite Like Q', p. 203; Burridge, *What are the Gospels?*, p. 63.

56. Cf. Kelber, *Oral and Written Gospel*, p. 65.

57. See A.B. Lord, 'The Gospels as Oral Traditional Literature', in W.O. Walker, Jr (ed.), *The Relationships among the Gospels: An Interdisciplinary Dialogue* (San Antonio, TX: Trinity University Press, 1978), pp. 33-91, esp. pp. 39-40; and C.H. Talbert, 'Oral and Independent or Literary and Interdependent? A Response to Albert B. Lord', in Walker (ed.), *The Relationships among the Gospels*, pp. 93-102, esp. p. 101.

5. *L's Place in Early Christianity*

Some necessarily tentative statements should be made here as to the probable date and place of composition of L. Obviously, the document must have been composed before Luke wrote his Gospel. Although the dating of the composition of Luke still varies among scholars, 80–90 CE has emerged as a consensus.[58] L's lack of any mention of the destruction of Jerusalem would probably push its date back, to before 70 CE.[59] Four more tentative observations may push its date back even further: 1) its almost complete lack of christological claims or titles for Jesus; 2) its extreme disinterest in any of the disciples, whose place is much more prominent in any of the complete Gospels;[60] 3) its high level of residual orality; and 4) its preservation of such a large number of sayings, especially parables, that are most often judged as originating from the historical Jesus, usually because of their lack of allegorization. L seems to lack the sort of christological, ecclesiastical, or allegorical developments that are found in later traditions; at the same time, it seems to stand quite close to the period of oral transmission of Jesus' sayings. These considerations taken together would indicate an early date for the source, probably before 60 CE, perhaps before 50 CE.[61]

Any statement as to the place of composition of L must be even more tentative than its dating.[62] The material seems Jewish–Christian throughout.[63] It also seems to have a better and more detailed knowledge of Palestine than other traditions, particularly when compared with Luke himself.[64] All of this would indicate Palestine as the most likely place of

58. Thus Fitzmyer, *Luke*, pp. 53-57 (80–85 CE); Bovon, *Lukas*, pp. 22-23 (80-90 CE). Dates at either extreme can still be found, however: see J. Wenham, *Redating Matthew, Mark, and Luke: A Fresh Assault on the Synoptic Problem* (London: Hodder & Stoughton, 1991), pp. 229-38 (early fifties CE); Nolland, *Luke*, pp. xxvii-xxxix (late sixties to late seventies CE); and Koester, *Ancient Christian Gospels*, p. 334 (early second century CE).

59. Note also the reference to the temple in Lk. 18.10-14a.

60. See above, Chapter 5, section 2.2.

61. Cf. Grant, *Gospels*, p. 63.

62. Cf. the tentative assertions as to the place of composition of Luke: Fitzmyer, *Luke*, p. 57; Nolland, *Luke*, p. xxxix.

63. See esp. Lk. 4.25-27; 7.11b-15; 10.30-37a; 13.10-17b; 14.2-5; 16.19-31; 17.12-18; 18.10-14a; 19.2-10. See also above, Chapter 4, section 3.4. Cf. Easton, *Luke*, p. xxvii; Manson, *Luke*, p. xx; Grant, *Gospels*, p. 63.

64. See above, Chapter 5, sections 2.3 and 2.4; note esp. Lk. 7.11b-15;

L's composition, though I would hesitate to specify the city.[65]

In sum, the evidence seems best explained if L was composed by Jewish–Christians in Palestine sometime between 40 and 60 CE. Some further observations on their probable life situation may be made here.

First, they differ from other early Christian communities in several ways. Although L is most formally similar to Q in its depiction of Jesus as a teacher, and by its lack of a Passion narrative, L does not share Q's interest in the itinerant mission of Jesus' disciples.[66] There is no indication that the community that produced L knows or approves of an itinerant missionary lifestyle for Christians; they seem rather to presuppose a settled existence in town or village.[67] L's Jesus is also not the aphoristic teacher of Wisdom found in Q;[68] the L community seems not to value the sapiential tradition. There seems to be no indication that the community is under any kind of persecution. Finally, as noted above, there is no emphasis on asceticism or renunciation of material wealth, but rather an exhortation to generosity and prudent use of goods for the benefit of oneself and others.[69]

Some observations may also be made on the positive side. The L community would appear to be of mixed economic backgrounds, as Jesus sometimes exhorts his listeners to identify with good and obedient ser-

---

10.30-37a; 13.1b-5, 6b-9; 15.11-32; 19.2-10.

65. The composition of L is located in Palestine by Easton, *Luke*, pp. xxvii-xxix; Manson, *Luke*, p. xx; and more recently, Giles, '"L" Tradition', p. 432. Streeter, *Four Gospels*, pp. 218-19, locates its composition in Caesarea for the totally different reason of fitting it into a chronology of Luke's life.

66. Cf. esp. the commissioning of Q 10.2-12; see also above, Chapter 5, section 2.2.

67. Indeed, even in traditions that acknowledge and approve of itinerant missionaries, their role in the community is problematic. In the *Didache*, this is dealt with by defining and limiting their activity and powers: see C.N. Jefford, *The Sayings of Jesus in the Teaching of the Twelve Apostles* (Leiden: Brill, 1989), pp. 108-13. Further, such missionaries cannot, by their very nature, serve as appropriate models for any community: see S.L. Davies, *The Revolt of the Widows: The Social World of the Apocryphal Acts* (Carbondale, IL: Southern Illinois University Press, 1980), p. 52. It is impossible now to determine whether the L community thinks of such missionaries as dangerous or irrelevant; they appear to be a non-issue for the community, for whatever reason.

68. Indeed, Lk. 12.19 seems like something of a negative comment on the sapiential tradition. Lk. 13.1b-5, 6b-9 may also be a negative judgment on the (broadly) sapiential idea of suffering being a sign of divine disapproval.

69. See above, Chapter 5, section 3.1.

vants (Lk. 12.35-38), while at other times he implies that they know what it is like to give large banquets (Lk. 14.12-14), or to own a significant amount of land (Lk. 14.28), or to be themselves the owners of slaves (Lk. 17.7-10). The prominence of stories about women and widows alongside stories about men would point to a community composed of both women and men.[70] As noted, the community expects and gives warnings of imminent judgment,[71] although they seem to conceive of it in individual rather than communal or apocalyptic terms. Finally, the community finds the center of Jesus' message in his seeking and bringing back the 'lost', who are welcomed joyously and have their status as 'children of Abraham' reaffirmed. The community therefore probably sees itself as also welcoming such outcasts, and an audience of recent or prospective converts seems likely.[72] In all this, however, the L community assumes a Jewish background: there is no mention of a gentile mission.[73] Within their Jewish–Christian community, however, they believe all boundaries are negative and should be broken down: the boundaries between Jews and Samaritans,[74] men and women,[75] rich and

70. Because the stories of women do not predominate, I would not speculate that the L community was a community of 'widows', as has been suggested for the apocryphal Acts: see Davies, *Revolt of the Widows*, p. 64. The function of the L stories of women would seem to be more akin to the balancing of exhortations to both sexes as found in Mark: see E.S. Malbon, 'Fallible Followers: Women and Men in the Gospel of Mark', *Semeia* 28 (1983), pp. 29-48.

71. Lk. 12.16b-20, 35-38; 13.1b-5, 6b-9; 16.19-31; see also above, Chapter 5, section 4.6.

72. Such welcoming is perhaps ironic in a community that does not emphasize missionary activity. Perhaps this could explain why the climactic 'lost' parable (Lk. 15.11-32) is the only one in which the 'lost' one actively works to come back, while the final L pericope, Zacchaeus (Lk. 19.2-10), also involves the 'lost' one trying hard to be 'found'. The prodigal son and Zacchaeus would therefore function as types of paradigmatic converts for the L community: 'lost' outcasts who are eager to return.

73. This is the more remarkable in the context of Luke's overall interest in universalism: see Fitzmyer, *Luke*, pp. 57-59, 190-91. One might argue that the accepting of heretical, syncretistic Jews such as the Samaritans would be considered more radical than the conversion of Gentiles, but the Samaritans are still 'children of Abraham' in a literal, biological sense: cf. the discussion in D. Ravens, *Luke and the Restoration of Israel* (JSNTSup, 119; Sheffield: Sheffield Academic Press, 1995), pp. 72-106. See also his discussion on Lk. 4.25-27 as not implying a gentile mission: Ravens, *Luke and the Restoration of Israel*, pp. 124-25.

74. Lk. 10.30-37a; 17.12-18.

75. Lk. 7.36-47; 10.39-42; 13.10-17b.

poor,[76] clean and unclean.[77] They therefore see their Jewish opponents, with their strict laws of exclusion, as particularly abominable, and often portray them as bitter opponents to Jesus' (and their own) inclusivity.[78]

The implications of the above reconstruction of L may be summarized as follows. Another pre-Gospel source, earlier than Mark and possibly as early as Q, has been argued as quite probable on several grounds. This source reveals to us an early community's vision of Jesus that differs markedly from others. L's Jesus is not the suffering Son of Man we have from Mark, nor is he Q's aphoristic teacher of Wisdom, nor is he Luke's universal savior. The L community revered and portrayed Jesus as a powerful ethical teacher who substantiated and revealed the authority of his teaching by acts of healing. They believed that Jesus had come to 'seek' and 'find' the 'lost', whom he had joyously reestablished as beloved 'children of Abraham'. The L community believed that Jesus had done this in their own lives, and they sought to carry on his message of divine acceptance, love, and joy.

76. Lk. 14.8-10, 12-14; 16.19-31; 19.2-10.
77. Lk. 7.11b-15; 13.10-17b; 14.2-5; 17.12-18.
78. Lk. 7.36-47; 10.30-37a; 13.10-17b; 14.2-5; 18.10-14a; see also above, Chapter 4, section 3.4.

Appendix

A Version of L

I conclude this work with a presentation of L as I have reconstructed it, so that the reader may experience it without the inconvenience of paging through his or her Bible.[1] I believe that Renan's estimation of Luke's Gospel with which I began this work may now be applied to L: 'C'est le plus beau livre qu'il y ait'.[2]

L: Jesus' Ministry to the Outcasts[3]

[And John the Baptist was baptizing and preaching.] And the crowds asked him, 'What then should we do?' He answered them, 'The one who has two coats should share with the one who has none; and the one who has food should do the same.' And tax collectors also came to be baptized, and they said to him, 'Teacher, what should we do?' He said to them, 'Collect no more than the amount designated for you.' Soldiers also asked him, 'And we, what should we do?' And he said to them, 'Extort money from no one, neither by violence nor by fraud, and be satisfied with your wages.'

[And Jesus was preaching. And he said to them,] 'But in truth, I say to you, there were many widows in Israel in the days of Elijah, when the sky was shut up three years and six months, so that a severe famine occurred in all the land; but Elijah was sent to none of them, but instead to a widow in Zarephath in Sidon. There were also many lepers in Israel in the time of the prophet Elisha, and none of them was cleansed; but instead, Naaman the Syrian.'

[And after this Jesus went to] Nain, and his disciples and a numerous crowd went with him. As he approached the gate of the city, a man who had died was being carried out, the only son of his mother, who was a widow; and a large crowd from the city was with her. And when the Lord saw her, he was moved with compassion for her and said

---

1.   The following is my translation. It is not shockingly different from the RSV, though in many places it is more wooden, as I have tried to convey some of L's verbal idiosyncracies ('a certain man', the abundant use of καί, etc.). Words in brackets are conjectures which I have supplied to provide smoother transitions between some of the pericopae; I have tried to keep these to a minimum.

2.   E. Renan, *Les Evangiles et la seconde génération chrétienne* (Paris: Calmaan-Lévy, 1877), p. 283; see above, Preface.

3.   Cf. Manson, *Sayings of Jesus*, p. 282, 'The L material in chapters 15–19 might be called in a special sense the Gospel of the Outcast'.

to her, 'Do not weep'. And having come forward, he touched the bier, and the bearers stood still. And he said, 'Young man, I say to you, rise!' And the dead man sat up and began to speak; and he gave him to his mother.

One of the Pharisees asked him to eat with him, and he went into the Pharisee's house and reclined at the table. And there was a woman there, a sinner in the city, and because she had learned that he was dining in the Pharisee's house, she had brought an alabaster jar of ointment; and standing behind him at his feet, weeping, she began to wet his feet with her tears, and she dried them with the hair of her head. And she kissed his feet and anointed them with the ointment. But when the Pharisee who had invited him saw it, he said to himself, 'If this man were a prophet, he would have known who and what kind of woman this is who is touching him, that she is a sinner.' And Jesus said to him, 'Simon, I have something to say to you.' 'Teacher', he said, 'speak.' 'A certain moneylender had two debtors; one owed him five hundred denarii, and the other fifty. When they could not repay their debts, he canceled the debts for both of them. Now which of them will love him more?' Simon answered, 'I suppose the one with the greater debt canceled.' And he said to him, 'You have judged correctly'. Then turning towards the woman he said to Simon, 'Do you see this woman? I came into your house; you gave me no water for my feet, but she has wet my feet with her tears and dried them with her hair. You gave me no kiss, but from the time I came in she has not stopped kissing my feet. You did not anoint my head with oil, but she has anointed my feet with ointment. Therefore I tell you, her sins, which are many, have been forgiven, because she has loved much. But the one who is forgiven little, loves little.'

[And] Jesus said, 'A certain man was going down from Jerusalem to Jericho. And he was surrounded by robbers, who, after stripping and beating him, went away, leaving him half dead. Now by chance a priest was going down that road; and when he saw him, he passed by on the other side. And likewise a Levite, when he came to the place and saw him, he passed by on the other side. But a Samaritan while traveling came upon him, and when he saw him, he was filled with compassion. And coming up to him, he bandaged his wounds, pouring on oil and wine. After putting him on his own mount, he brought him to an inn and took care of him. And the next day he took out two denarii, gave them to the innkeeper, and said, "Take care of him, and whatever more you spend, I will repay you when I come back". Which of these three, does it seem to you, was a neighbor to the man who fell among robbers?' He said, 'The one who showed mercy to him.'

[And later Jesus was dining with a woman named] Martha. And she had a sister named Mary, who, sitting at the Lord's feet, listened to his teaching. But Martha was distracted by much serving; so approaching him she said, 'Lord, do you not care that my sister has let me serve all by myself? Then tell her to help me'. But the Lord answered her, 'Martha, Martha, you are aggravated and distracted by many things; only one thing is necessary. Mary has chosen the good part, which will not be taken away from her.'

And he said to them, 'Is there any one of you who has a friend, and will go to him at midnight and say to him, "Friend, lend me three loaves of bread, because a friend of mine has arrived from a journey, and I have nothing to set before him"; and he will answer from within, "Do not bother me; the door has already been locked, and my children are with me in bed; I cannot get up and give you anything"? I tell you, even though he will not get up and give him anything because he is his friend, yet because of his persistence he will get up and give him whatever he needs.'

[And he said to them,] 'The land of a certain rich man produced abundantly. And he thought to himself, "What should I do, for I do not have a place to store my crops?" And he said, 'I will do this: I will pull down my barns and build larger ones, and there I will store all my grain and goods. And I will say to my soul, "Soul, you have ample goods laid up for many years; relax, eat, drink, be merry." But God said to him, "You fool! This night your soul is required of you; and the things you have prepared, whose will they be?"'

'Have your belts fastened and your lamps lit; and be like those who are waiting for their master to return from the wedding feast, so that when he comes and knocks they may immediately open the door for him. Blessed are those servants whom the master finds awake when he comes; truly, I tell you that he will fasten his belt and have them sit at table, and he will come and serve them. And if he comes during the second watch, or the third, and finds them so, blessed are those servants.'

[And some] told him about the Galileans whose blood Pilate had mixed with their sacrifices. And he replied to them, 'Do you think that these Galileans were worse sinners than all other Galileans because they suffered in this way? No, I tell you; but unless you repent, you will all likewise perish. Or those eighteen, killed when the tower of Siloam fell on them, do you think that they were worse offenders than all others living in Jerusalem? No, I tell you; but unless you repent, you will all perish in the same way.'

[And he said to them,] 'Someone had a fig tree planted in his vineyard; and he came looking for fruit on it and found none. So he said to the keeper of the vineyard, "See here! For three years I have come looking for fruit on this fig tree and I have not found any. Cut it down; why should it waste ground?" But he replied, "Sir, leave it alone for this year also, until I dig around it and put manure on it, and it might bear fruit next year; but if it does not, you can cut it down."'

Now he was teaching in one of the synagogues on the sabbath. And there was a woman who had had a crippling spirit for eighteen years; and she was bent over and was unable to stand up fully. When Jesus saw her, he called to her and said, 'Woman, you have been freed from your sickness.' And he laid his hands on her, and immediately she was made straight, and she praised God. But the leader of the synagogue, angry because Jesus had healed on the sabbath, said to the crowd, 'There are six days on which work ought to be done; come on those days and be healed, and not on the sabbath day.' But the Lord answered him and said, 'Hypocrites! Does not each of you on the sabbath untie his ox or his donkey from the stable, and lead it away to let it drink? Should not this woman, a daughter of Abraham whom Satan bound for eighteen years, be released from this bondage on the sabbath day?' And when he said this, all his opponents were put to shame.

[And some people] said to him, 'Get away from here, for Herod wants to kill you.' And he said to them, 'Go and tell that fox, "Behold, I cast out demons and perform cures today and tomorrow, and on the third day I am finished."'

[Later Jesus was teaching on another sabbath,] and behold, in front of him there was a certain man with dropsy. And Jesus said to the lawyers and Pharisees, 'Is it lawful to heal on the sabbath, or not?' But they were silent. And after taking a hold of him, he cured him and let him go. And he said to them, 'Which of you, if your donkey or ox falls into a well, will not immediately pull it out on a sabbath day?'

[And later when he was dining he said to them,] 'When you are invited by someone to a wedding feast, do not sit in the best seat, in case someone more honored than you has been invited by the host; and the one who invited both of you will come and say to you, "Give him your place", and then with shame you will start to take the lowest place. But when you are invited, go and take the lowest place, so that when your host comes, he may say to you, "Friend, go up higher"; then you will be honored in the presence of all who sit at the table with you.' He said also to the one who had invited him, 'When you give a meal or a dinner, do not invite your friends or your brothers or your relatives or rich neighbors, in case they may invite you in return and repay you. But when you give a banquet, invite the poor, the crippled, the lame, and the blind, and you will be blessed, because they cannot repay you; you will be repaid at the resurrection of the righteous.'

[And Jesus said to them,] 'For which of you, if he wants to build a tower, does not first sit down and calculate the cost, to see whether he has enough to complete it? Otherwise, when he has laid the foundation and is not able to finish, all who see it will begin to deride him, saying, "This man began to build and was not able to finish." Or what king, before he goes out to make war against another king, will not first sit down and consider whether he is able with ten thousand to fight the one who comes against him with twenty thousand? And if not, then, while the other is still far away, he sends a delegation and asks for the terms of peace.'

[And he said to them,] 'Which man of you, if he has a hundred sheep and loses one of them, does not leave the ninety-nine in the wilderness and go after the one which is lost until he finds it? And when he has found it, he lays it on his shoulders and rejoices. And when he comes home, he calls together his friends and neighbors, saying to them, "Rejoice with me, for I have found my sheep which was lost."'

'Or what woman, if she has ten drachmas and loses one of them, does not light a lamp and sweep the house and search carefully until she finds it? And when she has found it, she calls together her friends and neighbors, saying, "Rejoice with me, for I have found the drachma which I had lost."'

Then he said, 'There was a certain man who had two sons. And the younger of them said to his father, "Father, give me my appointed share of the property." So he divided his savings between them. And not many days later, the younger son gathered all that he had and traveled to a distant country, and there he squandered his property by living extravagantly. After he had spent everything, a severe famine occurred in that country, and he began to be in need. And he went and imposed on one of the citizens of that country; and he sent him into his fields to feed the pigs. And he longed to be fed from the pods that the pigs ate; and no one gave him anything. But when he came to himself he said, 'How many of my father's hired workers have more than enough bread, but I am here dying of hunger! I will get up and go to my father, and I will say to him, "Father, I have sinned against heaven and before you; I am no longer worthy to be called your son; treat me as one of your hired workers."' And he got up and went to his father. But while he was still far away, his father saw him and was filled with compassion, and after he had run up to him, he embraced him and kissed him. Then the son said to him, 'Father, I have sinned against heaven and before you; I am no longer worthy to be called your son.' But the father said to his slaves, 'Quickly, get out the best robe and put it on him; and put a ring on his finger and shoes on his feet; And bring the fatted calf and kill it, and let us eat and make merry; for this my son was dead and is alive again; he was lost and is found.' And they began to make merry.

'Now his elder son was in the field; and as he approached and drew near the house, he heard music and dancing. And he called one of the slaves and asked what was going on. He said to him, "Your brother has come, and your father has killed the fatted calf, because he has gotten him back safe and sound." But he became angry and did not want to go in. His father came out and begged him. But he answered his father, "Look—all these years I have worked for you, and I never disobeyed your command; yet you never gave me a young goat so that I might make merry with my friends. But when this son of yours came back, the one who has devoured your savings with prostitutes, you killed the fatted calf for him!" Then he said to him, "Son, you are always with me, and everything that is mine is yours. But it was necessary for us to make merry and rejoice, because this brother of yours was dead and is now alive; he was lost and has been found."'

[And Jesus said to them,] 'There was a certain rich man who had a manager, and charges were brought to him that this man was squandering his goods. And he summoned him and said to him, 'What is this that I hear about you? Give an account of your management, for you can no longer be my manager.' Then the manager said to himself, "What will I do, since my master is taking my job as manager away from me? I am not strong enough to dig, and I am ashamed to beg. I know what I will do, so that when I am dismissed as manager, people may welcome me into their homes." And summoning his master's debtors one by one, he said to the first, "How much do you owe my master?" He said, "A hundred measures of oil." He said to him, "Take your bill, sit down quickly, and write fifty." Then he said to another, "How much do you owe?" He said, "A hundred measures of wheat." He said to him, "Take your bill and write eighty." And the master praised the dishonest manager because he had acted shrewdly.'

[And he said to them,] 'There was a certain rich man, and he dressed in purple and fine linen. He feasted lavishly every day. Lying at his gate there was a certain poor man named Lazarus. He was covered with sores and he longed to be fed with what fell from the rich man's table; further, the dogs came and licked at his sores. It happened that the poor man died and was carried by the angels to Abraham's embrace; the rich man also died and was buried. And he was in torment in Hades. Lifting up his eyes, he saw Abraham far away and Lazarus in his embrace. And he cried out, "Father Abraham, have mercy on me and send Lazarus to dip the tip of his finger in water and cool my tongue, because I am suffering in this flame." But Abraham said, "Son, remember that you received your good things in your life, and likewise Lazarus received bad things; but now he is comforted here, while you are suffering. And besides all this, a great chasm has been placed between us and you, so that those who

wish to pass from here to you cannot do so, nor can they cross from there to us."
But he said, "Then I ask you, father, to send him to my father's house, for I have five
brothers, so that he might warn them, to keep them from also coming to this place of
torment." But Abraham said, "They have Moses and the prophets; let them listen to
them." But he said, "No, father Abraham, but if someone goes to them from the dead,
they will repent." But he said to him, "If they do not listen to Moses and the prophets,
then neither would they be persuaded if someone were to rise from the dead."'

[And Jesus said to them,] 'But which of you who has a servant plowing or tend-
ing sheep will say to him when he comes in from the field, "Come in quickly, sit down
at the table!"? Rather, will he not say to him, "Prepare my dinner, and tighten your belt
to serve me, until I have eaten and drunk; and after this you will eat and drink"? He
does not thank the servant because he did what was commanded, does he? So also
when you have done everything that was commanded, say, "We are unworthy servants; we have done what we were obligated to do."'

[And Jesus traveled throughout the area.] And as he entered into a certain town, ten
men with leprosy met him. They stood far away and raised their voices, saying,
'Jesus, master, show mercy to us.' And when he saw them he said to them, 'Go and
show yourselves to the priests.' And it happened that as they went, they were cleansed.
But one of them, when he saw that he was healed, turned back and praised God with a
loud voice. And he fell on his face at his feet, thanking him; and he was a Samaritan.
Then Jesus said, 'Were not ten cleansed? Where are the nine? Was no one found to
return to give praise to God except this foreigner?'

[And Jesus taught them,] saying, 'In a certain city there was a certain judge, who did
not fear God and did not respect people. There was a widow in that city; and she would
come to him, saying, "Take my side against my opponent." And for a while he did
not consent. But afterwards he said to himself, "Even though I do not fear God nor
respect people, yet because this widow harasses me, I will take her side; otherwise her
coming back will completely wear me out."' The Lord said, 'Listen to what the unjust
judge says. Will not God take up the side of his chosen ones, who cry out to him day
and night? I tell you that he will take up their side quickly.'

'Two men went up to the temple to pray; one was a Pharisee and the other was a tax
collector. The Pharisee stood and prayed to himself: "God, I thank you that I am not
like other people, extortioners, unjust, adulterers, or even like this tax collector. I fast
twice a week, I pay tithes on everything that I own." But the tax collector, standing far
away, did not want even to lift up his eyes towards heaven, but beat his chest, saying,
"God, be kind to me a sinner." I tell you, this man went down to his house more justified than the other.'

[And Jesus entered a certain town.] And there was a man named Zacchaeus; and he
was a chief tax collector, and he was rich. And he was trying to see who Jesus was;
and he was not able to because of the crowd, for he was short in height. And running
on ahead, he climbed a sycamore tree in order to see him, because he was about to pass
that way. And as he came to the place, Jesus looked up and said to him, 'Zacchaeus,
hurry up and come down, for it is necessary for me to stay in your house today.' And
hurrying he came down and welcomed him with joy. And all who saw it murmured,
'He has gone in to stay with a sinful man.' But Zacchaeus stood and said to the Lord,

'Lord, half of my possessions I give to the poor; and if I have gotten anything from anyone through fraud, I pay it back fourfold.' Jesus said to him, 'Today salvation has come to this house, since he also is a son of Abraham. For the Son of man came to seek and to save the lost.'

[Such is the story of Jesus, a teacher and healer powerful in word and deed. And we have seen and heard these things, and we tell them now to you.]

BIBLIOGRAPHY

Abel, E.L., 'The Psychology of Memory and Rumor Transmission and Their Bearing on
  Theories of Oral Transmission in Early Christianity', *JR* 51 (1971), pp. 270-81.
Achtemeier, P.J., 'Omne verbum sonat: The New Testament and the Oral Environment of
  Late Western Antiquity', *JBL* 109 (1990), pp. 3-27.
Attridge, H.W., 'Reflections on Research into Q', *Semeia* 55 (1991), pp. 223-34.
Bacon, B.W., 'The "Order" of the Lukan 'Interpolations', I. General Survey', *JBL* 34
  (1915) 166-79; 'II. The Smaller Interpolation, Lk. 6:20–8:3', *JBL* 36 (1917) 112-39;
  'III. The Longer Interpolation, Lk. 9:51–18:14', *JBL* 37 (1918), pp. 20-53.
Bailey, J.A., *The Traditions Common to the Gospels of Luke and John* (Leiden: Brill, 1963).
Bailey, K.E., *Poet and Peasant* (Grand Rapids: Eerdmans, 1976).
—*Through Peasant Eyes* (Grand Rapids: Eerdmans, 1980).
Barbi, A. 'Il Dio di Gesù nell'opera Lucana', *Scuola Cattolica* 117 (1989), pp. 167-95.
Barnett, A.E., *Paul Becomes a Literary Influence* (Chicago: University of Chicago Press,
  1941).
Barr, D.L., and J.L. Wentling, 'The Conventions of Classical Biography and the Genre of
  Luke–Acts: A Preliminary Study', in C.H. Talbert (ed.), *Luke–Acts: New Perspectives
  from the Society of Biblical Literature* (New York: Crossroad, 1984), pp. 63-88.
Bartlet, J.V., 'The Sources of St Luke's Gospel', in W. Sanday (ed.), *Studies in the Synoptic
  Problem by Members of the University of Oxford* (Oxford: Clarendon Press, 1911),
  pp. 313-63.
Bauckham, R., 'Synoptic Parousia Parables and the Apocalypse', *NTS* 23 (1977), pp. 162-
  76.
Beare, F.W., *The Earliest Records of Jesus* (Oxford: Basil Blackwell, 1964).
Berg, P., 'Die Quellen des Lukasevangeliums', *NKZ* 21 (1910), pp. 282-313, 337-52.
Bertram, G., 'ἄξιος,' *TDNT*, I, pp. 379-80.
Betz, H.D., 'The Cleansing of the Ten Lepers (Luke 17:11-19)', *JBL* 90 (1971), pp. 314-28.
Betz, O. and W. Grimm, *Wesen und Wirklichkeit der Wunder Jesu* (Bern: Peter Lang, 1977).
Beyer, H.W., 'βλασφημέω', *TDNT*, I, pp. 621-25.
—'διακονέω', *TDNT*, II, pp. 81-93.
Binder, H., 'Das Gleichnis vom barmherzigen Samariter', *TZ* 15 (1959), pp. 176-94.
Bishop, E.F.F., 'Local Colour in Proto-Luke', *ExpTim* 45 (1933–34), pp. 151-56.
Black, A., 'Women in the Gospel of Luke', in C.D. Osburn (ed.), *Essays on Women in
  Earliest Christianity* (Joplin, MO: College Press Publishing Co., 1993), I, pp. 445-69.
Blackburn, B., *Theios Aner and the Markan Miracle Traditions* (WUNT, 2.40; Tübingen:
  Mohr, 1991).
Blenkinsopp, J., *The Pentateuch: An Introduction to the First Five Books of the Bible* (AB
  Reference Library; Garden City, NY: Doubleday, 1992).

Blomberg, C.L., 'Midrash, Chiasmus, and the Outline of Luke's Central Section', in R.T. France and D. Wenham (eds.), *Gospel Perspectives: Studies in Midrash and Historiography* (Sheffield: JSOT Press, 1983), III, pp. 217-61.

—'When is a Parallel Really a Parallel? A Test Case: The Lucan Parables', *WTJ* 46 (1984), pp. 78-103.

—*Interpreting the Parables* (Downers Grove, IL: Inter-Varsity Press, 1990).

Boismard, M.E. *et al.*, *Synopse des quatre Evangiles en français* (3 vols; Paris: Editions du Cerf, 2nd edn, 1972).

Boismard, M.E., and A. Lamouille, *Le texte occidental des Actes des Apôtres: Reconstitution et réhabilitation. I. Introduction et textes. II. Apparat critique, index des caractéristiques stylistiques, index des citations patristiques* (Paris: Editions Recherche sur les Civilisations, 1984).

Bornhäuser, K., *Studien zum Sondergut des Lukas* (Gütersloh: Bertelsmann, 1934).

Bovon, F., 'Luc: Portrait et projet', *Lumière et Vie* 30 (1981), pp. 9-18.

—*L'Oeuvre de Luc: Etudes d'exégèse et de théologie* (LD, 130; Paris: Editions du Cerf, 1987).

—*Das Evangelium nach Lukas* (EKKNT; 2 vols.; Zürich: Benziger Verlag, 1989).

—'Studies in Luke–Acts: Retrospect and Prospect', *HTR* 85 (1992), pp. 175-96.

Braumann, G., 'Die Schuldner und die Sünderin Luk. vii. 36-50', *NTS* 10 (1963–64), pp. 487-93.

Brenner, A., 'Female Social Behaviour: Two Descriptive Patterns within the "Birth of the Hero" Paradigm', *VT* 36 (1986), pp. 257-73.

Brodie, T.L., *The Quest for the Origin of John's Gospel: A Source-Oriented Approach* (New York: Oxford University Press, 1993).

Brown, R.E., *The Gospel according to John* (AB, 29 and 29a; Garden City, NY: Doubleday, 1966).

—*The Birth of the Messiah: A Commentary on the Infancy Narratives in Matthew and Luke* (Anchor Bible Reference Library; Garden City, NY: Doubleday, rev. edn, 1993).

Bruce, F.F., *The Acts of the Apostles: The Greek Text with Introduction and Commentary* (rev. edn; Leicester: Apollos; Grand Rapids: Eerdmans, 1990).

Brun, L., 'Zur Kompositionstechnik des Lukasevangeliums', *SO* 9 (1930), pp. 38-50.

Bruners, W., *Die Reinigung der zehn Aussätzigen und die Heilung des Samariters Lk 17, 11-19: Ein Beitrag zur lukanischen Interpretation der Reinigung von Aussätzigen* (Forschung zur Bibel, 23; Stuttgart: Katholisches Bibelwerk, 1977).

Brutscheck, J., *Die Maria-Marta-Erzählung: Eine redaktionskritische Untersuchung zu Lk 10:38-42* (BBB, 64; Bonn: Peter Hanstein, 1986).

Buchanan, G.W., *Jesus: The King and His Kingdom* (Mercer, GA: Mercer University Press, 1984).

Bultmann, R., *The History of the Synoptic Tradition* (trans. J. Marsh; Oxford: Basil Blackwell, 1963).

—'αἰσχύνω', *TDNT*, I, pp. 189-91.

—'ἐλεέω', *TDNT*, II, pp. 477-87.

Burkill, T.A., 'The Notion of Miracle with Special Reference to St Mark's Gospel', *ZNW* 50 (1959), pp. 33-48.

Burkitt, F.C., *The Gospel History and its Transmission* (Edinburgh: T. & T. Clark, 1906).

Burridge, R.A., *What are the Gospels? A Comparison with Graeco–Roman Biography* (SNTSMS, 70; Cambridge: Cambridge University Press, 1992).

Burton, E.D.W., *Principles of Literary Criticism and the Synoptic Problem* (Chicago: University of Chicago Press, 1904).

Busse, U., *Die Wunder des Propheten Jesus: Die Rezeption, Komposition und Interpretation der Wundertradition im Evangelium des Lukas* (Forschung zur Bibel, 24; Stuttgart: Katholisches Bibelwerk, 1977).

Butts, J.R., 'The Chreia in the Synoptic Gospels', *BTB* 16 (1986), pp. 132-38.

Cadbury, H.J., *The Style and Literary Method of Luke* (HTS, 6; Cambridge, MA: Harvard University Press, 1920).

—'Lexical Notes on Luke–Acts. II. Recent Arguments for Medical Language', *JBL* 45 (1926), pp. 190-206; 'V. Luke and the Horse Doctors', *JBL* 52 (1933), pp. 55-65.

—*The Making of Luke–Acts* (New York: Macmillan, 1927; repr., London: SPCK, 1958).

—'Some Lukan Expressions of Time (Lexical Notes on Luke–Acts VII)', *JBL* 82 (1963), pp. 272-88.

—'Four Features of Lucan Style', in L.E. Keck and J.L. Martyn (eds.), *Studies in Luke–Acts* (Nashville: Abingdon Press, 1966), pp. 87-102.

Caird, G.B., *The Gospel of St Luke* (Pelican Gospel Commentaries; Harmondsworth: Penguin Books, 1963).

Capon, R.F., *The Parables of the Kingdom* (Grand Rapids: Zondervan, 1985).

—*The Parables of Grace* (Grand Rapids: Eerdmans, 1988).

Carlston, C.E., 'Reminiscence and Redaction in Luke 15:11-32', *JBL* 94 (1975), pp. 368-90.

Carlston, C.E., and D. Norlin, 'Once More—Statistics and Q', *HTR* 64 (1971), pp. 59-78.

Carroll, J.T., 'Luke's Portrayal of the Pharisees', *CBQ* 50 (1988), pp. 604-21.

—*Response to the End of History: Eschatology and Situation in Luke–Acts* (SBLDS, 92; Atlanta: Scholars Press, 1988).

Catchpole, D.R., 'The Son of Man's Search for Faith (Luke xviii.8b)', *NovT* 19 (1977), pp. 81-104.

— 'Q and "The Friend at Midnight" (Luke xi. 5-8/9)', *JTS* 34 (1983), pp. 407-24.

Cerfaux, L., 'A propos des sources du troisième évangile: Proto-Luc ou Proto-Matthieu?' *ETL* 12 (1935), pp. 5-27.

Chance, J.B., *Jerusalem, the Temple, and the New Age in Luke–Acts* (Macon, GA: Mercer University Press, 1988).

Charles, R.H. (ed.), *The Apocrypha and Pseudepigrapha of the Old Testament* (2 vols.; Oxford: Clarendon Press, 1963).

Clark, A.C., *The Acts of the Apostles: A Critical Edition with Introduction and Notes on Selected Passages* (Oxford: Clarendon Press, 1933; repr., 1970).

Conn, H.M., 'Luke's Theology of Prayer', *Christianity Today* 17 (1972), pp. 290-92.

Conzelmann, H., *The Theology of St Luke* (trans. G. Buswell; New York: Harper & Row, 1961).

Cope, O.L., 'On the History of Criticism of the Gospel of Luke', *USQR* 42 (1988), pp. 59-61.

Creed, J.M., *The Gospel according to St Luke: The Greek Text with Introduction, Notes, and Indices* (London: Macmillan; New York: St Martin's, 1930).

—' "L" and the Structure of the Lucan Gospel: A Study of the Proto-Luke Hypothesis', *ExpTim* 46 (1934–35), pp. 101-107.

—'The Supposed "Proto-Lucan" Narrative of the Trial before Pilate: A Rejoinder', *ExpTim* 46 (1934–35), pp. 378-79.

Crossan, J.D., 'Parable and Example in the Teaching of Jesus', *NTS* 18 (1972), pp. 285-307.

—*In Parables: The Challenge of the Historical Jesus* (New York: Harper & Row, 1973).
—'The Servant Parables of Jesus', *Semeia* 1 (1974), pp. 192-221.
—*Cliffs of Fall: Paradox and Polyvalence ᵢₙ the Parables of Jesus* (New York: Seabury, 1980).
—*In Fragments: The Aphorisms of Jesus* (San Francisco: Harper & Row, 1983).
—*The Historical Jesus: The Life of a Mediterranean Jewish Peasant* (San Francisco: HarperCollins, 1991).
Crump, D.M., *Jesus the Intercessor: Prayer and Christology in Luke–Acts* (WUNT, 2.49; Tübingen: Mohr [Paul Siebeck], 1992).
Daly, L.W. (ed. and trans.), *Aesop without Morals: The Famous Fables, and a Life of Aesop* (New York: Thomas Yoseloff, 1961).
D'Angelo, M.R., 'Women in Luke–Acts: A Redactional View', *JBL* 109 (1990), pp. 441-61.
Daniélou, J., 'Le bon Samaritain', in *Mélanges bibliques rédigés en l'honneur de André Robert* (Paris: Bloud et Gay, 1957), pp. 457-65.
Davies, S., 'Women in the Third Gospel and the New Testament Apocrypha', in A.-J. Levine (ed.), *'Women Like This': New Perspectives on Jewish Women in the Greco–Roman World* (SBL Early Judaism and Its Literature, 1; Atlanta: Scholars Press, 1991), pp. 185-97.
Davies, S.L., *The Revolt of the Widows: The Social World of the Apocryphal Acts* (Carbondale, IL: Southern Illinois University Press, 1980).
Dawsey, J.M., *The Lukan Voice: Conflict and Irony in the Gospel of Luke* (Macon, GA: Mercer University Press, 1986).
—'The Literary Unity of Luke–Acts: Questions of Style—A Task for Literary Critics', *NTS* 35 (1989), pp. 48-66.
Delobel, J. (ed.), *Logia: Les paroles de Jésus—The Sayings of Jesus: Mémorial Joseph Coppens* (Leuven: Leuven University Press, 1982).
Delobel, J., 'L'onction de Jésus par la pécheresse', *ETL* 42 (1966), pp. 415-75.
—'La rédaction de Lc., IV, 14-16a et le "Bericht vom Anfang" ', in F. Neirynck (ed.), *L'Evangile de Luc: The Gospel of Luke* (rev. edn; BETL, 32; Leuven: University Press, 1989), pp. 113-33, 306-12.
Denaux, A., 'L'hypocrisie des Pharisees et le dessein de Dieu: Analyse de Lc., XIII, 31-33', in F. Neirynck (ed.), *L'Evangile de Luc: The Gospel of Luke* (rev. edn; BETL, 32; Leuven: University Press, 1989), pp. 155-95, 316-23.
Derrett, J.D.M., 'Positive Perspectives on Two Lucan Miracles', *Downside Review* 104 (1986), pp. 272-87.
Diamond, G., 'Reflections upon Recent Developments in the Study of Parables in Luke', *AusBr* 29 (1981), pp. 1-9.
Dibelius, F., 'Die Herkunft der Sonderstücke des Lukas-evangeliums', *ZNW* 12 (1911), pp. 325-43.
Dibelius, M., *From Tradition to Gospel* (trans. B.L. Woolf; New York: Charles Scribner's Sons, 1965).
Dickie, E.P., 'The Third Gospel: A Hidden Source', *ExpTim* 46 (1934–35), pp. 326-30.
Dillon, R.J., *From Eye-Witness to Ministers of the Word: Tradition and Composition in Luke 24* (Rome: Biblical Institute Press, 1978).
Diogenes Laertius, *Lives of Eminent Philosophers* (trans. R.D. Hicks; LCL; 2 vols.; Cambridge: Harvard University Press; London: Heinemann, 1925).
Dodd, C.H., *The Parables of the Kingdom* (New York: Charles Scribner's Sons, 1961).

Donahue, J., *The Gospel in Parable: Metaphor, Narrative, and Theology in the Synoptic Gospels* (Philadelphia: Fortress Press, 1988).

—'Two Decades of Research on the Rich and the Poor in Luke–Acts', in A. Knight and P.J. Paris (eds.), *Justice and the Holy: Essays in Honor of Walter Harrelson* (Atlanta: Scholars Press, 1989), pp. 129-44.

Downing, F.G., 'Quite Like Q—a Genre for Q: the Lives of the Cynic Philosophers', *Bib* 69 (1988), pp. 196-225.

—*Christ and the Cynics: Jesus and other Radical Preachers in First Century Tradition* (Sheffield: Sheffield Academic Press, 1988).

—*Cynics and Christian Origins* (Edinburgh: T. & T. Clark, 1992).

Drury, J., *Tradition and Design in Luke's Gospel: A Study in Early Christian Historiography* (Atlanta: John Knox, 1976).

—*The Parables in the Gospels: History and Allegory* (New York: Crossroad, 1985).

Dundes, A., *Interpreting Folklore* (Bloomington: Indiana University Press, 1980).

Dupont, J., *Les Béatitudes: Le problème littéraire, le message doctrinal* (Bruges: Editions de l'Abbaye de Saint-André, 1954).

—*Les sources du livre des Actes: Etat de la question* (Bruges: Desclée de Brouwer, 1960).

—'Renoncer à tous ses biens (Luc 14, 33)', *NRT* 93 (1971), pp. 561-82.

Easton, B.S., 'Linguistic Evidence for the Lucan Source L', *JBL* 29 (1910), pp. 139-80.

—'The Special Source of the Third Gospel', *JBL* 30 (1911), pp. 78-103.

—*The Gospel according to St Luke: A Critical and Exegetical Commentary* (New York: Charles Scribner's Sons, 1926).

—*Christ in the Gospels* (New York: Charles Scribner's Sons, 1930).

Eddy, P.R. 'Jesus as Diogenes? Reflections on the Cynic Jesus Thesis', *JBL* 115 (1996), pp. 449-69.

Edmonds, P., 'The Lucan Our Father: A Summary of Luke's Teaching on Prayer?' *ExpTim* 91 (1979–80), pp. 140-43.

Edwards, R.A., *A Theology of Q: Eschatology, Prophecy, and Wisdom* (Philadelphia: Fortress Press, 1976).

Ellis, E.E., *The Gospel of Luke* (NCB; London: Nelson, 1966).

—*Eschatology in Luke* (Facet Books, Biblical Series, 30; Philadephia: Fortress Press, 1972).

Enslin, M.S., 'Luke and Matthew, Compilers or Authors?', (*ANRW* II.25.3; Berlin: de Gruyter, 1985), pp. 2357-88.

Esler, P.F., *Community and Gospel in Luke–Acts: The Social and Political Motivations of Lucan Theology* (SNTSMS, 57; Cambridge: Cambridge University Press, 1987).

Evans, C.F., 'The Central Section of St Luke's Gospel', in D.E. Nineham (ed.), *Studies in the Gospels: Essays in Memory of R.H. Lightfoot* (Oxford: Basil Blackwell, 1955), pp. 37-53.

—*Saint Luke* (TPI New Testament Commentaries; London: SCM, 1990).

Farmer, W.R., 'Notes on a Literary and Form-Critical Analysis of some of the Synoptic Material Peculiar to Luke', *NTS* 8 (1961–62), pp. 301-16.

—*The Synoptic Problem: A Critical Analysis* (New York: Macmillan, 1964).

—'Source Criticism: Some Comments on the Present Situation', *USQR* 42 (1988), pp. 49-57.

—'The Passion Prediction Passages and the Synoptic Problem: A Test Case', *NTS* 36 (1990), pp. 558-70.

Farrar, F.W., *The Bible: Its Meaning and Supremacy* (London: Longmans, Green, & Co., 1897).

Farrell, H.K., 'The Structure and Theology of Luke's Central Section', *Trinity Journal* 7.2 (1986), pp. 33-54.

Farrer, A.M., 'On Dispensing with Q', in D.E. Nineham (ed.), *Studies in the Gospels: Essays in Memory of R.H. Lightfoot* (Oxford: Basil Blackwell, 1955), pp. 55-88.

Farris, S., *The Hymns of Luke's Infancy Narratives: Their Origin, Meaning and Significance* (JSNTSup, 9; Sheffield: JSOT Press, 1985).

Feine, P., *Eine vorkanonische Überlieferung des Lukas in Evangelium und Apostelgeschichte* (Gotha: Perthes, 1891).

Finegan, J., *The Archeology of the New Testament: The Life of Jesus and the Beginning of the Early Church* (Princeton, NJ: Princeton University Press, rev. edn, 1992).

Fitzmyer, J.A., 'Memory and Manuscript: The Origins and Transmission of the Gospel Tradition', *TS* 23 (1962), pp. 442-57.

—*The Gospel according to Luke* (AB, 28 and 28a; Garden City, NY: Doubleday, 1981–1985).

Foerster, W., 'ἐμπαίζω', *TDNT*, pp. 630-35.

Foulkes, F., *The Epistle of Paul to the Ephesians: An Introduction and Commentary* (Grand Rapids: Eerdmans, 1963).

Fournier, W.J., 'The Third Gospel: A Hidden Source', *ExpTim* 46 (1934–35), p. 428.

Frankenmölle, H., 'Die Makarismen (Mt 5, 1-12; Lk 6, 20-23): Motive und Umfang der redaktionellen Komposition', *BZ* (n.f.) 15 (1971), pp. 52-75.

Franklin, E., *Christ the Lord: A Study in the Purpose and Theology of Luke–Acts* (Philadelphia: Westminster Press, 1975).

Freed, E.D., 'The Parable of the Judge and the Widow (Luke 18:1-8)', *NTS* 33 (1987), pp. 38-60.

Fuller, R.H., *Interpreting the Miracles* (Philadelphia: Westminster Press, 1963).

—'Die neuere Diskussion über das synoptische Problem', *TZ* 34 (1978), pp. 129-48.

Funk, R.W., 'The Good Samaritan as Metaphor', *Semeia* 2 (1974), pp. 74-81.

—*Parables and Presence: Forms of the New Testament Tradition* (Philadephia: Fortress Press, 1982).

Garrett, D., *Rethinking Genesis: The Sources and Authorship of the First Book of the Pentateuch* (Grand Rapids: Baker Book House, 1991).

Geldenhuys, N., *Commentary on the Gospel of Luke* (NICNT; Grand Rapids: Eerdmans, 1951).

George, A., 'Le miracle dans l'oeuvre de Luc', in X. Léon-Dufour (ed.), *Les miracles des Jésus selon le Nouveau Testament* (Paris: Editions du Seuil, 1977), pp. 249-68.

Gerhardsson, B., 'The Good Samaritan—The Good Shepherd?', *ConNT* 16 (1958), pp. 1-31.

—*Memory and Manuscript: Oral Tradition and Written Transmission in Rabbinic Judaism and Early Christianity* (Lund: Gleerup, 1961).

Giles, K., ' "L" Tradition', in J.B. Green, S. McKnight, and I.H. Marshall (eds.), *Dictionary of Jesus and the Gospels* (Leicester: Inter-Varsity Press, 1992), pp. 431-32.

Gilmour, S.M., 'A Critical Re-examination of Proto-Luke', *JBL* 67 (1948), pp. 143-52.

—'The Gospel according to St Luke' (IB, 8; New York: Abingdon Press, 1952), pp. 1-434.

Glöckner, R., *Neutestamentliche Wundergeschichten und das Lob der Wundertaten Gottes in den Psalmen: Studien zur sprachlichen und theologischen Verwandtschaft zwischen neutestamentlichen Wundergeschichten und Psalmen* (Walberger Studien; Theologische Reihe, 13; Mainz: Grünewald, 1983).

Goguel, M., 'Luke and Mark: With a Discussion of Streeter's Theory', *HTR* 26 (1933), pp. 1-55.

Gollwitzer, H., *Das Gleichnis vom Barmherzigen Samariter* (BS, 34; Neukirchen–Vluyn: Neukirchener, 1962).

Gooding, D., *According to Luke: A New Exposition of the Third Gospel* (Leicester: Inter-Varsity Press; Grand Rapids: Eerdmans, 1987).

Goulder, M.D., and M.L. Sanderson, 'St Luke's Genesis', *JTS* NS 8 (1957), pp. 12-30.

Goulder, M.D., *Luke: A New Paradigm* (2 vols.; JSNTSup, 20; Sheffield: JSOT Press, 1989).

—'Is Q a Juggernaut?', *JBL* 115 (1996), pp. 667-81.

Grant, F.C., *The Growth of the Gospels* (New York: Abingdon Press, 1933).

—*The Gospels: Their Origin and Their Growth* (New York: Harper & Row, 1957).

Grayston, K., and G. Herdan, 'The Authorship of the Pastorals in the Light of Statistical Linguistics', *NTS* 6 (1959–60), pp. 1-15.

Grobel, K., '… Whose Name Was Neves', *NTS* 10 (1963–64), pp. 373-82.

Guthrie, D., *New Testament Introduction* (Leicester: Apollos; Downers Grove, IL: Inter-Varsity Press, rev. edn, 1990).

—*The Pastoral Epistles: An Introduction and Commentary* (rev. edn; Tyndale New Testament Commentaries; Leicester: Inter-Varsity; Grand Rapids: Eerdmans, 1990).

Haenchen, E., *Die Apostelgeschichte* (MeyerK Abt. 3; Göttingen: Vandenhoeck & Ruprecht, 13th edn, 1961).

Hanson, A.T., *The Pastoral Epistles* (NCB Commentary; Grand Rapids: Eerdmans; London: Marshall, Morgan, & Scott, 1982).

Hanson, R.P.C., 'Does δίκαιος in Luke xxiii. 47 explode the Proto-Luke Hypothesis?', *Hermathena* 60 (1942), pp. 74-78.

Harnack, A., *The Sayings of Jesus: The Second Source of St Matthew and St Luke* (trans. J.R. Wilkinson; London: Williams & Norgate; New York: Putnam's Sons, 1908).

—*Luke the Physician* (trans. J.R. Wilkinson; London: Williams & Norgate, 1911).

Harrington, W.J., *The Gospel according to St Luke: A Commentary* (New York: Newman Press, 1967).

Harris, L.O., 'Prayer in the Gospel of Luke', *Southwestern Journal of Theology* 10 (1967), pp. 59-69.

Harrison, P.N., *The Problem of the Pastoral Epistles* (Oxford: Oxford University Press, 1921).

Havelock, E.A., *The Muse Learns to Write: Reflections on Orality and Literacy from Antiquity to the Present* (New Haven: Yale University Press, 1986).

Havener, I., *Q: The Sayings of Jesus* (Wilmington, DE: Michael Glazier, 1987).

Hawkins, J.C., *Horae Synopticae: Contributions to the Study of the Synoptic Problem* (Oxford: Clarendon Press, 2nd edn, 1909).

Hendriksen, W., *New Testament Commentary: Exposition of the Gospel according to Luke* (Grand Rapids: Baker Book House, 1978).

Hendrickx, H., *The Infancy Narratives* (Studies in the Synoptic Gospels; London: Geoffrey Chapman, rev. edn, 1984).

—*The Parables of Jesus* (London: Geoffrey Chapman; San Francisco: Harper & Row, 1986).

—*The Miracle Stories of the Synoptic Gospels* (London: Geoffrey Chapman; San Francisco: Harper & Row, 1987).

Hicks, J.M., 'The Parable of the Persistent Widow (Luke 18:1-8)', *ResQ* 33 (1991), pp. 209-23.

Hiroishi, N., 'Die Gleichniserzählung vom verlorenen Sohn (Lk 15, 11-32): Eine form- und traditionsgeschichtliche Untersuchung der Gleichniserzählung Jesu im lukanischen Sondergut', *AJBI* 16 (1990), pp. 71-99.

Hobart, W.K., *The Medical Language of St Luke* (Dublin: Hodges, Figgis, & Co., 1882).

Hock, R.F., and E.N. O'Neil, *The Chreia in Ancient Rhetoric*. I. *The Progymnasmata* (Texts and Translations, 27; Graeco–Roman Religion Series, 9; Atlanta: Scholars Press, 1986).

Hockey, S., *A Guide to Computer Applications in the Humanities* (Baltimore: The Johns Hopkins University Press, 1980).

Horn, F.W., *Glaube und Handeln in der Theologie des Lukas* (Göttingen: Vandenhoeck & Ruprecht, 1983).

Hunkin, J.W., 'The Composition of the Third Gospel, with Special Reference to Canon Streeter's Theory of Proto-Luke', *JTS* 28 (1926-27), pp. 250-62.

Ireland, D.J., *Stewardship and the Kingdom of God: An Historical, Exegetical, and Contextual Study of the Parable of the Unjust Steward in Luke 16:1-13* (NovTSup, 70; Leiden: Brill, 1992).

Jefford, C.N., *The Sayings of Jesus in the Teaching of the Twelve Apostles* (Leiden: Brill, 1989).

Jeremias, J., 'Perikopen-Umstellungen bei Lukas?' *NTS* 4 (1957–58), pp. 115-19.

—*The Parables of Jesus* (trans. S.H. Hooke; New York: Charles Scribner's Sons, 1963).

—*Die Sprache des Lukasevangeliums: Redaktion und Tradition im Nicht-Markusstoff des dritten Evangeliums* (Göttingen: Vandenhoeck & Ruprecht, 1980).

Johnson, L.T., *The Literary Function of Possessions in Luke–Acts* (SBLDS, 39; Missoula, MT: Scholars Press, 1977).

—*Sharing Possessions: Mandate and Symbol of Faith* (Overtures to Biblical Theology, 9; Philadelphia: Fortress Press, 1981).

—*The Gospel of Luke* (Sacra Pagina Series, 3; Collegeville, MN: Liturgical Press, 1991).

Johnson, M.D., *The Purpose of the Biblical Genealogies with Special Reference to the Genealogies of Jesus* (SNTSMS, 8; Cambridge: Cambridge University Press, 1969).

Johnson, P.F., 'The Use of Statistics in the Analysis of the Characteristics of Pauline Writings', *NTS* 20 (1973–74), pp. 92-100.

Kariamadam, P., *The Zacchaeus Story (Lk. 19, 1-10): A Redactional–Critical Investigation* (Kerala, India: Pontifical Institute Publications, 1985).

Kee, H.C., *Miracle in the Early Christian World: A Study in Sociohistorical Method* (New Haven: Yale University Press, 1983).

Kelber, W.H., *The Oral and Written Gospel* (Philadelphia: Fortress Press, 1983).

Keller, J.E., and L.C. Keating (trans. and eds.), *Aesop's Fables, with a Life of Aesop* (Lexington, KY: University Press of Kentucky, 1993).

Kenny, A., *The Computation of Style: An Introduction to Statistics for Students of Literature and Humanities* (New York: Pergamon Press, 1982).

—*A Stylometric Study of the New Testament* (Oxford: Clarendon Press, 1986).

Kilpatrick, G.D., 'A Theme of the Lucan Passion Story and Luke xxiii. 47', *JTS* 43 (1942), pp. 34-36.

—'Scribes, Lawyers, and Lucan Origins', *JTS* (NS) 1 (1950), pp. 56-60.

Klein, G., 'Die Berufung des Petrus', *ZNW* 58 (1967), pp. 1-44.

Kloppenborg, J.S., *The Formation of Q: Trajectories in Ancient Wisdom Collections* (Studies in Antiquity and Christianity; Philadelphia: Fortress Press, 1987).

—*Q Parallels: Synopsis, Critical Notes, and Concordance* (Foundations and Facets Reference Series; Sonoma, CA: Polebridge, 1988).

—'Literary Convention, Self-Evidence and the Social History of the Q People', *Semeia* 55 (1991), pp. 77-102.

Knox, W.L., *The Sources of the Synoptic Gospels*. II. *St Luke and St Matthew* (Cambridge: Cambridge University Press, 1957).

Koester, H., *Ancient Christian Gospels: Their History and Development* (London: SCM Press; Philadelphia: Trinity Press, 1990).

Kuhn, T.S., *The Structure of Scientific Revolutions* (Chicago: University of Chicago Press, 1962).

Lagrange, M.J., 'Les sources du troisième Evangile', *RB* 4 (1895) 5-22; *RB* 5 (1896) 5-38.

—*Evangile selon Saint Luc* (Paris: Gabalda, 1921).

Lambrecht, J., *Once More Astonished: The Parables of Jesus* (New York: Crossroad, 1981).

Latourelle, R., *The Miracles of Jesus and the Theology of Miracles* (trans. M.J. O'Connell; New York: Paulist Press, 1988).

Leaney, A.R.C., *A Commentary on the Gospel according to St Luke* (Black's New Testament Commentaries; London: A. & C. Black, 1958).

Lentz, T.M., *Orality and Literacy in Hellenic Greece* (Carbondale, IL: Southern Illinois University Press, 1989).

Lindberger, J.M., 'Ahiqar', in J.H. Charlesworth (ed.), *The Old Testament Pseudepigrapha* (2 vols.; Garden City, NY: Doubleday, 1985), II, pp. 479-507.

Linnemann, E., *Jesus of the Parables: Introduction and Exposition* (trans. J. Sturdy; New York and Evanston: Harper & Row, 1966).

Linss, W.C., 'Example Stories?' *CurTM* 17 (1990), pp. 447-53.

Loisy, A., *L'Evangile selon Luc* (Paris: Emile Nourry, 1924).

—*Les origines du Nouveau Testament* (Paris: Emile Nourry, 1936).

Lord, A.B., *The Singer of Tales* (Cambridge, MA: Harvard University Press, 1960).

—'The Gospels as Oral Traditional Literature', in W.O. Walker, Jr (ed.), *The Relationships among the Gospels: An Interdisciplinary Dialogue* (San Antonio: Trinity University Press, 1978), pp. 33-91.

—*Epic Singers and Oral Tradition* (Ithaca, NY: Cornell University Press, 1991).

Lührmann, D., *An Itinerary for New Testament Study* (trans. J. Bowden; London: SCM; Philadelphia: Trinity Press, 1989).

Mack, B.L., 'The Anointing of Jesus: Elaboration within a Chreia', in B.L. Mack and V.K. Robbins (eds.), *Patterns of Persuasion in the Gospels* (Foundations and Facets: Literary Facets; Sonoma, CA: Polebridge Press, 1989), pp. 85-106.

Malbon, E.S., 'Fallible Followers: Women and Men in the Gospel of Mark', *Semeia* 28 (1983), pp. 29-48.

Malina, B.J. and J.H. Neyrey, 'Honor and Shame in Luke–Acts: Pivotal Values of the Mediterranean World', in J.H. Neyrey (ed.), *The Social World of Luke–Acts: Models for Interpretation* (Peabody, MA: Hendrickson Publishers, 1991), pp. 25-65.

Manson, T.W., *The Sayings of Jesus* (London: SCM Press, 1949).

—'John the Baptist', *BJRL* 36 (1953–54), pp. 395-412.

Manson, W., *The Gospel of Luke* (MNTC, 3; New York and London: Harper & Brothers, 1927).

Marshall, I.H., *Luke: Historian and Theologian* (Grand Rapids: Zondervan, 1976).

—*The Gospel of Luke: A Commentary on the Greek Text* (NIGTC; Grand Rapids: Eerdmans, 1978).

—'The Present State of Lucan Studies', *Themelios* 14 (1989), pp. 52-57.

Marxsen, W., *Introduction to the New Testament: An Approach to its Problems* (trans. G. Buswell; Philadelphia: Fortress Press, 1968).

März, C.P., '"Feuer auf die Erde zu werfen, bin ich gekommen ..."': Zum Verständnis und zur Entstehung von Lk 12, 49', in *A cause de l'Evangile: Etudes sur les Synoptiques et les Actes: Mélanges offerts à Jacques Dupont* (Paris: Cerf, 1985), pp. 479-511.

Meeûs, X. de, 'Composition de Lc., XIV et genre symposiaque', *ETL* 37 (1961), pp. 847-70.

Menken, M.J.J., 'The Position of σπλαγχνίζεσθαι and σπλάγχνα in the Gospel of Luke', *NovT* 30 (1988), pp. 107-14.

Metzger, B.M., 'A Reconsideration of Certain Arguments Against the Pauline Authorship of the Pastoral Epistles', *ExpTim* 70 (1958–59), pp. 91-94.

Michaelson, S., and A.Q. Morton, 'Last Words: A Test of Authorship for Greek Writers', *NTS* 18 (1971–72), pp. 192-208.

—'The New Stylometry: A One-Word Test of Authorship in Greek Writers', *Classical Quarterly* 22 (1972), pp. 89-102.

Miller, R.J., *The Complete Gospels: Annotated Scholars Version* (Sonoma, CA: Polebridge, 1992).

Minear, P., 'A Note on Luke 17:7-10', *JBL* 93 (1974), pp. 82-87.

Minear, P.S., 'Luke's Use of the Birth Stories', in L.E. Keck and J.L. Martyn (eds.), *Studies in Luke–Acts* (Nashville : Abingdon Press, 1966), pp. 111-30.

Mitton, C.L., *The Epistle to the Ephesians: Its Authorship, Origin, and Purpose* (Oxford: Clarendon Press, 1951).

Moffatt, J., *An Introduction to the Literature of the New Testament* (International Theological Library; New York: Charles Scribner's Sons, 1911).

Montefiore, H., 'Does "L" Hold Water?', *JTS* 12 (April 1961), pp. 59-60.

—'A Comparison of the Parables of the Gospel according to Thomas and of the Synoptic Gospels', in H.E.W. Turner and H. Montefiore, *Thomas and the Evangelists* (London: SCM Press, 1962), pp. 40-78.

Morris, L., *Luke: An Introduction and Commentary* (The Tyndale New Testament Commentaries; Leicester: Inter-Varsity Press; Grand Rapids: Eerdmans, 1988).

Morton, A.Q., *Literary Detection: How to Prove Authorship and Fraud in Literature and Documents* (New York: Charles Scribner's Sons, 1978).

Morton, A.Q., and J. McLeman, *Paul, the Man and the Myth: A Study in the Authorship of Greek Prose* (London: Hodder & Stoughton, 1966).

Neill, S., and T. Wright, *The Interpretation of the New Testament 1861–1986* (Oxford: Oxford University Press, 2nd edn, 1988).

Nietzsche, F., *The Antichrist* (trans. E. Haldmean-Julius; New York: Arno Press, 1972).

Neirynck, F., and F. Van Segbroeck, 'Le texte des Actes des Apôtres et les caractéristiques lucaniennes', *ETL* 61 (1985), pp. 304-39.

Neirynck, F., 'Luke 14, 1-6: Lukan Composition and Q Saying', in C. Bussmann and W. Radl (eds.), *Der treue Gottes trauen: Beiträge zum Werk des Lukas* (Freiburg, Basel, Wien: Herder, 1991), pp. 243-63.

Neyrey, J., *The Passion according to Luke: A Redaction Study of Luke's Soteriology* (Theological Inquiries; New York: Paulist Press, 1985).

Nolland, J., *Luke* (WBC, 35a, 35b, and 35c; Dallas, TX: Word Books, 1989–1993).

O'Brien, P.T., 'Prayer in Luke–Acts', *TynBul* 24 (1973), pp. 111-27.

O'Hanlon, J., 'The Story of Zacchaeus and the Lukan Ethic', *JSNT* 12 (1981), pp. 2-26.

Olrik, A., 'Epische Gesetze der Volksdichtung', *Zeitschrift für deutsches Altertum* 51 (1909), pp. 1-12.

Ong, W.J., *Orality and Literacy: The Technologizing of the Word* (London: Methuen, 1982).

O'Rourke, J.J., 'Some Notes on Luke xv. 11-32', *NTS* 18 (1971–72), pp. 431-33.
—'Some Considerations about Attempts at Statistical Analysis of the Pauline Corpus', *CBQ* 35 (1973), pp. 483-90.
Ott, W., *Gebet und Heil: Die Bedeutung der Gebetsparänese in der lukanischen Theologie* (Munich: Kösel, 1965).
Paffenroth, K., 'Romans 12:9-21—A Brief Summary of the Problems of Translation and Interpretation', *IBS* 14 (1992), pp. 89-99.
Parker, P., 'A Proto-Lukan Basis for the Gospel according to the Hebrews', *JBL* 59 (1940), pp. 471-78.
Parrott, D.M., 'The Dishonest Steward (Lk 16.1-8a) and Luke's Special Parable Collection', *NTS* 37 (1991), pp. 499-515.
Pascal, B., *Pensées* (trans. A.J. Krailsheimer; Harmondsworth: Penguin Books, 1966).
Patsch, H., 'Der Einzug Jesu in Jerusalem: Ein historischer Versuch', *ZTK* 68 (1971), pp. 1-26.
Patterson, S.J., 'Fire and Dissension: Ipsissima Vox Jesus in Q 12:49, 51-53?', *Forum* 5.2 (1989), pp. 121-39.
Patton, C.S., *Sources of the Synoptic Gospels* (New York: Macmillan, 1915).
Paulsen, H., 'Die Witwe und der Richter (Lk 18,1-8)', *TGl* 74 (1984), pp. 13-39.
Perkins, P., *Hearing the Parables of Jesus* (New York: Paulist Press, 1981).
Perrin, N., *Rediscovering the Teaching of Jesus* (New York: Harper & Row, 1976).
Perry, A.M.,' "Proto-Luke" and the "Chicago Theory" of the Synoptic Problem', *JBL* 47 (1928), 91-116.
—'An Evangelist's Tabellae: Some Sections of Oral Tradition in Luke', *JBL* 48 (1929), pp. 206-32.
—'A Judaeo–Christian Source in Luke', *JBL* 49 (1930), pp. 181-94.
—'Luke's Disputed Passion Source', *ExpTim* 46 (1934–35), pp. 256-60.
Perry, B.E. (trans. and ed.), *Secundus the Silent Philosopher* (APA Philological Supplements, 22; Ithaca, NY: Cornell University Press, 1964).
Perry, B.E. (ed.), *Aesopica* (Urbana, IL: University of Illinois Press, 1952).
Pesch, R., *Der reiche Fischfang: Lk 5, 1-11/Jo 21, 1-14. Wundergeschichte–Berufungs-erzählung–Erscheinungsbericht* (Düsseldorf: Patmos, 1969).
—*Jesu, ureigene Taten? Ein Beitrag zur Wunderfrage* (QD, 52; Freiburg: Herder, 1970).
Petrie, C.S., 'The Proto-Luke Hypothesis', *ExpTim* 54 (1942–43), pp. 172-77.
—'The Proto-Luke Hypothesis: Observations on Dr Vincent Taylor's Rejoinder', *ExpTim* 55 (1943–44), pp. 52-53.
Petzke, G., *Das Sondergut des Evangelium nach Lukas* (Zürcher Werkkommentare zur Bibel; Zürich: Theologischer Verlag, 1990).
Pilgrim, W.E., *Good News to the Poor: Wealth and Poverty in Luke–Acts* (Minneapolis: Augsburg, 1981).
Piper, R.A., *Wisdom in the Q-tradition: The Aphoristic Teaching of Jesus* (Cambridge: Cambridge University Press, 1989).
Plummer, A., *A Critical and Exegetical Commentary on the Gospel according to St Luke* (ICC, 28; Edinburgh: T. & T. Clark, 5th edn, 1922).
Plymale, S.F., *The Prayer Texts of Luke–Acts* (New York: Peter Lang, 1991).
Powell, M.A., 'Are Sands Still Shifting? An Update on Lukan Scholarship', *Trinity Seminary Review* 11 (1989), pp. 15-22.
—*What Are they Saying about Luke?* (New York: Paulist Press, 1989).

Ramsay, W.M., *Luke the Physician and Other Studies in the History of Religion* (London: Hodder & Stoughton, 1908).

Ravens, D.A.S., 'Zacchaeus: The Final Part of a Lukan Triptych?' *JSNT* 41 (1991), pp. 19-32.

Ravens, D. *Luke and the Restoration of Israel* (JSNTSup, 119; Sheffield: Sheffield Academic Press, 1995).

Rehkopf, F., *Die lukanische Sonderquelle: Ihr Umfang und Sprachgebrauch* (WUNT, 5; Tübingen: Mohr, 1959).

Reicke, B., *The Roots of the Synoptic Gospels* (Philadelphia: Fortress Press, 1986).

Renan, E., *Les Evangiles et la seconde génération chrétienne* (Paris: Calmann–Lévy, 1877).

Rengstorf, K.H., *Das Evangelium nach Lukas* (NTD, 3; Göttingen: Vandenhoeck & Ruprecht, 1967).

Rese, M., 'Einige Überlegungen zu Lukas XIII, 31-33', in J. Dupont (ed.), *Jésus aux origines de la christologie* (BETL, 40; Leuven: Leuven University Press, 1975), pp. 201-25.

—'Das Lukas-Evangelium. Ein Forschungsbericht' (*ANRW* II.25.3; Berlin: de Gruyter, 1985), pp. 2258-328.

Rhoads, D., and D. Michie, *Mark as Story: An Introduction to the Narrative of a Gospel* (Philadelphia: Fortress Press, 1982).

Richard, E., 'Luke—Writer, Theologian, Historian: Research and Orientation of the 1970's', *BTB* 13 (1983), pp. 3-15.

Rigaux, B., *Témoignage de l'évangile de Luc* (Paris: Desclée de Brouwer, 1970).

Robbins, V.K., 'The Chreia', in D.E. Aune (ed.), *Greco–Roman Literature and the New Testament: Selected Forms and Genres* (SBLSBS, 21; Atlanta: Scholars Press, 1987).

Robinson, J.M., 'LOGOI SOPHON: On the Gattung of Q', in J.M. Robinson and H. Koester (eds.), *Trajectories through Early Christianity* (Philadelphia: Fortress Press, 1971), pp. 71-113.

Robinson, W.C., Jr, *Der Weg des Herrn* (Hamburg–Bergstedt: H. Reich, 1964).

Rochais, G., *Les récits de résurrection des morts dans le Nouveau Testament* (SNTSMS, 40; Cambridge: Cambridge University Press, 1981).

Rosché, T.R., 'The Words of Jesus and the Future of the "Q" Hypothesis', *JBL* 79 (1960), pp. 210-20.

Sabourin, L., *The Names and Titles of Jesus* (trans. M. Carroll; New York: Macmillan, 1967).

—*L'Evangile de Luc: Introduction et commentaire* (Rome: Editrice Pontificia Università Gregoriana, 1985).

Sahlin, J., 'Die Früchte der Umkehr: Die ethische Verkündigung Johannes des Täufers nach Lk 3:10-14', *ST* 1 (1948), pp. 54-68.

Salazar, A.M., 'Questions about St Luke's Sources', *NovT* 2 (1958), pp. 316-17.

Sanders, E.P., *The Tendencies of the Synoptic Traditions* (SNTSMS, 9; Cambridge: Cambridge University Press, 1969).

Sanders, J.T., 'Tradition and Redaction in Luke xv.11-32', *NTS* 15 (1968–69), pp. 433-38.

Scheffler, E.H., 'The Social Ethics of the Lukan Baptist (Lk 3:10-14)', *Neot* 24 (1990), pp. 21-36.

Schenk, S., *Synopse zur Redenquelle der Evangelien: Q-Synopse und Rekonstruktion in deutscher Übersetzung mit kurzen Erläuterungen* (Düsseldorf: Patmos, 1981).

Schlatter, A., *Das Evangelium des Lukas* (2nd edn; Stuttgart: Calwer Verlag, 1960).

Schnackenburg, R., 'Der eschatologische Abschnitt Lk 17, 20-37', in A. Descamps and A. de Halleux (eds.), *Mélanges bibliques en hommage au R.P. Beda Rigaux* (Gembloux: Duculot, 1970), pp. 213-34.

Schneider, G., *Das Evangelium nach Lukas* (Ökumenischer Taschenbuchkommentar zum Neuen Testament, vols. 3/1-2; Gütersloh: Gerd Mohn; Würzburg: Echter, 2nd edn, 1984).

Schneider, J., 'ὄνειδος', *TDNT*, V, pp. 238-42.

Schottroff, L., 'Das Gleichnis vom verlorenen Sohn', *ZTK* 68 (1971), pp. 27-52.

—'Die Erzählung vom Pharisäer und Zöllner als Beispiel für die theologische Kunst des Überredens', in H.D. Betz and L. Schottroff (eds.), *Neues Testament und christliche Existenz: Festschrift für Herbert Braun zum 70 Geburtstag* (Tübingen: Mohr–Siebeck, 1973), pp. 439-61.

Schramm, T., *Der Markus-Stoff bei Lukas: Eine literarkritische und redaktionsgeschichtliche Untersuchung* (Cambridge: Cambridge University Press, 1971).

Schreck, C.J., 'The Nazareth Pericope: Luke 4, 16-30 in Recent Study', in F. Neirynck (ed.), *L'Evangile de Luc. The Gospel of Luke* (BETL, 32; Leuven: Leuven University Press, rev. edn, 1989), pp. 399-471.

Schulz, S., *Q: Die Spruchquelle der Evangelisten* (Zürich: Theologischer Verlag, 1972).

Schürmann, H., 'Protolukanische Spracheigentümlichkeiten? Zu Fr. Rehkopf, Die lukanische Sonderquelle. Ihr Umfang und Sprachgebrauch', *BZ* 5 (1961), pp. 266-86.

—'Das Thomasevangelium und das lukanische Sondergut', *BZ* 7 (1963), pp. 236-60.

—'Der "Bericht vom Anfang": Ein Rekonstruktionsversuch auf Grund von Lk. 4, 14-16', *TU* 87 (1964), pp. 242-58.

—*Traditionsgeschichtliche Untersuchungen zu den synoptischen Evangelien* (Düsseldorf: Patmos, 1968).

—*Das Lukasevangelium* (HTKNT, Band III, t. 1-3; Freiburg, Basel, Wien: Herder, 1969).

—'Zur Traditionsgeschichte der Nazareth-Perikope Lk. 4, 16-30', in A. Descamps and A. de Halleux (eds.), *Mélanges bibliques en hommage au R.P. Béda Rigaux* (Gembloux: Duculot, 1970), pp. 187-205.

—'Die Redekomposition wider "dieses Geschlecht" und seine Führung in der Redenquelle (vgl. Mt. 23, 1-39 par Lk. 11, 37-54): Bestand-Akoluthie-Kompositionsformen', *SNTU* 11 (1986), pp. 33-81.

Schüssler Fiorenza, E., *In Memory of Her: A Feminist Theological Reconstruction of Christian Origins* (New York: Crossroad, 1983).

—'A Feminist Critical Interpretation for Liberation: Martha and Mary. Luke 10:38-42', *Religion and Intellectual Life* 3 (1986), pp. 21-36.

Schweizer, E., 'Eine hebraisierende Sonderquelle des Lukas?', *TZ* 6 (1950), pp. 161-85.

—*The Good News according to St Luke* (trans. D.E. Green; Atlanta: John Knox, 1984).

Scott, B.B., *Hear Then the Parable: A Commentary on the Parables of Jesus* (Minneapolis: Fortress Press, 1989).

Scott, J.A., *Luke: Greek Physician and Historian* (Evanston, IL: Northwestern University Press, 1930).

Segal, M.H., *The Pentateuch: Its Composition and its Authorship* (Jerusalem: Hebrew University, Magnes Press, 1967).

Sellew, P., 'Interior Monologue as a Narrative Device in the Parables of Luke', *JBL* 111 (1992), pp. 239-53.

Shaw, G.B., 'Back to Methuselah: A Metabiological Pentateuch', in D.H. Laurence (ed.), *Bernard Shaw: Collected Plays with their Prefaces* (7 vols.; New York: Dodd, Mead, & Co., 1972), V, pp. 255-715.

Siker, J., '"First to the Gentiles": A Literary Analysis of Luke 4:16-30', *JBL* 111 (1992), pp. 73-90.

Sim, D.C., 'The Women Followers of Jesus: The Implications of Luke 8:1-3', *HeyJ* 30 (1989), pp. 51-62.

Sloan, R.B., *The Favorable Year of the Lord: A Study of Jubilary Theology in the Gospel of Luke* (Austin, TX: Schola Press, 1977).

Smalley, S., 'Spirit, Kingdom and Prayer in Luke–Acts', *NovT* 15 (1973), pp. 59-71.

Smith, D.M., *John among the Gospels: The Relationship in Twentieth-Century Research* (Minneapolis: Fortress Press, 1992).

Soards, M.L., *The Passion according to Luke: The Special Material of Luke 22* (JSNTSup, 14; Sheffield: Sheffield Academic Press, 1987).

Solages, B. de, *La composition des évangiles de Luc et de Matthieu et leurs sources* (Leiden: Brill, 1973).

Stanton, V.H., *The Gospels as Historical Documents. II. The Synoptic Gospels* (Cambridge: Cambridge University Press, 1909).

Steele, E.S., 'Luke 11:37-54: A Modified Hellenistic Symposium?', *JBL* 103 (1984), pp. 379-94.

Stephenson, T., 'Fresh Light on the Synoptic Problem', *JTS* 23 (1922), pp. 250-55.

Sterling, G., *Historiography and Self-Definition: Josephos, Luke–Acts, and Apologetic Historiography* (Leiden: Brill, 1991).

—'"Athletes of Virtue": An Analysis of the Summaries in Acts (2:41-47; 4:32-35; 5:12-16)', *JBL* 113 (1994), pp. 679-96.

Steyn, G.J., 'Die Manifestering van Septuaginta-invloed in die Sondergut-Lukas', *Hervormde Teologiese Studies* 45 (1989), pp. 864-73.

Streeter, B.H., 'On the Original Order of Q', in W. Sanday (ed.), *Oxford Studies in the Synoptic Problem* (Oxford: Clarendon Press, 1911), pp. 141-64.

—'Fresh Light on the Synoptic Problem', *HJ* 20 (1921–22), pp. 103-12.

—*The Four Gospels: A Study of Origins. Treating of the Manuscript Tradition, Sources, Authorship, and Dates* (London: Macmillan; New York: St Martin's, 1924).

—'Die Ur-Lukas-Hypothese', *TSK* 102 (1930), pp. 332-40.

Strobel, A., 'Die Passa-Erwartung als urchristliches Problem in Lc 17, 20f.', *ZNW* 49 (1958), pp. 157-96.

Swidler, L., *Biblical Affirmations of Women* (Philadelphia: Westminster Press, 1979).

Talbert, C.H., *Literary Patterns, Theological Themes, and the Genre of Luke–Acts* (SBLMS, 20; Missoula, MT: Scholars Press, 1974).

—'Shifting Sands: The Recent Study of the Gospel of Luke', *Int* 30 (1976), pp. 381-95.

—'Oral and Independent or Literary and Interdependent? A Response to Albert B. Lord', in W.O. Walker, Jr (ed.), *The Relationships among the Gospels: An Interdisciplinary Dialogue* (San Antonio: Trinity University Press, 1978), pp. 93-102.

—*Reading Luke: A Literary and Theological Commentary on the Third Gospel* (New York: Crossroad, 1982).

Tannehill, R.C., 'The Mission of Jesus according to Luke iv. 16-30', in W. Eltester (ed.), *Jesus in Nazareth* (BZNW, 40; Berlin: de Gruyter, 1972), pp. 51-75.

—*The Narrative Unity of Luke–Acts: A Literary Interpretation* (2 vols.; Minneapolis: Fortress Press, 1986).

Taylor, V., 'Proto-Luke', *ExpTim* 33 (1921-22), pp. 250-52.

—'The Value of the Proto-Luke Hypothesis', *ExpTim* 36 (1924–25), pp. 476-77.

—*Behind the Third Gospel: A Study of the Proto-Luke Hypothesis* (Oxford: Oxford University Press, 1926).

—'The First Draft of Luke's Gospel', *Theology* 14 (1927), pp. 131-64.

—*The First Draft of St Luke's Gospel* (London: SPCK, 1927).
—'The Proto-Luke Hypothesis: A Reply to Dr W.K. Lowther Clarke's Queries', *Theology* 14 (1927), pp. 72-76.
—'Is the Proto-Luke Hypothesis Sound?' *JTS* 29 (1927–28), pp. 147-55.
—*The Formation of the Gospel Tradition* (London: Macmillan, 1933).
—'Professor J.M. Creed and the Proto-Luke Hypothesis', *ExpTim* 46 (1934–35), pp. 236-38.
—'The Proto-Luke Hypothesis: A Rejoinder', *ExpTim* 54 (1942–43), pp. 219-22.
—'The Order of Q', *JTS* 4 (1953), pp. 27-31.
—'Important Hypotheses Reconsidered: The Proto-Luke Hypothesis', *ExpTim* 67 (1955–56), pp. 12-16.
—'The Original Order of Q', in A.J.B. Higgins (ed.), *New Testament Essays: Studies in Memory of T.W. Manson* (Manchester: Manchester University Press, 1959), pp. 246-69.
—*The Names of Jesus* (London: Macmillan; New York: St Martin's Press, 1962).
—'Rehkopf's List of Words and Phrases Illustrative of Pre-Lukan Speech Usage', *JTS* (1964), pp. 59-62.
Tetlow, E., *Women and Ministry in the New Testament* (New York: Paulist Press, 1980).
Theissen, G., *The Miracle Stories of the Early Christian Tradition* (trans. F. McDonagh; Edinburgh: T. & T. Clark; Philadelphia: Fortress Press, 1983).
—*The Gospels in Context: Social and Political History in the Synoptic Tradition* (trans. L.M. Maloney; Minneapolis: Fortress Press, 1991).
Thiering, B., 'The Three and a Half Years of Elijah', *NovT* 23 (1981), pp. 41-55.
Tiede, D.L., *Luke* (Augsburg Commentary on the New Testament; Minneapolis: Augsburg, 1988).
Tinsley, E.J., *The Gospel according to Luke* (Cambridge: Cambridge University Press, 1965).
Trites, A.A., 'The Prayer Motif in Luke–Acts', in C.H. Talbert (ed.), *Perspectives on Luke–Acts* (Danville, VA: Association of Baptist Professors of Religion, 1978), pp. 168-86.
Trocmé, A., *Jesus and the Nonviolent Revolution* (trans. M.H. Shank and M.E. Miller; Scottdale, PA: Herald Press, 1973).
Trudinger, L.P., 'Once Again, Now "Who Is My Neighbour?"', *EvQ* 48 (1976), pp. 160-63.
Tuckett, C.M., 'Luke 4, 16-30, Isaiah, and Q', in J. Delobel (ed.), *Logia: Les paroles de Jésus—The Sayings of Jesus: Mémorial Joseph Coppens* (Leuven: Leuven University Press, 1982), pp. 343-54.
—'A Cynic Q?', *Bib* 70 (1989), pp. 349-76.
—'On the Stratification of Q: A Response', *Semeia* 55 (1991), pp. 213-22.
Turner, H.E.W., and H. Montefiore, *Thomas and the Evangelists* (Naperville, IL: Alec R. Allenson; Chatham, UK: W. & J. MacKay & Co., 1962).
Tyson, J.B., 'Sequential Parallelism in the Synoptic Gospels', *NTS* 22 (1975–76), pp. 276-308.
—'Source Criticism of the Gospel of Luke', in C.H. Talbert (ed.), *Perspectives on Luke–Acts* (Danville, VA: Association of Baptist Professors of Religion, 1978), pp. 24-39.
Vaganay, L., *Le problème synoptique: Une hypothèse de travail* (Bibliothèque de Théologie, Série III, Théologie Biblique, vol. 1; Tournai, Belgium: Desclée, 1954).
Vansina, J., *Oral Tradition: A Study in Historical Methodology* (trans. H.M. Wright; Chicago: Aldine Publishing, 1965).

Via, D.O., *The Parables: Their Literary and Existential Dimension* (Philadelphia: Fortress Press, 1967).

Via, E.J., 'Women in the Gospel of Luke', in U. King (ed.), *Women in the World's Religions* (New York: Paragon House, 1987), pp. 38-55.

Wegner, U., *Das Hauptmann von Kafarnaum* (WUNT, 2.14; Tübingen: Mohr, 1985).

Weiser, A., *Die Knechtsgleichnesse der synoptischen Evangelien* (SANT, 29; Munich: Kösel, 1971).

Weiss, B., *Lehrbuch der Einleitung in das Neue Testament* (Berlin: W. Hertz, 1886).

—*Die Quellen des Lukasevangeliums* (Stuttgart: J.G. Cotta'schen Buchhandlung Nachfolger, 1907).

—*Die Quellen der synoptischen Überlieferung* (Leipzig: J.C. Hinrichssche Buchhandlung, 1908).

Wellhausen, J., *Das Evangelium Lucae: Übersetzt und erklärt* (Berlin: Georg Reimer, 1904).

Wenham, J., *Redating Matthew, Mark, and Luke: A Fresh Assault on the Synoptic Problem* (London: Hodder & Stoughton, 1991).

Wenham, J.W., 'Synoptic Independence and the Origin of Luke's Travel Narrative', *NTS* 27 (1981), pp. 507-15.

Wilckens, U., 'Vergebung für die Sünderin', in P. Hoffmann, N. Brox, and W. Pesch (eds.), *Orientierung an Jesus: Zur Theologie der Synoptiker. Für Josef Schmid* (Freiburg: Herder, 1973), pp. 394-424.

Willcock, J., 'Cainan (Luke III, 36)', *ExpTim* 30 (1918–19), pp. 86-87.

Williams, D.S., *Stylometric Authorship Studies in Flavius Josephus and Related Literature* (Lewiston, NY: Edwin Mellen, 1992).

Winter, P., 'The Treatment of his Sources by the Third Evangelist', *ST* 8 (1954), pp. 138-72.

—'On Luke and Lucan Sources', *ZNW* 47 (1956), pp. 217-42.

—'Lucan Sources', *ExpTim* 68 (1956-57), p. 285.

—'Sources of the Lucan Passion Narrative', *ExpTim* 68 (1956–57), p. 95.

Witherington, B., 'On the Road with Mary Magdalene, Joanna, Susanna, and Other Disciples—Luke 8, 1-3', *ZNW* (1979), pp. 243-48.

Witherington, B., III, *Women in the Ministry of Jesus* (SNTSMS, 51; Cambridge: Cambridge University Press, 1984)

—*Women in the Earliest Churches* (SNTSMS, 58; Cambridge: Cambridge University Press, 1988).

Yoder, J.H., *The Politics of Jesus* (Grand Rapids: Eerdmans, 1972).

Young, N.H., 'Once Again, Now "Who Is My Neighbour?": A Comment', *EvQ* 49 (1977), pp. 178-79.

Zeller, D., *Kommentar zur Logienquelle* (Stuttgarter Kleiner Kommentar Neues Testaments, 21; Stuttgart: Katholisches Bibelwerk, 1986).

INDEXES

INDEX OF REFERENCES

OLD TESTAMENT

NEW TESTAMENT

Mark (cont.)		5.43	87	8.34-38	48
3.5	89	6.1-6	34, 106,	8.37	100
3.7-8	120		107, 112	8.38	79
3.9-14	87	6.6-13	46	9.2-8	89
3.13-19	89, 125	6.7-13	89	9.5	75
3.17	119	6.8	87, 123	9.9	87
3.22-30	106	6.12	87	9.12	87
3.31-35	47, 106,	6.13	75, 120	9.14-29	110
	107, 112	6.17	119	9.16	99
3.32	89	6.25-33	48	9.19	100
3.33-34	112	6.25	87	9.21-29	99
3.33	100	6.31	99	9.22	77, 87
4.1	120	6.32-44	89	9.27	107
4.2-9	97	6.34	77	9.28-29	110
4.8	90	6.35	89	9.30-32	31
4.13	100	6.37-38	99	9.30	120
4.15-17	105	6.37	90	9.33	99, 120
4.19	123	6.38	75	9.36	89
4.20	90	6.40	90	9.38-41	106
4.21	87	6.41	87	9.38-40	112
4.22	87	6.42	83	10.1-12	106
4.26-29	97	6.43	75	10.13-16	112
4.30-32	97	6.44	75	10.17-31	87, 106
4.30	100	6.56	87	10.17-22	37, 48,
4.35-41	89	7.1-23	106		90
4.38	112	7.6	82	10.17	87
4.39	99	7.9	87	10.18	83, 89
4.40	89, 100	7.24-31	110	10.21	89, 122
5.1-43	125	7.24-30	97	10.24	99
5.2	80	7.26	87	10.29	89
5.6	82	7.27	83	10.30	90
5.8	99	7.31-37	97, 107,	10.31	32, 43
5.9	99		108	10.32-34	32
5.12	99	7.32-37	108	10.32-33	32
5.13	90	7.32	87	10.32	120
5.18	87	7.36	87	10.33-34	32
5.20	120	8.2	77	10.34	135
5.21-43	89	8.3	82	10.35-45	106
5.21-24	107, 108	8.4	83	10.35	87
5.21	120	8.6	87	10.37	87
5.23	87, 99	8.8	83	10.38	43
5.26	80	8.15	38	10.46	119
5.28	99	8.22-26	97, 107,	10.47	81, 89
5.31	119		108	10.48	81
5.34	89	8.22	87	10.49	99
5.35-43	108	8.27	120	10.52	89
5.36	89	8.29	89	11.1-10	32
5.37	119	8.30	87	11.9-10	33

The Story of Jesus according to L

	149	18.38	81		99, 101,
18.2	131	18.39	81		103
18.4	46, 89,	18.40	55, 99	19.12-13	70
	131	18.42	89	19.12	79, 87
18.5	76, 87,	18.43–19.10	13, 30,	19.13	75
	131		53, 64	19.14-44	93
18.6	64	18.43	64	19.14	75
18.8	63, 64	19.1-10	14, 64,	19.15-26	70
18.9-14	13, 14,		78	19.15	88
	30, 64	19.1	64	19.17	75
18.9	57, 64	19.2-10	64, 65,	19.23	100
18.10-14	64, 65,		85, 87,	19.28-38	32
	89, 93-		93, 94,	19.29	55
	95, 97,		111, 115,	19.33	75
	98, 100,		116, 118-	19.34-44	30
	101, 103,		21, 123,	19.34-40	31
	104, 115,		128, 130,	19.36	32
	116, 118,		134, 136,	19.37-44	13, 30
	121, 123,		145, 146,	19.37-40	32
	126, 131,		155-58	19.37-38	32
	145, 147,	19.2-8	85	19.37	55, 81
	149, 155,	19.2-7	65, 95,	19.39-44	14
	158		139	19.39-40	32, 33,
18.13	82, 128	19.2-3	87		65, 95
18.14	59, 64,	19.2	134	19.41-44	38, 39,
	88, 102,	19.3	118, 135		57, 65,
	128	19.4	87, 118,		70, 78,
18.15-43	70		121		87, 95
18.15-17	70, 112	19.5	112, 128	19.41	39, 55
18.16	39	19.6	84, 128,	19.43-44	39, 87
18.17	39		136	19.45-48	106, 107,
18.18-30	87, 106	19.7	112, 128		112
18.18-23	89	19.8	65, 78,	19.45	87, 120
18.18	87		95, 112,	19.47-48	13, 30,
18.19	83, 89		123, 128,		31, 33
18.22	39, 59,		139	20.1-8	106
	61, 89,	19.9-10	112	20.1	120
	122, 123	19.9	65, 95,	20.2	87
18.24	99		134, 137,	20.6	100
18.29	89		139	20.7	99
18.30	90	19.10-14	85	20.9-19	103
18.31-34	13, 30-	19.10	65, 95,	20.9	57, 77
	32, 64		136, 137,	20.13	98
18.31	120		139	20.14	88
18.35	55, 64,	19.11-28	13, 30,	20.15	100
	119		39	20.16	91
18.36	91	19.11-27	14, 53,	20.17	100
18.37	57, 89		76, 90,	20.19	57, 58

INDEX OF AUTHORS